A WATCH OVER MORTALITY

SUNY Series in Latin American and Iberian
Thought and Culture

Jorge J. E. Gracia, Editor

A WATCH OVER MORTALITY

THE PHILOSOPHICAL STORY OF JULIÁN MARÍAS

HAROLD RALEY

STATE UNIVERSITY OF NEW YORK PRESS

Published by
State University of New York Press, Albany

© 1997 State University of New York

For information, address State University of New York Press,
State University Plaza, Albany, N.Y. 12246

Production by M. R. Mulholland
Marketing by Dana E. Yanulavich

Library of Congress Cataloging-in-Publication Data
Raley, Harold C., 1934–
    A watch over mortality : the philosophical story of Julián Marías
    Harold Raley.
        p.   cm.—(SUNY series in Latin American and Iberian
    thought and culture)
      Includes bibliographical references and index.
      ISBN 0-7914-3153-3 (alk. paper).—ISBN 0-7914-3154-1 (pbk. :
    alk. paper)
      1. Marías, Julián, 1914–   . I. Title. II. Series.
    B4568.M374R35   **1997**
    196'.1—dc20   97-3773
                                            CIP
                                            Rev

10 9 8 7 6 5 4 3 2 1

CONTENTS

Introduction to a New Philosophy

In the faith that looks through death,
In years that bring the philosophic mind.
....
The Clouds that gather round the setting sun
Do take a sober colouring from an eye
That hath kept watch o'er man's mortality.

—Wordsworth, *Intimations of Immortality*

In 1973–74, I wrote *Responsible Vision: The Philosophy of Julián Marías*. After a series of editorial delays, the book appeared in 1980, which allowed the Spanish translation by Espasa-Calpe to precede it in 1977. This odd chronology was to have an unfortunate effect on both versions of the book in this country. Many university libraries do not buy translations, and since it was not clear which was which, in many cases neither was acquired. As a result, while *La visión responsable* has enjoyed a generous reception in the Spanish-speaking world, *Responsible Vision* is nearly unknown here.

Yet my disappointment with these circumstances in no way detracted from the satisfaction I felt about the book itself. Even today, more than two decades later, there is very little I would change if I were going to write a similar book. I believe that *Responsible Vision* continues to be responsible, that within the margins of my limited knowledge and probable error it is still a reasonably accurate vision of important portions and trajectories of Marías's way of thinking.

But this is precisely the point that needs to be made here: I do not intend simply to extend or rectify or reflect on what I wrote many years ago. This book will be, I hope, complementary to that work, but if it goes as envisioned it will also be launched from a different personal plane and life stage, as a reflection of altered external circumstances, and, internally, of life lived, of time gone by for both Marías and me.

What I have just stated as a commonplace pattern of life takes on a special significance in the case of Marías. At an age when most people retire or decline and have "had their say," Marías accelerated his pace. Since 1977, he has written many of his best books, participated in the public arena in new and unique ways, and suffered some of the most wrenching personal ordeals of his life. I call it his "second voyage" into philosophy.

Yet it would be a mistake to conclude from these statements that 1977 marks a personal break with his earlier views and that a "new" Marías has emerged. If anything, he has become more himself without renouncing or denying who he was and what he thought in earlier times. His life and work display a remarkable congruence that makes it unnecessary for him to deny or conceal portions of his past. What he wrote more than fifty years ago bears his inimitable stamp and style, and blends smoothly with his latest efforts.

He writes with enormous power, displaying an elegant synthesis of the classic *gravedad española* [translatable perhaps as "sober Spanish composure"], clarity, cordiality, and veracity. And never was Buffon's dictum truer: style is the man. For these are also personal traits. Seemingly without effort he goes immediately for the heart of problems, and once centered on his theme he swiftly pursues it with remarkable linguistic economy and efficiency. To read Marías is to see truth emerge in one of its handsomest forms, and it is to wonder afterward why it never occurred to anyone else, ourselves included, to say truthful things with such grace and precision. As in the case of all great writers, there seems to be no stylistic alternative, no better way to tell the things he has told. There are no superfluous elements in his writings, no concessions to trivialities, and no interest in exhibitionist pedantry or intramural cleverness. Concentrated, incisive, and supple, the style of his rich repertory of ideas, discoveries, and fascinating *aperçus* furnishes countless examples of what he has described as "page quality." Enrique Lafuente Ferrari describes Marías's prose as *diamantina,* "diamond-like."[1] Later we shall see that, far from being an incidental feature of thought, style itself is an essential dimension of philosophy as Marías understands it.

Marías speaks of an urgency to complete tasks and leave things well done in all sectors of his life. But as he has redoubled his efforts, he has sharpened his aim. This allows him to work rapidly but without haste. In recent years, Marías has restated his major premises with even greater elegance and precision and, at the same time, he has extended his methods and insights into new areas.

This process of simultaneous summation and extension may seem paradoxical, but if so it is the classic paradox of philosophy itself that must ever call its contentions into question and seek constant rejustification and redirection. Philosophy involves more than simply telling the truth. For as Ortega y Gasset once pointed out, the truth merely told soon lapses into formula and dogma; in order to remain truth it must be retold, that is, reinvented, as circumstances change, or perhaps so that they can change.

As Marías sees it, authentic philosophy involves the human search for radical certainty from a starting point of fundamental uncertainty. In simple terms, it is a peculiarly human need for a certain kind of truth from which to live life. Real philosophical problems are the problems of real people. This is why at this level truth assumes a redemptive power that transcends mere verbal congruence and verifiable fact.

Nor can we ignore the aesthetic dimensions of truth that come into play here. Ortega observed that unless words were beautiful and rousing, Mediterranean peoples would not accept them as being truthful. Marías appears to subscribe to a similar view. For him truth has to be, prior to its content and doctrinal weight, attractive and efficacious—in order to be truth at all. These prerequisites, which the Germanic or Anglo-Saxon thinker would probably take to be nice though not necessary addenda, are for Marías and Ortega the *sine quibus non* of effective philosophy. At bottom, they point to nothing less than two apparently very different intuitions of truth: to the Northern mind, truth has nearly always been understood essentially as a supine and passive verbal congruence between word and external reality. Truth is seen, therefore, as an extrapersonal quality passively awaiting discovery and, once discovered, as a docile predictor of behavior in things. This is why, generally speaking, sincerity and honesty summarize the extent of our personal responsibility toward truth.

On the other hand, truth in the Southern, "Mediterranean" sense seems to exhibit a redemptive note that has a bearing and leaves an imprint on one's personal destiny. We could say that the Northern mind thinks of truth as a feature of the objective, external world and, when developed to the full, tends toward impersonal science, logic, and social norm. From a very different perspective, the Southerner personally appropriates truth by creating it in a sense, and expresses it natively as aesthetics, art, philosophy, and religion. For the Northerner, truth is simply there, verbalized or not, as an incidental feature of things; for the Southerner, it must be told, and told well, to be truth in the first place.[2] For truth, far from being an incidental attribute of things, is, as Machado puts it, ". . . also a creation."

Furthermore, because of its redemptive dimension, its ability to guide and keep us afloat in our oceanic existence, truth is not a luxury or an addendum but a matter of primary human urgency and need. And, as Marías sees it, this urgency and need must be reflected in all authentic philosophy. Even though the answers to our pressing questions may be problematical or even impossible, this alone is no valid reason for avoiding their pursuit. In any case, we have no advance way of knowing whether they are unanswerable, and to pronounce them so beforehand, as modern thought is in the habit of doing, amounts to uninformed prejudice. And, I was going to add, intellectual heresy. Even if they should prove to be beyond our capabilities, authentic philosophy progresses by posing the questions, and not by predetermining the certainty of its answers. This is why Marías has scant sympathy for the fabricated problems and metaphysical phobias that pass for contemporary philosophy.

Marías comments on all these points in many of his writings and, in the

Memorias, explains his posture in much more personal ways than I can go into here. On the other hand, I am interested in the dramatic and *therefore* philosophical impact this biographical trajectory has had on his thinking.

Here a preliminary explanation is in order. Otherwise, within an Anglo-American philosophic context and mindset this appeal to personal drama and philosophy in the same breath would be taken as a descent to theatrics and a sure sign that we are about to get off track. Three initial points offer us guidance: first, human life is dramatic, not primarily because of dramatic scenes or plots but because it consists of an inner and essential personal drama. Shakespeare understood this. Many of his scenes are trite or contrived, and his plots second-hand stories from an assortment of sources. Of course these externals have their importance, but they are decidedly secondary when compared to the inner drama of all his characters from kings and nobles to villains and varlets. It is the same dramatic intuition that enlivens the novels of Cervantes.

If this is true of imperishable art, then there is a good chance that it corresponds to an imperishable truth of human life. And this means that in order to philosophize in a coherent and responsible way about life, which is to say at the level and in the way we really live it, we must acknowledge its dramatic quality, and philosophy must assume a form and adopt a method that reflect it. There is more. In the line of thought to which Ortega y Gasset and Marías belong (and also Unamuno in his own disjunctive way) life is the foundational reality of philosophy, for other realities appear and are knowable *to us*—it is important to stress this point—only from our personal life perspective. This means, in summary, that philosophy devolves on a metaphysics of human life.

This brings us to the third point. The motionless categories and rigid genres of traditional philosophy, to say nothing of their weak-spirited contemporary versions, are not up to this narrative task. Life moves and they stand still, losing any chance of grasping its dramatic flight. Conventional philosophy cannot narrate life's story, and yet its truth is in the telling. How can the human tale be told? To begin with, as it always has been: by literature, art, and history. This is why, in order to develop an adequate form, Spanish philosophy moved in full theoretical regalia toward those genres already sensitized to the inherent drama of life. By a happy coincidence, the exceptionally high quality of Spanish literature produced in the first decades of the twentieth century by the Generation(s) of 1898 facilitated this convergence of new theory and adequate form. Until recent relapses traceable most likely to the importation of philosophies obedient to older and more primitive impulses, to do philosophy at all in Spain presupposed an extraordinarily high literary style equal to, and often better than, the best that novelists and poets could produce.

For his part and from another starting point, Unamuno argued that even the most cerebral books (and he proposed Kant's *Critique of Pure Reason* as an example) are "novels" of human experience. Perhaps this is what he meant.

At least it is what I mean. Which brings me to the nature of this book. It is neither a biography of Marías nor an intellectual treatise indifferent to his life. Perhaps the most approximate description would be that it is a philosophical biography or story, but this definition can also mislead us unless we are willing to understand these terms in a new way that will be clearer as we proceed. Initially, it is enough to say that to approach philosophy from this vantage point is to find ourselves also engaged in the philosophical process.

But the factual account of our life is never the whole story. As Marías himself teaches, the real narrative of human life is more than the sum of its documentable episodes and phases. Modestly, behind the factual content of our lives trail the unreal images of who we could have been and what we could have done. And only in view of what we have said no to—and what has said no to us—can we begin to understand human life, including our own. Carlyle said that history does not reveal its alternatives. Perhaps not, but they remain in an ideal way nonetheless as lingering reminders of the magnitude of their sacrifices. The roads not taken, the chances missed or denied, are not mere nostalgic anecdotes of ancient renunciations but an abiding moral and explanatory justification of those we chose to follow and to actualize. Each of us is a constellation of real and rejected lives. At varying distances from the dramatic center of our being, shining with faint or splendid luminosity, our chosen or forfeited ideals trace our way through life. Paradoxically, who we are includes who we could not or would not be.

This is one reason why, as Marías notes, all biographies are susceptible to utopian exaggerations, for every human life, even the lives of our closest friends, has recesses and secret places we cannot penetrate. On the other hand, we run the risk of falling into dehumanized abstractions the moment we separate thought from its living origins. Thinkers so treated cease being men and women in a real world and become names in a so-called and probably misleading "history of ideas." Marías himself makes this very clear: ". . . philosophy is *dramatic theory,* and as such, intrinsically personal and biographical; considered apart from the real life of the philosopher it is not intelligible and, strictly speaking, is not philosophy. Philosophy is meaningful only as something that emanates from the life of a specific person, with a *free inevitability* that only the theory of human life renders understandable."[3]

In my case, another consideration must be added to this general equation: my personal contacts with Marías have been necessarily sporadic; great distances normally separate us, to say nothing of cultural and linguistic differences. For although we speak each other's language and admire each other's culture, we are "installed"—as Marías would probably say—firmly and irrevocably in our own.

I am interested in the real genesis, vitality, and range of this way of thinking, and despite the contentions of conventional logic this involves an

argumentum ad hominem, an appeal to the man himself, or to be more specific, to the trajectories, vectors, tensions, and passions of his life, however
imperfectly known and appreciated they may be. This means that, in order to
understand what Marías has said, we must, as Ortega would argue, tell his
story, not a random tale but an intellectual story obedient to the rules of rigorous analysis—and synthesis—which, far from scorning the personal content
of his life, takes its cues from its pace. For it rests on the abiding Spanish intuition that life constitutes the true system, that is, the internal coherence and
sense of philosophy. This points to the dramatic nature of philosophy I referred to earlier and to which I shall return several times in this book.

In this sense, this philosophical biography becomes an experiment in the
very philosophy Marías espouses. It is an effort to see whether these methods
of analysis, argumentation, application, and justification work at a primary
level and with a real person. Marías claims to have been guided by its principles in his own writings, especially in his *Memorias.* In our case, we will see
what transpersonal use can be made of this approach.

There are constants in this process. The first is my conviction, grown
stronger over the years, that this way of thinking efficiently combines a fertile
understanding of the material world with an uncommon respect for the real
human condition. In our day, as we struggle, often crudely and ineptly, to understand our relationship and responsibility to the world, we would do well to
learn from this pioneering philosophy that lovingly and aesthetically has
coaxed so many secrets from life and its circumstances. There is nothing cumbersome or heavyhanded in its methods, nothing ugly or hateful in its finalities, and this is probably the best clue that we are dealing with superior truths.

To my way of understanding, these features offer the best chance for an
intelligent and moral "watch over mortality." The adjectives are not casual; we
have abundant proof that only the moral has the possibility of being truly intelligent and, conversely, that the immoral reduces ultimately—and often immediately—to error. We have learned the hard way that intellect alone cannot
be trusted to chart human destiny.

Consider the conventional picture of our time. According to philosopher
Gabriel Marcel, ours is a *Monde cassé,* a broken world. Things fall apart, yet
despite our remedial efforts nothing we do seems to slow the erosion of
human values or stop the destruction of the natural world. To make matters
worse, our customary instruments and old approaches fail us: philosophy has
become the precious algebra of trite paradoxes and contrived problems; ethics
languishes a prisoner of situational existentialism; science has turned myopi-
cally indifferent to all but its own image, while its offspring technologies pro-
liferate in uncontrolled and dangerous abandon; art continues in reckless free
fall toward spiritual and thematic impoverishment; and religious faith is taken
to be a quaint echo of a bygone age.

But is this our real condition, or our opinion of it? Naturally, what we believe becomes a decisive part of reality. In fact, opinion becomes the foremost dimension, the facial appearance, as it were, of things and affects in a primary way our behavioral relationship with all the other dimensions, hidden, realized, or potential. We seem to have fallen into the habit of speaking ill of our contemporary world, of seeing dark conspiratorial evils in nearly everything. A heavy-handed pessimism has become stylish; we routinely discount not only present reality but also its historical dimensions and, most importantly, its future possibilities.

It is not easy to see past this morbid web of opinion and discover the hidden face of things. But the task is not impossible. For instance, if we talk to our neighbors and friends and take stock of their lives, we often find that even though at the drop of a hat they repeat the conventional pessimism about the world, their own lives tell a different story of morality, spontaneity, trust, good will, and intelligence. We begin to suspect that a whole category of truth exists beyond our customary perceptual modes. For contrary to the popular adage, words nearly always speak louder than actions. This is why for the most part we see not what really is but what we have been told to see. Normally, therefore, we overlook these visible, everyday truths in the mistaken belief that reality has another configuration. We assume that important truth must be abstract, global, and grandiose and that anything less is a trifle.

Two principal features emerge from this attitude: first, an extraordinary number of what Marías calls "negative beliefs." We do not think the world as constituted is trustworthy. From this fundamental attitude derive several remarkable consequences. One is the extraordinarily high level of cynicism and boredom, for we tend to think that nothing is really worthy or interesting in itself, and only if it threatens us in some way or perhaps offers a momentary gratification can it claim our attention. In other words, nothing is sacred, which means that lacking intrinsic value everything is relative and open to debate. Hence the inordinate insistence on dialogue as a universal panacea for problems.

We find another aspect of these negative beliefs in our immoderate passion for security. At one level this is perfectly understandable; for if the world consists primarily of threats and dangers and the final annihilation of death, the temptation is to turn away from them and seek whatever temporary refuge we can. Even philosophy—perhaps most of all philosophy—has yielded to this urge for security by turning its back on the questions of death and personal destiny and busying itself with contrived problems and secondary questions.

The second consequence of this attitude is much more positive and promising. As Marías puts it, "The indifference toward remote things has been replaced by a strong feeling of *solidarity* with everything human."[4] It seems that we are becoming aware that our search for personal security is illusory if it is based on indifference to what goes on about us. There is a renewed willingness to admit that everything and everybody affects us, and though understood only in the most nebulous way, this Donnesque realization could lead to a new cycle of philosophical inquiry.

Our conventional pessimism and cynicism are probably justifiable up to a point, and perhaps this is why they have such a hold on us and why it has been so hard for us to move beyond them. But to point out what is wrong, or false, or untrustworthy in things is to establish the primary moral and dialectical preconditions for launching a search for truth that is both radical and livable. And when broadened to a responsible, systematic, and sustained encounter with all reality within our experience, this search for "livable truth" may mature into philosophy. Naturally, these preconditions alone determine very little. It is likely that in most cases they will not lead to philosophy, which, historically speaking, is a rather rare occurrence. Marías points out two other unlikely factors that render the process problematic: on the one hand, there is the responsibility of the philosopher, which involves both an active truthfulness and a gift of expression—signs of a genuine philosophic calling—and on the other, a high degree of receptivity and an authentic desire for truthfulness on the part of the public. Only rarely do both conditions converge.

Marías often refers to philosophy as "responsible vision" and as the alertness that he calls *no poder dormir* ("unable to sleep"). But such vision and alertness would be impossible in a truly dull and uninteresting world. In order for philosophy to exist at all reality has to be worth the enormous effort it demands. Otherwise we must forego philosophy and settle for sophistry. For Marías this means that we must transcend our modern indifference to reality and rediscover its essential enchantment. Failing this, we do not have to await some future apocalyptical end of the world; it will have disintegrated already, long since dead and drained of human life and hope.[5]

Once we begin to see that, far from being supine and indifferent, our relationship to reality is dramatic and, in theory at least, inexhaustible, this appeal to enchantment starts to make sense. Naturally, this appeal cannot be made with dead language, inelegant jargon, and lifeless style. Here Marías can help us. Not only does he have very important truths to tell us but, more importantly perhaps, he also makes available to us philosophical and moral methods that allow us to strike out responsibly on our own toward other truths and toward the radical certainties that mark the real origin and end of philosophy. I see in his thought the chance to begin a timely reconquest of our surrendered world.

This process might be simpler if Marías were a single clear voice in our modern wilderness. But we hear a cacophony of proposed "salvations." How do we "distinguish the voices from the echoes," as Spanish poet Antonio

Machado once said? I wish I knew. But this I do know: it is important to tell the truth, for it registers in our life in a mysterious way decidedly different from falsehood.

Not that the truth comes easily. For if the world is often historically perverse, it is always metaphysically modest. Heraclitus said that reality likes to conceal itself. Heidegger wrote that it hides its secrets, and that each reluctant revelation becomes in turn the condition of a further concealment. Yet we cannot avoid running the tricky gamut the world stretches before us. For we are indigent beings and cannot live solely with the familiar. We also, and perhaps primarily, need the hidden recourses of reality; we are privileged—or to some condemned—to probe beyond the first reach of light and enlightenment. And the world takes advantage of this uncertain venture through evasive strategies of concealment. Shadow and substance do not easily separate but seem to delight in their fugitive deception. Perhaps this is why the revelation of truth, what Heidegger and Ortega called *aletheia,* always contains an exhilarating hint of unexpected human triumph. Ortega acknowledged this condition in his Prologue to *Veinte años de caza mayor* [Twenty Years of Big Game Hunting] by pointing out the subterranean links between the hunter's alertness and perils of the chase and the vigilance of the philosopher in the risky pursuit of elusive truth.

Our generation (and several before us) was urged to think for itself and discover its own truth. But we accepted the dictum without obeying it. The result is that essentially we have done neither, for thinking is harder work than we are accustomed to, and we got no further than assuming that the discovery of new truths consisted simply of disqualifying the old ones. In the process, we came to the simplistic conclusion that truth is a matter of chronology, making the calendar an automatic disqualifier of reality. In other words, we began to prefer trend to truth, to assume that the new and untried is always better and the old and tested ever suspect. Hence the more pernicious notions of evolutionary "progress." The result has been that in many cases we have neither old truths nor new ones. Hence one of the primary conditions for the anguish of modern life. With his usual perspicacity, Ortega noticed this phenomenon many decades ago, pointing out that twentieth-century generations believe themselves to be superior to all their predecessors but radically inferior to their own internal image of who they ought to be.

In our day, we are engaged in a great debate over the nature of modernity. Art, philosophy, education, feminism, government, ideology, religion, abortion, politics, environment, these are some of the dimensions of this massive squabble. But as deep as our disagreements are, they arise from a prior and tacit agreement: we cannot reasonably be expected to continue in sheer indeterminacy. We hear a clamor for profound changes. The question is, what kind of changes must we seek and where do we find the truth about our world?

For our spiritual doubts and ontological dissatisfactions have not translated so far into intelligent advancements of the human cause, much less worthy substitutes for lost faith and shattered moralities. Genuine needs have not automatically generated genuine solutions, at least not acceptable ones. For it is not enough that solutions work, for us to accept them they must conform to our fashionable expectations. Beggars, we still insist on being choosers.

For scores of years, even centuries, we have sought our solutions and pursued our art and science within a general mode of rebelliousness. Since the rise of Jacobin revolution, orthodoxy in all its forms has had a bad name, or at least a bad press, whereas mere dissidence in the many forms it has assumed from that time until now has enjoyed increasing respect. Personal creativity and authenticity have come to be thought of as little more than forms of protest against an established and essentially sinister "system."

In art especially, this has taken the form of a frantic search for "originality," that is, for ways to oppose system and orthodoxy. In fact, this automatic and presumptive opposition has itself become a sort of neo-orthodoxy, complete with its own conventions, rules, politically correct postures, and punishments for violations.

In simpler terms, we have sought to be original by discrediting our origins. Lately, this oxymoronic paradox seems to be taking its toll among us. Dissension can easily be taken to an extreme, but seldom far enough to establish foundational truths. Customarily, it ends in a cynical trivialization of life and values, a tendency we note with increasing frequency. For we face the evident principle that to vilify who we have been and where we have come from is to diminish who we are and who we can be. In the inexorable economy of life, the truths we scorn sooner or later return to scorn us.

Marías points to a different pathway. Instead of spiritual dysfunction, there is the way of inner renewal. Instead of condemning the world, there is always the nobler chance of saving it. For him, true originality means being true to one's origin, which must never be mistaken for mere conformity to the expedient and imperfect. It means going back—or perhaps forward—to the source; it means restating what is real and viable, not declaring it null and void. Authentic innovation means the creation of something new within what is old, and this means respecting and making use of what is historically real so as to discover our future possibilities.

Historian Eugen Rosenstock-Huessy traces the incremental creation of the modern world to five hundred years of "clerical" or intellectual revolution, while thinkers like Julien Benda and Ortega foresaw its demise in a *trahison des clercs,* to use Benda's expression, "a betrayal by clerks," that is, an unwillingness on the part of intellectuals to shoulder the burdens of life, society, or even intellect itself.[6]

Looking at the phenomenon from another perspective, and for the moment divesting the terms "catholic" and "protestant" of their unhappy histori-cal contentiousness, I would say that in this context Marías may be understood as a "catholic" thinker. (Who also happens to be Catholic as well.) Yet notwithstanding our initial clarification, the adjective is still risky and possi-bily misleading, so let us understand it exactly. By "catholic" I mean that his thought presupposes the underlying unity of European culture. In the name and spirit of what he once called a "European patriotism"—which he then ex-tended to include the American cultures—he claims as his heritage the British, French, Italian, and German cultures even though he remains firmly rooted in his Spanish circumstance. Indeed, it is by being so thoroughly Spanish that he can be truly European, for in radical commitment to who we are we discover our profound fellowship with others. On the other hand, by persuading us that we are at home everywhere, most forms of cosmopolitanism guarantee that we belong nowhere.

If "modern" Europe and America have been essentially "protestant," meaning that they have conceived of invention and innovation as a rebellious attitude toward their civil norms and canons and a belief that what can be must necessarily be at odds with what has been, Marías represents a way of think-ing, lately ignored and scorned, that finds an innovative and liberating spirit within that heritage. No wonder then that, unlike the "protestant" moderns, he has never been embarrassed by the richness of his heritage. To the culturally protestant mind, the imperfections of this heritage justify its rejection; for Marías, they stand as an agenda of perfectability. He does not make the mis-take of despising the good in the name of the utopian. He believes in straight-forward fashion that real history, science, art, theology, and philosophy are superior to and thus more interesting than the unsubstantial ideological schemes to which modernity has rendered homage.

This is why, or so I think, his way of thinking seems oddly familiar even to those of us steeped in the secular "protestantism" I have just described. For he brings us back to our deeper heritage, as a melody returns us ideally to fond things long past. Perhaps this is one reason, too, why we can describe his thought as "responsible." For unlike the "protestant" intellectual or artist who stands in splendid or sordid isolation from the main, obedient only to personal whims or private demons and finally indifferent to all else, Marías "re-sponds"—in the dual sense of response and responsibility—to the august tra-dition within which he moves.

Meanwhile, our "protestant" intellectuals, artists, and celebrities of the modern age busily work to undermine almost every orthodoxy but their own, yet often seem nonplussed and perplexed when others are willing to take them seriously. One sometimes suspects that they fear ultimate responsibility.

Nothing could be more unlike Marías than what I have just described. He grew to intellectual maturity in a cultural milieu organized and modulated by philosophy, and this sense of social and civic responsibility has always permeated his thought. Furthermore, by assuming responsibility for his time he joins a fraternity of thinkers over the ages who were also responsible for theirs. He always speaks for himself, but in his words we hear the further resonance and measured wisdom of a bimillennial world.

For all these reasons and others yet to come, it seems important for us to hear this responsible thinker and take possession of his message. Yet the process involves more than I have said. All authentic thought becomes a collaborative enterprise as soon as we appropriate it. As Marías puts it: "It must be *relived* and *rethought* . . . that is, incorporated into our own life and viewed from our irrevocable perspective and at the temporal level of each person. This is the only way that free fidelity permits us to take possession of another's creation, which ceases to be alien as it continues to live in other people."[7]

This is why, when taken in the spirit in which it is offered, the philosophy we find in Marías invites our cordial participation. It is a system but an open system. If we truly respond to it, that is, if we are truly responsible, then we cannot remain aloof from its inherent human drama, nor can we remain unaware of its implications for us. It is possible, of course, to ignore these dramatic enticements and simply "study" this philosophy in a detached manner that would document concepts and miss the point. The historical and personal level from which we consider a thinker may remain unmentioned, but if Marías is right it will continue to be implicit in what we say or do not say. For this reason, it seems wiser, or at least more honest, to acknowledge this philosophic "communicability of circumstances," as Marías might call it, and to admit from the first that to tell the story of his method and strategy is also to reveal much about our own situation. The ancient saying proves true here: *De te fabula narratur,* "the story is about you."

In a profound sense, Marías calls us homeward, for his is an invitation to return to our intellectual roots and begin a spiritual and historical reconciliation with our heritage. To our prodigal generation so jealous of its rights, so vigilant of its prerogatives, this involves perhaps the greatest and most often denied right of all: to be original by remaining true to our origins and attentive to our real problems. Over against the rebellious irresponsibility and desertion of the modern "clerks," Marías seeks to inaugurate a new cycle of intellectual authority by the straightforward and courageous strategy of facing the world and giving the most reasonable account possible of what it means and can mean.

This sounds simple. It is, in fact, the most arduous of tasks, for it presupposes the firmest moral and mental resolve to meet reality on its own terms and to resist with equal tenacity the seduction of fad and the shortcuts of expediency. Under these conditions, the *homo theoreticus,* the man of theory that

Marías is, finds that he can take nothing for granted but must account for every step if he is to stay on solid ground.

To most people, as always, this will appear to be either an excessively tedious or thoroughly superfluous task. Why should we be bothered with philosophy when the world is destabilized to the point of calamity? Marías would say, precisely for that reason. The dangerous melodrama of our time needs as perhaps never before the corrective example of a superior philosophic drama. In this sense, true philosophy is for neither the fainthearted nor the fanatical but for those who, as Goethe said, from the darkness aspire to light.

All this may have a noble ring to it, but can any good thing come out of Europe these days, to say nothing of Spain? Not if we can believe the general claims of the international and overwhelmingly dominant network of "canon bashers," minimalist deconstructionists, and sinecured radical critics. Among them, there has existed in recent years a consensus that the subversions of language itself, like a cultural AIDS virus, infect all our mental constructs and inexorably demolish all realms of absolute truths and ideals. A Derrida or Lyotard would likely tell us there is really no defense against its ravages; the best we can hope for is a sort of absolute and absolutely negative irony that frees us from all the great myths of the past even as it restricts us to a life of axiological or solipsistic relativism marked by our inability to remedy our condition. Human history becomes a transparent parody of annihilated mythic constructs. We may call it farce or tragedy, for the terms attach to nothing transcendent but are arbitrary ways of describing the closed circularity of our condition.

This sounds very grim indeed and has either intimidated many otherwise intelligent people into silence or frightened them out of their wits. But we need to remember that although the deconstructionists and their recent protégés have made the case for their minimalist anti-philosophy, they have yet to prove it. Or to look at the matter from another perspective, if language cannot be trusted, why should we believe what the minimalists tell us? After all, they resort to the same linguistic instruments they disparage. Naturally this paradox has not been lost on the minimalist writers themselves, who have responded self-consciously to their exegetical awkwardness, adding tricks and turns of their own either to ease their embarrassment or simply to reassure us of their cleverness. But either way, to understand their dilemma is no reason to condone their strategies or accept their conclusions. We have no business mistaking these maneuvers for intelligence. We need only wait until these tactics fall victim to their own dialectical trap.

Thus this minimalist philosophy, or as I have referred to it, anti-philosophy, collapses in paradox, and this is probably a sure sign that we are in the presence of a falsehood with nothing to recommend it save possibly the playing out of its internal contradictions. In the end these minimalist ideologies, like their existential, deterministic, and relativistic ancestors, limp away defeated from their skirmishes with reality and tell us that further effort is futile. For them, only this certainty remains: reality has lost its virginal enchantment, and we must renounce all our old transcendent hopes. The world does not end for us in a spectacular bang or even a pathetic whimper but fizzles out in a babble of word games.

Or does it? It seems more reasonable to expect that life and the world will go on but deconstructionism, minimalism, neohistoricism, and their assorted variants most likely will not. The wiser course for us appears to be to accept the modest evidence of our eyes and ears and conclude that words can still have meaning, because we continue to understand and live reality through language, that truthful things can still be told (or not), because we see it happen every day, that some things are better than others, because we chart our lives by our preferences, and that responsible philosophy remains a possibility because it remains a historical fact.

This book begins with the premise that Marías reveals a graceful exit from minimalism. His way of thinking has outlasted several hostile ideologies in his own land. Yet candor obliges me to add that his philosophy remains largely unknown, or at least underutilized in most of the world, even in Spain itself. Optimistically, this may mean, as Marías says in his *Razón de la filosofía* (1993), that it represents a future possibility to be attained and utilized; if not a philosophy for the twentieth century, perhaps it will be for the twenty-first. Or to look at things from a gloomier point of view, if we fail to reach the level implied in this thought it could mean that we are condemned to remain naively archaic in our thinking, up to date in fad but behind the times in fact, that is, behind the real innovations and highest levels possible in our age. Perhaps there is truth in both views. In any case, now that we sense a certain weariness in our own prodigal infatuation with the minimalist trivialities that pass for philosophy, perhaps the time is coming when a tolerance for a genuine philosophic enterprise will be reborn in us.

There is really no reason not to enjoy the prospect. In Marías we find a soberer version of the youthful Ortegan exuberance about the world. He would not deny that grim problems customarily beset us. Enormous sadness may figure in our personal fate, yet there is in the genuine philosophic calling a certain vital resiliency that resists mere pessimism. A residue of happiness lies at its core. Although almost everything can be wrong at any given moment, Marías seems to agree with poet Jorge Guillén's verse: "The world is well made."

The philosophy we discover in Marías is the system of this "well-made world." We sense in him a belief, or better a faith, in the ultimate sanity of the world that is translated into a concern for the muted clamor of things to be understood. By developing an anthropology on the "amorous condition" of human life, Marías has expanded on Ortega's early pronouncement that philosophy is "the general science of love."

This chapter bears the title "Introduction to a New Philosophy." Yet initially, history seems to contradict the newness. After all, certain components and premises of Marías's philosophy date from Ortega's thought early in this century, especially his *Meditations on Quixote* (1914). How then can a philosophy be "new" if in one form or another it has existed for several decades? If by "new" we mean recent, then we are in contradiction. But if we mean "unused" or perhaps "underutilized," then the claim makes more sense. The radical truths of life follow their own chronology with only oblique references to calendar reckonings. For it is not a matter of being up to date but of being up to a certain philosophic level. Even though this philosophy has existed as a possibility for many years, it is still new to most and represents a level yet to be reached.

Ortega called this level "the height of the times." Marías adds that it is also "the depth of the times." Both expressions partially summarize their governing philosophic intuition that not only does our life constitute an unmistakable historical and circumstantial profile at any given moment but also that, complemented by its perfective and dramatic future thrust, it can be coaxed into revealing an intelligible structure of an order and magnitude previously unknown in philosophy. For the greater part of the twentieth century Marías has kept watch over this mortal and radical reality, tirelessly pointing out many of its dimensions, applications, and implications. It is a vast work and here I can barely even hint of its extent. For now I will say only that it is the theme of this book and that it seems a story worth telling.

PART I

Marías and his Philosophical Circumstances

1

The Biographical Setting

Julián Marías was born June 17, 1914, in the city of Valladolid in Old Castile, Spain.[1] His father, Julián Marías de Sistac (1870–1949), was Aragonese; his mother, María Aguilera Pineda (1874–1938), Andalusian. Three sons were born to the family: Pablo (1907–1910), Adolfo (1911–1930), and Julián.

A precocious child, Marías taught himself to read and by age seven had learned a considerable amount of French by leafing through his father's catalog of arms. (Ortega y Gasset once called Marías the most intelligent man ever born in Valladolid.)

In 1919, his family settled in Madrid, where eventually Marías began his studies at the Institute of Cardinal Cisneros, soon displaying an especial affinity for the sciences: mathematics, physics, and chemistry. He also excelled in Latin and geography. Philosophy would come later. School was relatively easy for him, which gave him time to read voraciously, explore the streets of Madrid, and indulge his life-long habit of collecting books.

Following an early graduation from the Institute, at seventeen he enrolled in the University of Madrid in both the Faculty of Sciences and the School of Philosophy and Letters, but by 1932 he yielded to his philosophic urgings and decided to continue only in Philosophy and Letters.

The University of Madrid had entered its most brilliant phase, and Marías flourished under illustrious professors: Manuel García Morente, José Gaos, Xavier Zubiri, and, above all, José Ortega y Gasset. It may be that Marías shares Ortega y Gasset's conviction that in normal times universities are the most reliable barometer of the social and intellectual well-being of countries. In any case, he has never become reconciled to the decline of the University of Madrid during the Franco regime. In 1936 when he received his baccalaureate, it seemed only natural that in time he would join his mentors as a colleague and help carry on the twentieth-century Spanish renaissance.

It was not to be. Not long after his graduation the Civil War broke out and he joined the Army of the Republic. Though by his own definition and in the context of the time a liberal and a Republican, Marías recognized the shortcomings of the Republic and considered the war itself to be a colossal historical blunder that could have been prevented. He noted after the war that probably neither side deserved to win, but he inclined to the Republic because of its legitimate claims to political authority.

To Marías's great relief, his military activities, minimal as such, did not cause anyone's death. One of his assignments consisted of broadcasting government releases in French. His real hope and purpose, which he shared with such high-minded Spaniards as Julián Besteiro, former president of the *Cortes* (Parliament), was to help bring an end to the fratricidal slaughter and prepare both sides for a national reconciliation.

After the Republican defeat in 1939, Marías experienced one of the most precarious times of his life. Falsely denounced by a former friend, he was imprisoned from May until August 1939. Given a provisional release, he took stock of his remaining options: "I could not be a professor, a deep and undeniable calling, in the official Spanish institutions. I could perhaps write essays in the few journals that could accept a person in my situation. Newspapers were inaccessible to me and remained so for a dozen years, until 1951. What was left? My philosophic vocation was imperative, and no less so was my calling to be a writer. The only authentic recourse was to write books of philosophy."[2]

But if much had been taken from Marías, much remained. To begin with, during those fateful and difficult years his religious faith never wavered. And his intellectual calling persisted even though official doors were closed to him, as he had foreseen. It helped immensely that a handful of friends stood by him. Most of all, he refused to give up and sink into rancorous recrimination and indulgent self-pity. As he remarked later, if he could not do what he wanted he would do what he could. This attitude has always been one of his most characteristic traits.

He made other fundamental decisions as well: he would stay in Spain and in whatever honorable ways open to him he would set about to earn a living. And there was still one more life-altering move for him to make: on August 14, 1941, he married Dolores Franco, his college classmate. Five sons were born of the marriage: Julián (Julianín) (deceased in 1949), Miguel, Fernando, Javier, and Alvaro.

Before the Holy Sepulchre, which he visited in 1933 on a student cruise of the Mediterranean, Marías had asked in a simple prayer that he be allowed to live ". . . an intense life . . . full of Christian meaning." To judge by what he has done, the request was granted, for indeed his has been an incredibly intense life of work and faith. His personal motto reveals his attitude: "Por mi que no quede," loosely equivalent to "I'll do my part."

His part was to be a major force in the continuing intellectual renaissance of twentieth-century Spain. In May 1939, shortly before his imprisonment, Marías received a letter from Ortega, at the time exiled and living in

Lisbon. In it, Ortega proposed the rebuilding of Spain by first recapturing the classic serenity known as *gravedad española,* which had so astonished Europeans in the sixteenth century. On this moral and psychological foundation, Ortega urged, Spain and the private lives of Spaniards must be restructured. Marías's reaction was characteristic: "I took his advice seriously: to rebuild Spain and my own life."[3]

His first book, *Historia de la filosofía* [History of Philosophy] (1941), served both purposes. Not only was it an early sign that intellectual Spain had survived the war but also a powerful demonstration of his own capabilities. His *Miguel de Unamuno* (published in 1943 but written earlier) was among the first of many efforts he would make to save the legacy of the Generation of 1898. This work was followed by *Introducción a la filosofía* [Introduction to Philosophy] (1947). In 1948, he joined Ortega in the founding of the Institute of the Humanities in Madrid. His *Generations: A Historical Method* (1949) was based on one of the courses he offered.

In 1951, he was allowed to receive his doctorate. That same year, he was invited to Lima, Peru, and almost simultaneously to the United States, as Visiting Professor at Wellesley College. He accepted both invitations. These trips were to be the first of many to the Americas as visiting professor and lecturer in such universities as Harvard, Yale, Wellesley, Indiana, Oklahoma, UCLA, the University of Puerto Rico, and others too numerous to name.

His writing continued apace: *Idea de la metafísica* [Idea of Metaphysics] and *La estructura social* (translated as *The Structure of Society*), both in 1955. In 1956, he published *Los Estados Unidos en escorzo* [The United States in Perspective], and in 1960, *Ortega I. Circunstancia y vocación* [Ortega: Circumstance and Vocation]. *Imagen de la India* [Image of India] (1961), *Meditaciones sobre la sociedad española* [Meditations on Spanish Society] (1966), *Consideración de Cataluña* [Consideration of Catalonia] (1966), *Nuestra Andalucía* [Our Andalusia] (1966), *Análisis de los Estados Unidos* [Analysis of the United States] (1968), and *Israel: una resurrección* [Israel: A Resurrection] (1968), preceded the watershed work *Antropología metafísica* [Metaphysical Anthropology] (1970). This work, which Marías referred to at the time as his "most personal book," is undoubtedly one of his most original contributions to philosophy. Building on Ortegan and Heideggerian foundations, Marías launched into the unexplored area of human reality he called the "empirical structure of life."

The end of the Franco era prompted his *La España real* [Real Spain] (1976), the first of a trilogy of best-selling works that included *La devolución de España* [Spain Returned] (1977) and *España en nuestras manos* [Spain in our Hands] (1978). In 1977, he was appointed senator to the *Cortes* by King Juan Carlos, to assist in drafting a new Spanish constitution.

During all these years, he also wrote countless essays and articles in newspapers and journals and collected many prestigious awards (Fastenrath Prize, John F. Kennedy Prize, Juan Palomo Prize, Gulbenkian Essay Award, Ramón Godó Lallana Prize for Journalism, the León Felipe Prize, among others). In 1964, he was elected to the Royal Spanish Academy. His two-volume work *Visto y no visto* [Seen and Unseen] (1970), is an incomplete compilation of his film reviews.

Following the death of his wife in December 1977, Marías paused in certain projects for nearly two years as he reassessed his life. While he honored other "transpersonal" commitments—his senatorial duties, essays, editorial work, the Royal Academy, lectures, etc.—he suspended more personal writings.

Then, in 1979, he began again with *Problemas del cristianismo* [Problems of Christianity]. On what we will call his "second voyage" the intensity he asked for in his youth reappears but internalized in a deeper way and at the same time raised to a higher power. He describes the experience: "Strictly speaking, when I was truly able to write again I had to do so from my deepest inner levels, not from the peripheral zones of my being but from the very core after I had come to a final accounting with myself. I can say that after it became possible for me to write again in recent years I became more profoundly a writer than I had ever been before."[4]

The results of his efforts seem humanly close to the impossible: after decades of exceptional production and in what for most people are declining years, many of his best works started to pour forth: *La mujer en el siglo XX* [Woman in the Twentieth Century] (1980); *Ortega. Las trayectorias* [Ortega. The Trajectories] (1983); *España inteligible* (translated as *Understanding Spain*) (1985); *La mujer y su sombra* [Woman and her Shadow] (1986); *La felicidad humana* [Human Happiness] (1987); the three volumes of *Una vida presente. Memorias* [A Present Life. Memoirs] (1988–89); *Cervantes clave española* [Cervantes, A Spanish Key] (1990); *La educación sentimental* [The Education of Sentiment] (1992); *Razón de la filosofía* [The Reason of Philosophy] (1993), *Mapa del mundo personal* [Map of the Personal World] (1993), and *Tratado de lo mejor* [Treatise on the Best] (1995). And lest one think this is all, there are shorter works as well: *Breve tratado de la ilusión* [Brief Treatise on *Ilusión*] (1984), *Cara y cruz de la electrónica* [Heads and Tails of Electronics] (1985), uncounted essays yet to be collected, and other writings still flowing from his pen.

Which brings us up to date and to the question, what now for Marías? The ancient Greeks believed, very sensibly it seems to me, that no one's biography could be considered definitive during the life of that person. In the case of Marías the point needs to be taken as something more than a classic caveat. His opponents have been eager to dismiss him since his youth, and even his most devoted friends have been amazed by the surge of productivity of his "second voyage." Probably this creative energy is the best sign that Marías keeps close company with the truth. And this leaves a wide margin for surprises. For as C. S. Lewis once noted, falsehood and those who incline to it follow drearily predictable patterns, while truth, far from limiting us, confers a marvelous freedom of style.

In our time there is a strange haste, perhaps not unmixed with a secret rancor, to declare people finished and their life story over. Marías himself has always resisted the urge and now he stands as good proof that there is wisdom in this opposition. So let us decline to make final pronouncements on what is not final and in a gesture of cordiality and respect give Marías the freedom to tell at his own pace and in his inimitable way the future chapters of his life.

2

CIRCUMSTANCE AND VOCATION

The Philosophical Setting

In his *The Tragic Sense of Life* (1913), Unamuno asked, is truth to be lived or to be understood? For he saw reason and life as being antithetical to each other. To which Ortega y Gasset soon answered, in his *Meditations on Quixote* (1914), that it is to be understood by living, for life in the Ortegan sense was reason in its highest and most clarifying mode. Naturally, this did not settle the matter at hand; the plot of this philosophic crisis of reason was to thicken and unfold for decades to come in Spanish philosophy, just as it had been forming for many years in the works of other thinkers such as Kierkegaard, Nietzsche, James, Bergson, Dilthey, and Spengler.

Although as far as we know, Ortega made no direct references to *The Tragic Sense of Life,* there is reason to believe that its publication alarmed him and roused him to respond. Long displeased with the direction Unamuno had taken and already dissatisfied with his own philosophic grounding, by 1913 Ortega seemed to think he had no choice but to wrest the notions of life and reason away from the irrationalists on the one hand and the proponents of *Lebensphilosophie* on the other so as to counteract what he took to be their irresponsible posturings and dubious premises.[1] And there was yet a third challenge: what Ortega considered to be the defective phenomenology in Husserl's *Ideen zu einer reinen Phänomenologie und phänomenologischen Philosophie* [Ideas for a True Phenomenology and Phenomenological Philosophy], which appeared the same year as *The Tragic Sense of Life* (1913).

As for Unamuno, *The Tragic Sense of Life* would prove to be his definitive philosophic statement. By 1912–14, his anti-rational philosophy had peaked and he would have little of substantive to add to his arguments. Thereafter he seemed content to rehash his arguments, turning to fictional and poetic profit the glaring antinomies of his ideology, which he claimed were the main features of the human condition.[2]

On the other hand, whereas *Meditations on Quixote* was Ortega's first mature statement of his philosophy, it was by no means his final or definitive posture. As Marías puts it, "In 1914–16 Ortega was in possession of the nucleus of his philosophy. Its expansion, extension, and articulation would occupy the rest of his life, some forty years of creative effort."[3]

This was the philosophical setting into which Julián Marías was born in 1914 as a member of the "Generation of 1916."[4] In time, he would join in the Ortegan enterprise of overcoming the crisis of reason that stimulated the debate between Ortega and Unamuno. And like Ortega, he would devote his life to exploring and fleshing out this new way of understanding reality, a process which necessarily meant surpassing Ortega's own positions in several instances. He would agree with Ortega's contention that in its reduction to rationalism the modern world had been built on a fertile and perhaps necessary error. And while respecting Unamuno, he would oppose the Unamunean notion that pure reason could only be counteracted with pure irrationality. From the first, he subscribed to the Ortegan premise that reason is a form and function of life. As a modern or, better, postmodern imperative this meant in exegetical and methodological terms that the Cartesian era of pure reason must give way to an unnamed age of vital and historical reason. From his standpoint, far from representing a relapse into primitive forms of reasoning, vital reason is a step beyond both biological spontaneity and rationalism. For it means that life, which until now was regarded as a bare fact and accident of the cosmos, henceforth becomes a principle and the basis of right.[5]

For a brief historical moment in 1911–12, Husserlian phenemenology seemed to be a way of transcending the rational crisis and surpassing the neo-Kantianism of Germany and the positivism that predominated in the rest of Europe. Ortega says of himself and his classmates at Marburg: ". . . phenomenology for us was not a philosophy: it was . . . a stroke of good fortune."[6] But then he goes on to say within the same context that no sooner had he discovered phenomenology than he abandoned it.

The problem for Ortega, which led to the radical intuition on which his philosophy came to be based, was that Husserl's celebrated *epoche* called for the suspension of the very reality to which his method led him, leaving only the *Erlebnis,* or so-called pure experience, and consciousness. Ortega considered this maneuver to be an obvious tactical mistake: "As I create for myself the illusion that I *abandon* my position of my former 'primary consciousness' I merely place in its stead a new and fabricated reality: 'suspended consciousness', one that has been anesthetized."[7] For Ortega it was a question of going in precisely the other direction: instead of suspending the discovered reality, it was necessary to recognize it for what it truly was phenomenologically: a living person who searches for pure reality, for the given: ". . . in summary, *life* in its uncoercible and insuperable spontaneity and ingenuity."[8]

The persistent error of modern philosophy, which Husserl came close to transcending only to fall back into Cartesianism, had been to insist on discovering reality according to the dictates of rational thought. Descartes's *cogito* ("I think, therefore I am") was the prototype that would resonate in one tonality or another throughout all the rational approaches to being. But Ortega argued that if phenomenology is honest with itself, it must acknowledge that the reality of life *precedes* one's thought about it, and this means that the terms of philosophy must be inverted. Life is not a secondary reality discovered subsequently as a function of rational instrumentality but the primary or "radical" reality in which in one way or another all others appear or are "rooted," even those that absolutely transcend it, for instance, God. In other words, I live and therefore think, act, love, suffer, enjoy, etc., and all other realities occur to me as I live. Marías summarizes: "In point of fact, things inevitably appear *in life*. My life is the area or ambit in which I encounter all things, including myself as a man, as a reality rooted in the radical reality of my life."[9]

But for all its limitless radicality as the prime reality, the personal, physical life we live reveals itself to be limited and mortal. We are restricted in location and time, to say nothing of our physical and sexuate nature. Yet this very limitation points to an access to reality. Hitherto, rationalistic philosophy had always tried to reach a point of view apart from place, time, history, and what it saw as the "accidents" or "properties" of personhood. Cartesian rationalism essentially denies historical increments to knowledge. Through reason, Adam supposedly had the same access to reality as we do. But the discovery of radical reality meant that now it had to perceive the world from a localized standpoint in history, that is, from a personal perspective. Conversely, the false perspective is the one that claims impartiality, that is, a denial of its part in any specific time and place. And as Ortega argued in consequence, the most reasonable conclusion is that perspective is a peculiar component of reality.[10] From this human perspective, the only one we have access to, reality is never merely "there." It is, instead, reality as lived and interpreted in a certain way, and this "wayness" is inherent and inescapable, *as far as human life is concerned*. For interpretation is the real manifestation, the functional meaning, of perspectivistic reality.

To illustrate, a bolt of lightning and clap of thunder are usually interpreted by modern people to be "natural phenomena." But to other cultures they may be taken as certain evidence of divine wrath. In other words, our understanding of such phenomena comes not primarily from the events themselves but from history, from inherited, generic interpretations. Usually we understand things in the ways we have been taught to understand them. Louis J. Halle was right when he said that the nominal is more real to us than the real itself.

The Limits of Objectivism

Perhaps the most persistent fallacy of rationalistic thought has been to assume that such interpretations could simply be set aside in favor of an "objective" explanation which was touted as the "real truth." It would be more jective" explanation which was touted as the "real truth." It would be more correct to say with greater modesty that the objective perspective is *one* aspect of truth without warrant to discredit others. The human perspective that recognizes itself as such also acknowledges the justification of other perspectives (without necessarily falling into the fallacy of subscribing to them). In this way it can be said, as Marías has stated on occasion, that no one interpretation alone is reality but that all perspectives partake of the real. The objective bias causes us to discredit all other perspectives, yet the objective viewpoint itself fares no better from other standpoints that manifest their own justification and seeming invulnerability. It is important to remember that no particular viewpoint enjoys privileged unassailability on its own merits. Its validity relates ultimately to the historical dialectic that made it possible and necessary at a given time and place. As such, it is the product of reason itself, not necessarily the rationalistic reason that at a moment of history also was justified, but the inclusive, free-ranging reason of human life. The historical accumulation of these viewpoints, the interpretative solutions to life problems, is what we call culture. In this sense, rationalism is but another in the series of historical perspectives, valid certainly, but by that same mark unauthorized to claim absoluteness. We could say that rationalism itself is a discovery made through the instrumentality of "vital reason." Ortega believed that by 1900 the modernity based on Cartesian rationalism and its alter ego relativism was moribund, and that a new era, to be dominated by vital reason, was in the making. When he spoke of the "theme of our time," he had in mind nothing less than modernity transcended. Having formulated the nucleus of his own philosophy with this superior rationality as its methodological centerpiece, Ortega could describe himself in 1916 as *nada moderno y muy siglo XX* ("not at all modern and very much twentieth-century.")[11]

This does not mean, as the relativists might claim, that each perspective is arbitrary, nor that it is simply a function of my location. Instead, reality itself, *as we know it and insofar as it is humanly knowable,* relates and is thus "relative" to each life point of view. And what each discovers is absolutely true as far as it goes. Not that all perspectives are intellectually equal. Obviously, some are extremely limited, but it is important to acknowledge their justification, that is, to understand the human circumstances to which they correspond.

Returning to the theme of personal life, the life of each person, we can say now that it offers a view and gives a reason, a true view and a real reason, of perspectivistic reality. It is a limited view with universal significance, and far from being a distortion of reality, as the old rationalists might claim, the perspective of life is the only effective human way of realizing the organization of the world. And as Ortega boldly puts it, "Our truth is also truth for God."

Radical Reality and Vital Reason

Ortega discovered that life is the radical reality capable of rendering the only authentic human verdict on the world. Before a mystery, a need, a project, that is, in the relationship of things to life, it assumes an explicative mode that we identify in the philosophy of Ortega and Marías as *vital reason,* which in its execution becomes, as we shall see, narrative, dramatic, and historical.

The primary and perhaps clearest application of vital reason is to human life itself. It begins with Ortega's early injunction: in order to understand anything human we must tell a story. Consider three "realities": a circle, a tiger, and the man called Marías. In order to comprehend a circle, a definition and perhaps a diagram will suffice. A tiger requires a zoological classification and a description of its attributes and habitat. But to understand the human person "Marías" we must switch modes, from "what" to "who." For human life is not a thing, not even an animate, thinking, or spiritual thing, but a "personal" reality of an entirely different order and level, a truth that ordinary language has recognized for thousands of years. Human life consists of executive, futuristic doing and deeds with an aim or project of humanizing and personalizing circumstance so as to convert it into "my world" and thereby realize "my life." As Marías himself puts it, "Human life is strictly personal, not a *what* but a *who,* a projective, or as I call it a *future-tending (futurizo),* task. As such, it is at once real and unreal. It is a drama, that which I do with things in order to be who I strive to be."[12] This means that in order to understand "Marías" we must tell "who" (not "what") he is, and this involves a personal name and an account of what he has done—and tried to do. We will relate that he was born in a particular place and time, that he entered into certain personal relationships (which alerts us to yet other aspects of life beyond the "intrinsic theory"), that specific things happened to him. In other words, his human reality is primarily *biographical* and *historical* rather than *biological.* If we remove his name and biographical data and describe him as a mammalian animal with a certain zoological pedigree we may be factually correct but still remote from the person, the man, we set out to know. This does not mean that biology and other forms of knowledge may not function sub*sequently* as adjuncts to the "story" we are telling, only that they cannot usurp and replace it.

However, it should be noted in passing that the interpretative range of these three realities cannot be restricted to the suggested interpretations. A circle may also be, in other cultural circumstances, a religious symbol, a covert communication, a political emblem, an aesthetic possibility, a geometric design, a psychological hint, etc. Just as a tiger may appear to a shaman as a symbol of power, or to a stockman as a menace to cattle, or to environmentalists as an endangered species, or as combinations of these and other possibilities. As for the man Marías, he may appear as friend or foe, as someone enlightened or deluded, or as a help or hindrance in our pathway, to mention only a few possible interpretations. In other words, his biography "communicates" with ours and appears in the light of who we are—or are not. To put it another way, in telling his story we also reveal something of our own. This is the primary reason why we cannot describe philosophy as Marías understands it without "doing" philosophy to some degree ourselves.

Orteganism as a System

Can this way of thinking be understood as a "philosophic system"? If by this term we mean a textual corpus and a progression of doctrines, the answer would probably be no in the case of Ortega. On the other hand, Marías offers a much more complete textual compilation of Ortegan themes. Unlike Ortega, who for all his brilliance customarily abandoned themes and books before they were finished, Marías has the talent for writing books and completing tasks that his mentor lacked.

But in either case, Marías would argue that to understand "system" in this way is to miss the point entirely. Simply put, both Ortega and Marías understand that because life itself is systematic, *therefore* so is philosophy. The case is compelling, yet it must be admitted that the traditional concept of philosophic system as an imposed or textual construct cannot be ignored, especially in view of the tenacity with which the Ortegan model has been resisted or rejected. However, we ought to note that even though Marías is fully in agreement with Ortega on this point, his own work satisfies both sets of criteria. As Juan López-Morillas astutely notes: "We find therefore in this work the conceptual unity that is indispensable in philosophy. Yet it would be a serious mistake to suppose that by proving its internal cohesion one would obtain an adequate basis for proceeding to a critical consideration of his work. To the conceptual unity must be added necessarily the biographical unity. For what sets the philosophy of Marías apart is the fact that, in addition to being conceptual system it is also temporalized, vitalized thought: in a word, biography."[13]

This new understanding of system is one reason why it is a mistake to seek the sources of Ortega's philosophy in Germany, even though he was the first to acknowledge his debts to Germanic culture. As Ernst Robert Curtius states: "Ortega is something totally different from a mere disciple and offshoot or follower of German philosophy. From Leibniz to Husserl, from Kant to Scheler, Ortega has received it [German philosophy] as a stimulus, and I use the term 'stimulus' in a physiological sense. The stimulus causes a reaction, a response by the organic system. Through the encounter with the German intellectual world Ortega's thought has come into its own."[14]

For similar reasons, Marías's philosophy cannot be "reduced" to Ortega, even though his loyalty to Ortega is beyond question. Authentic philosophy is always a personal matter; it arises primarily not from isolated ideas (although naturally it makes use of them as it does other elements), but ultimately from the circumstantial tensions, aspirations, and restrictions of private human life. The adjective "authentic" is a necessary reminder of its real origin, for there is always a temptation to convert philosophy into an abstract discipline or history of ideas (hence the notion of *philosophia perennis,* or "perennial philosophy"), which almost invariably has preceded its demise. Because of this customary oversight it is often forgotten that Marías forged his personal philosophy on his own, in isolation from Ortega himself, long after the latter had ceased to be his teacher. In 1960, he wrote: "In those eight years in which I neither saw Ortega nor received any guidance from him, when I remained alone with his books, class notes, and memories and had to mobilize my personal thought, I made the progressive discovery of the truth and richness of Ortegan thought. . . . Each day I felt myself more deeply installed, at a different level, in a philosophy that had been rethought, relived, and projected in directions that my own calling took me."[15]

In comparison to Ortega's formative years, Marías's own circumstances were approximately reversed. Ortega found in Marburg a dramatic sense of philosophy. In the German university, he discovered tradition, trappings, and teachers—everything *except* philosophy itself, that is, a philosophy he could sink his teeth into, ingest, and live by.

On the other hand, Marías found in Ortega (and to a lesser degree in his other teachers) a livable doctrine but one he had to digest and appropriate on his own. Marías was a faithful disciple, but because of circumstances, his was a loyalty forged at a distance and in complete independence. This in no way lessened his admiration and friendship for his mentor, but it did allow him to retain a certain vital objectivity and introspective awareness about his relationship to Ortega.

It is interesting to speculate on what a closer association would have brought about. Perhaps it would have pulled Marías too near Ortega's gravitational tug; his own perspective might have been warped. It has not been emphasized enough that Marías was both disciple *and* friend to Ortega. And in order to be a true friend he had to retain his own standpoint, develop his own style, and set his own course. Unless I am mistaken, this is the sense in which Ortega came to refer to "our philosophy," that is, a doctrine in which both thinkers worked and acted independently but which also linked them in a deep and personal way. The loyalty of Marías to Ortega stands as a splendid example of human integrity and generosity, and to understand it fully is to catch a glimpse of the moral underpinnings of Marías's personal attitudes and philosophical orientation.

This personal centering is necessary if we are to understand the real genesis of thought. Only when philosophy is understood as an academic discipline rather than a personal vocational commitment can it be thought of in terms of influences, borrowings, or occasional pilferings. Its real nature becomes clearer if we compare it analogously to love and religious faith, two other radical forms of human calling. Neither pure love nor real faith can be learned or taught (though we can point to examples and perhaps stir an inchoate calling); much less can they be borrowed or stolen. Similarly, philosophy involves a personal calling, and even though it may be influenced, shaped, or even debilitated to varying degrees by subsequent factors of circumstance and opportunity, without such a vocation deeply and freely accepted it cannot truly exist. At the most fundamental level, it is a function not of what one knows or reads but of who one is, or as Unamuno would probably say, who one tries to be. Marías would argue that it is a part of the same life drama it describes. In this sense—and it is an enormous one—it is a self-conscious and autobiographical endeavor.

For Marías, then, his circumstance and calling pointed him to Ortega. Of these he notes: "There are two radical ingredients in human life that are not the object of choice. The first is *circumstance;* the second is *vocation.*"[16] We are born into a set of latent historical and individual circumstances with an inert center and periphery defined by reference to the "I" that each person is. (We are speaking of what Marías will call the "general" or "intrinsic" theory of life, which begins not as a theory at all but an acknowledgment of empirical reality, that is, the everyday phenomenological evidence of our eyes and experience.) This is generally equivalent to the scientific meaning of "environment" perhaps, but at a remove from the human meaning of circumstance as Marías understands it.

For this circumstance becomes a world, my world, in the dialogue between my circumstance and me. My circumstance is therefore not merely the place wherein I am located, nor is it simply a network of things, potential or realized. Instead, it is a "setting" in much the same way in which we use the term in literature. And this means that it corresponds to a plot or argument of life. It is where we do things and where things happen to us. This is what Ortega meant when he described life as a poetic task and stated that we are the novelists of ourselves. My circumstance becomes my world whenever I impose on it my personal series of projects, desires, efforts, and longings, in a word my "plot," that is, the plan of life I try to place in execution so as to become myself. A fundamental fidelity is involved if I am authentic: only by being myself can I become myself.

System as Narrative

This *logos* of life, or better, the *logos* of which living consists, converts our cosmic circumstance into human significance which is understandable as a narrative, or more formally, as narrative reason. Marías accepts and expands on the Ortegan argument that life must be understood biographically. Life becomes a twice-told tale, first in the living, then in the recounting that releases its significance for others—and me—to understand. In this en-livening and narrative sense there is no unalterable continuity of circumstance. The recounted truth of each generation, and, strictly speaking, of each person, becomes, as Ortega pointed out, the recipes and formulas of the next, useful perhaps but prone to congeal into dogma. For the circumstantial setting derives its significance not from the continuity of physical externals or even psychic internal states, but from the "plot" that defines and lends structure to individual human life. This is another way of saying that, far from being a mere cosmic fact, human life is a historical reality. Indeed, as Ortega argued, history as the story of why human reality is as it happens to be must be understood as the system of human life—and in an extended but necessary sense, as the system of philosophy.

There are several examples of this narrative insight in Ortega, most notably the "forest" (*bosque*) in *Meditations on Quixote* (1914), *Veinte años de caza mayor* (1942), and *Aventuras del Capitán Alonso de Contreras* (1943). But perhaps the most plot-like is a short essay written in 1924 and published in Volume V of *El Espectador.*[17] It begins with a bit of disconcerting news: "Soledad," the lady with whom the narrator is in love, has left Madrid. And in her absence he finds the city curiously changed and diminished. Although physically and geographically the city seems the same, its organizing principle in the person of Soledad has vanished. His eyes tell him it is the same, but his heart knows differently. For the narrator realizes how his love for Soledad flowed out over the city, touching and transforming even the remotest things, lending them story and speculation in relation to her in a network of significances.

What does this mean? to begin with, what we said before: that realities reveal their human significance only within a circumstantial setting, that is, within the plot, or argument, of my life. In the human sense there is no city in itself, just as there was no forest in itself in *Meditations on Quixote,* as the simple-minded and the realist might contend. On the other hand, neither the city nor the forest exists "in me" (in my mind), as the idealists used to argue.

But there is an important difference between the forest and the city, even though both contain a narrative reference to my life. The forest of the *Meditations* was a natural reality and therefore independent of me, even though as such the sum of my possible deeds or actions that I could take in relationship to it. In other words, the vital being of the forest consisted of being my life possibilities. This is one of the great ontological discoveries by Ortega: realities that consist of being possibilities—for themselves and me through me.

In the case of the city, Ortega takes a step beyond his position of 1914. To begin with, far from being a natural reality, the city is intrinsically human;

it was made by men for mankind. Therefore, the reference to human acts is not merely possible or potential but immediate and essential. In reality, this is not just any city—as the forest was potentially any forest—but a specific city: Madrid. Nor are we dealing with generic life, as in the case of *Meditations,* but with a particular man defined by his love of Soledad, that is, by a particular and irreplaceable woman.

In other words, we have transcended the descriptive account of his earlier *Meditations* and entered into a narrative of living persons who do things within a specific human circumstance and in the pursuit of certain aims that make logical sense to us. This could be a portion of a novel; in fact, it is a part of a theory that because of the reality it deals with—the specifically human—can only be treated narratively.

Here, circumstantial setting appears for perhaps the first time with much of the rigor that it will acquire in Marías's work. It is important to show that as a narrative theory it was not initially conceived extemporaneously and abstractly in essential indifference to its own internal demands and structures, but that it, too, assumes a narrative structure and is, in fact, an example of obedience to its own premises. As Marías himself puts it, "The 'dramatization' of this passage is the theoretically adequate form of 'enlivenment' of the doctrine."[18]

Let us probe deeper into the theory. I said earlier that we are dealing with the life of a particular man defined by his love of Soledad. This must be understood in both a theoretical and dynamic way. For Soledad is not simply another element in the circumstantial hierarchy of his life, but the one reality that gives meaningful structure to all the others. Even the supposedly "objective" topographical and spatial structure of the city depends on her. Her attraction acts as an organizing magnetic field for the lover so that the physical elements of the city assume an order according to his vital disposition and situation at each moment.

The realist would object that this reordering is purely psychic or psychological and that in an ancient city like Toledo or Venice, the physical elements have scarcely changed over the centuries. This may be true, but it is not the point and certainly not the story to be told. For it would be fair to say that the projects of the modern citizens of Toledo or Venice have little in common with those of imperial Spain or the Venice of the Doges. This means that the order of these enduring and static elements has varied repeatedly, and therefore that the structure referred to as Toledo or Venice has obeyed a historic cycle of successive changes. To overlook the human origins of this structural modification is to misread the very meaning of circumstantial reality.

The point is that Soledad—or her equivalent in another life—does not function simply as another element in "my" circumstance. Bear in mind that even the remotest things are transfigured or magnetized by her presence. But as we shall see, this is precisely the organizing function of the "I" that allows my circumstance to assume its circular stance, that is *circum me,* about me. In a formal sense, circumstance is the object and aim of my projects, and it immediately divides them into possible and impossible categories. On the other hand, I allow circumstance to be itself, that is, I allow its latent portions to come to the foreground as actualized reality or I leave them unrealized through my indifference to them. Circumstance, therefore, is not simply an addendum to my life, nor am I merely a creature of physical milieu, as the nineteenth-century naturalistic determinists like Bernard or Zola thought. In any case, I cannot be I without it and it is not circumstance without me. Circumstance and I need each other in order to be ourselves. The world and I have a mutual dependency, and this means, as Marías notes, that any substantial variation of my circumstance—corporality, soul, country, time, family, friends, geography, society, etc.—would bring about an alteration of my reality. For according to Ortega's celebrated *cogito* in *Meditations on Quixote:* "I am I and my circumstance."

But this circumstantial dialogue, the projection of my aims on a world that responds with varying degrees of resistance or complicity, also creates in us a sense of confronting or facing the world. As Ortega would say in his *Vitalidad, alma, espíritu:* "We feel ourselves to be individuals thanks to this mysterious eccentricity of our souls. Because in the face of nature and spirit, soul is this: eccentric life." [19]

Here lies the root of isolation and weariness of life. There comes a moment when we tire of the eccentric duality of our existence. We long to be raptured out of ourselves, to find repose from our consuming circumstantial task. Is it possible? In an absolute sense the answer may be no, yet at different levels of our being religious faith and human love offer remedies. For example, says Ortega, in love we may transfer our center of gravity to another soul and virtually or vicariously overcome the eccentricity of our life.

Let us take time to anticipate a question that is also an objection. Is this philosophy? Does love have anything to do with the perennial themes we have come to associate with philosophic thought? It does when we consider that it is a matter of examining the actual structure of life and of identifying the dynamic features that give it narrative significance. With other aims in mind, Ortega once defined philosophy as "the general science of love." But it remained for Marías to discover the human and therefore philosophic implications of love in relation to the real structure of life.

In his theories on love, Ortega always insisted on the notion of "amorous fusion," which even though not evident in the passage referred to *(Geometría sentimental),* indeed appears as a theme of his *Estudios sobre el amor.* While he treated the topic of woman with unwavering enthusiasm, he subscribed to Dante's belief that the feminine function is essentially normative.[20] The supreme mission of woman, he tells us, is ". . . to demand perfection of man."[21] When woman is purely woman, that is, when her life transcends the feminine precipitates of mother, wife, daughter, or sister, she serves as the "concrete ideal" of man.

For his part, Marías faults Ortega for failing to see the plot-like nature of love: "It would be sufficient to take seriously the idea of project and follow it to its ultimate consequences when an individual life is indissolubly linked to another also in its full individuality. This would require the full use of *vital reason.* But this is precisely the great philosophic discovery of Ortega: the theory that is constituted as such only in its exercise, in its function of *giving a reason* for diverse realities . . ."[22]

As Marías sees it, without this plot-like structure the Ortegan theories of love suffer from a certain superficiality. Ortega insisted on the element of attention in love, but in the view of Marías, much more is demanded. It remains doubtful whether women or men reveal themselves fully in mere flirtation, as Ortega claimed, and most certainly it is not the proper setting for the *fondo insorbornable,* the "incorruptible depths" which Ortega insisted on when he was more serious about the reality of life.

In later works, among them *Antropología metafísica* [1970], Marías would go on beyond Ortega to develop a theory of love as our deep calling, as vocation in the most primary sense.[23] He begins by rejecting the classic notion of "fusion" with the beloved. The beloved woman—Soledad or her equivalent—is always a separate person. Her being is not merged with mine. In fact, I would not change her for the world, else my hopes of escaping from my circumstantial isolation would be dashed. Far from being absorbed into my life, "Soledad" lifts me out of my bleakness by transfiguring my world.

How does this occur? Marías discovers that when a man and woman love each other there occurs a special case of what he calls the "communicability of circumstances": "Thanks to this communicability, I find other lives in my circumstance that are not wholly alien to me, since their circumstances 'communicate' with mine, and I have access to them not only as 'things' but as lives. This is the basis of the possibility of love, of friendship, and all relations that are characteristically human—that is, personal."[24]

We are getting a bit ahead of our story. Marías is now moving into an area of philosophy, what he calls the "empirical structure of life," that is inherently Ortegan yet not to be found in Ortega's own writings. Here, love becomes a case of reciprocal reference and fulfillment. The beloved person becomes my life project. To put it another way, as I consider my life and the life project of which my life consists, I find myself to be inexorably involved with my beloved. However, this does not mean simply that I project myself *toward* her, but that I project myself *with* her through life. And therefore, without her I am not really myself. Being in love means that my life undergoes an ontological shift. I become a changed person. But changed to what or whom? Any lover can tell you: to the person I was meant to be. Later we shall explore this in more detail.[25]

Two other preliminary points need to be restated, always reserving the possibility of returning to them later. The first is that even though the beloved reorders my circumstantial world she cannot be thought of as a circumstantial element. Instead, she is included in the foundational project of self-realization that I attempt to impose on my circumstance. And second, she is a part of my becoming myself by being myself. In other words, she constitutes my calling to be myself.

Further Implications

Marías considers certain final implications of "Soledad's absence" that will appear later in his philosophy of "empirical structure." What happens when she does not merely depart for another city but perhaps for the next world and the next life? The emptiness of the Madrid she has abandoned is transferred to the whole world. What happens to life, to the projective nature of living and to the contents of my projects when their reason for being no longer exists? There are without doubt personal echoes from Marías's own experience in his questions about death, but they are intrinsic also in his anthropological analysis of human life. Unamuno treated the theme of death because of personal predilection, while Ortega avoided the topic by choice. For Marías, it was to be a matter of doctrinal necessity because it was first a part of the personal experience in which his philosophy is rooted.

Let us summarize the points we have covered and point out certain implications. By means of a tactical turn in phenomenological philosophy, Ortega discovered the radical reality of human life. My life is neither a thing nor a rational postulation but a dramatic task that unfolds historically and futuristically, that is, perspectivistically and circumstantially as a projective and biographical "story." In my life, and only in my life, I encounter (in one form or another and in one manner or another) all other things (that is, "realities" and "non-realities" of whatever stripe) including the physical person that I am and the realities that transcend it absolutely. Therefore life is the "radical" reality. On the other hand, I can say that other realities are 'rooted' in it (bearing in mind the Latin etymologies of *radical* and *radicadas*—"root" and "rooted," respectively). Living is doing something with things in order to live as the person I am called to be. And this means making sense of things in some fashion, a fashion that accumulates individually as biography and collectively as culture. Therefore, life itself is reason in a living, total way that includes its limited forms (rational, mathematical, political, etc.).

Because life makes sense of things, we can make sense of it through narration, that is, by a verbal approximation of its mode of happening in the world. But my life which is mine alone does not happen alone. As Marías puts it, ". . . *my* life appears at once as a coexistence with 'other lives,' and for this reason I discover myself in the presence of a *you;* I find that life has a *disjunctive* nature (that it is this life *or* this one *or* that one), and this leads to a new notion, 'life' [as such], which is not a species or kind but *the life of each one.* It turns out, therefore, that *my life* as a reality implies an 'intrinsic theory,' without which there can be no interpretation or imaginative projection of itself as life *as such.*" [26] This self-discovery through others, which involves the "communicability of circumstances" mentioned earlier, opens the door to a whole range of human relationships, including love, friendship, and social life.

We have partially penetrated the first level of theory that will guide us toward other aspects of Marías's life and thought. But only partially. Like a sculptor who must make an initial indentation in the marble that contains his eventual statue or the artist who outlines his work with preliminary brush strokes, it was necessary for us to establish a base and achieve a working control of certain fundamental concepts in order subsequently to double back and illuminate other areas of Marías's work. The unitary nature of his thought made this approach an arduous one, and as it is, we have barely scratched the surface of this finely articulated philosophy.

There are certain other acknowledgments that need to be made. The first, already apparent, is Marías's continuing dialogue with Ortega. Perhaps the most formidable exegetical task in dealing with Marías is to keep both thinkers in balanced perspective. As Marías himself has said, his relationship to Ortega may be thought of as filial, that is, inconceivable without him but at the same time irreducible to him.

At the same time, it must be remembered that Ortega is not the only circumstantial factor at work in Marías. At concentric removes from the immediate planes of reference, he lays claim to more extended realities: the generations that preceded his—especially the Generation of 1898—historical Spain, Europe, the Classical world, the Americas, the Western world, among others. To put it another way, the very fact that Spain was to be the focus of his life and his work meant that he had to concentrate on the actual circumstances of his country, and these included an extended context. He took to heart Ortega's warning: "[It is] a grave oversight, a wretched awkwardness, to restrict ourselves to just a few circumstances, when the truth is that everything surrounds us!" [27]

The temptation has always been to insert Marías within the general trajectory of Ortegan thought and show how he continued within that species of philosophy. To do the same here would have been an exercise in erudition perhaps but something less than philosophy. For the key is not that Marías simply continues within Orteganism but that Orteganism continues within the life and thought of Marías *toward something else*. For what Marías calls *alteridad* ("otherness") to describe the situation of the early Greek thinkers applies also to his relationship to the thought of Ortega. "After the initial moment has passed, the philosopher finds an existing philosophy but, for one reason or another, it does not suffice for him. He must create *another*. Thus a relationship of "alterity" [*alteridad*] defines his philosophy. He starts from an existing philosophy but only so that he can diverge from it and seek another. But it must be remembered that in order to do this he must keep the former philosophy in mind and verify its inadequacy."[28] Naturally, the philosophy of Marías includes an essential reference to Ortega, but it does not end there. For as Marías often says, one must keep on thinking, and we could add the corollary, because life goes on.[29] And this dramatic movement determines the trajectory of real thought. On the other hand, philosophy that stops becomes mere scholasticism. And this means that in order to understand this protean aspect of philosophy we had to refer his thought to his life. For the life of a thinker is really the "plot" of his thought that we have been insisting on all along.

Therefore, this reference to Marías's life is not a perfunctory courtesy but a way of illuminating his philosophy. We can make sense of it only if we discover the sense that gave rise to it. For as Marías himself has always insisted, theory becomes understandable in a deep and usable way only when we see it arise as a possibility and a need from the life of the thinker.

3

METAPHYSICAL REALITY AND
THE THEORY OF GENERATIONS

A bold assertion by Helio Carpintero sets the tone for this chapter: "Julián Marías is one of those Spaniards who have made the firmest decision not to renounce the promise of a Spain that the men of [the Generation of] 1898 first began to reveal. His vast intellectual effort is aimed at giving substance to a Spanish possibility . . . within the lines of a tradition which, beginning in our time, we can already call 'classic.'"[1]

In 1949, when Marías published his first work on the generations theory, a decade had passed since the end of the Civil War. Ortega had returned to Spain in 1945 from nine years of exile, beginning a period of intense collaboration and friendship with Marías who at thirty-one was half his age. Not long after his return, in his first address at the Ateneo in Madrid, Ortega struck the note of historical and intellectual continuity that had been the norm for Marías since the war. In the decade to come, the last one of Ortega's life, the two philosophers held long discussions, usually twice a day during walks through Retiro Park, and if one or the other was away from Madrid, they exchanged letters. There were, says Marías, ". . . constant adjustments of philosophy or friendship, and always projects, projects, and more projects."[2] The most notable of their collaborative efforts was the Institute of Humanities (1948–50). It was there, at the suggestion of Ortega, that Marías gave a course on the generations theory.

But the generations theory is also a chapter in the larger story of Marías's efforts to save the Spanish possibilities referred to above. For Marías, this was first of all an imperative of understanding, or to put it another way, given his vocation and circumstance, to understand his world was a primary way of "saving" and putting to use its inherent possibilities, initially in a personal way. Ortega once remarked that the writers of the Generation of 1898 had looked at Spanish reality from a catastrophic perspective. Marías himself alludes to their "literary temper," complemented by the "philosophical temper" of Ortega's generation. From Marías's standpoint it was a matter of reconciling and thus saving—to the degree he could—his entire heritage, of carrying out at the highest theoretical and moral level the "reabsorption of cir-cumstance" which Ortega described as the concrete destiny of man.

It is worth noting that Marías understands this attitude to be far removed from an exercise in pedantic scholarship. Enormously erudite like Ortega and Unamuno, like them also he shows little patience with self-serving pedantry. In his view, erudition alone often becomes the refuge of the non-theoretical mind, which seems to prefer the docility of the extraneous or the escapism of the esoteric to the responsibilities of the essential. This may be why, as Marías has also hinted, a disheartening number of scholars do studies on books no longer read and topics no longer vital.

History and Human Life

As Marías sees it, history is not primarily an archival and scholarly ac-tivity (although naturally at an entirely different level archives and scholarship have their own importance), nor does it have to be written, documented, and footnoted by historians to be real. For its importance is not primarily that it happened and died but that it survived and remains as a resource and possibil-ity for our life, that is, our future, for living is a frontal, futuristic task. Real history is not what passed away but what has been passed on, and, far from being the exclusive province of our chronicles, it is much more certainly the stuff of our life. This is why its real story happens on Main Street, not in mu-seums. The rest is anecdote. For the past, which according to the Ortegan for-mula persists in the peculiar form of "having been," *is* our truth, but of course not our whole truth and not our whole story. For life is always an unfinished task, always a work "in progress." And because of our essential imperfection, what could be called our vital indigence, we have no authentic choice, if we are to go on living, but to surpass our history in search of completion. The fu-ture is the only possible, though uncertain, arena of that completion. In this sense, if we can say with Ortega that the past continues to exist in the form of "having been," then the future also exists here and now as possibility, as the "not yet." In other words, the present consists of both the past and the future, and to remove or forget either of its dimensions is to invalidate the one that remains.

Therefore, we could say that our life is a "surpassing" endeavor because we have a transcendent purpose (taking care in this context not to mistake this vital transcendence for the eschatologically transcendent). In everyday lan-guage we say, perhaps stoically but with age-sanctioned wisdom, that "life goes on," and so must our collateral enterprises such as philosophy if they are to keep pace and remain authentic.

On the other hand, the merits and genius of the past do not necessarily guarantee its survival. All human things are susceptible to loss, to regression and ruin. Because human reality can be more than it is, it can also be less—even to the point of materially ceasing to be. Marías would be the first to admit that this protean quality appears in our life as an essential ontological riskiness. Everyone knows that living is dangerous, and modern philosophers and writers have commented endlessly—and almost always gloomily—on the doubts, strategies, agonies, and implications that radiate from this condition. The risks of mortality are sobering, of course, but perhaps we ought also to remember, as Plato reminds us, that the risks of being immortal are beautiful.

In either case, this mortal risk calls for vigilance, or to recall the title of this book, for "a watch over mortality," that is, the mortal task of living. In the most primary way, this describes our personal condition, but it is also true at the social and cultural level. Marías could not rest easy, could not sleep philosophically, as he might put it, with the awareness that the superior work of several generations could be lost or abandoned. This sense of urgent responsibility for preserving and surpassing the viable past, especially the recent past with its valuable insights and methodologies, is transparent in the following comment on the theme of death in Ortega and Unamuno: "It seems important, it seems to me to be necessary, *to go farther than both* by posing the problem [of death], the problem of Unamuno (which is not his alone), in the light of the intellectual resources that we owe principally to Ortega."[3] A listing of these "resources" would certainly include the generations theory.

There is another important factor to consider: Marías's own generational situation, which placed him at a crucial personal distance from this tradition but which was by no means a detachment from it, established the conditions necessary for him to make the attempt. To the degree he has succeeded it has been of course a matter of his perseverance and intellect.

The Generations Theme

As Marías observes in his *Generations: A Historical Method,* the generations theme itself may be thought of as extremely ancient or quite new, depending on the rigor and scope of the consideration. As a constant of ordinary experience it is probably as old as humanity itself, but as a general historiographical concept it is essentially a modern discovery, and as a precise exegetical method based on a comprehensive metaphysics or theory of human life, is restricted, as far as I know, to Ortega, Marías, and their school.[4]

Taken as a whole, the development of the generations theory is one of the most revealing examples of the manner in which Marías insists on an empirical reference to historical reality as both a corrective and verification of his philosophy. Hear how he explains it: "Since the theory of generations is intrinsically methodical, this means that it is modified and enriched by contact with socio-historical reality. It is always reality that decides, that imposes rectifications if they are needed, and that reclaims the complements of an always developing theory, which in turn is but an instrument for conceptually apprehending and dominating that same reality."[5]

In a related sense, the generations theory also stands as a typical example of how, as Ferrater Mora observes, Marías ". . . has developed many of the themes that Ortega himself only initiated or hinted at in his writings or oral teachings . . ."[6] And in yet a more extended and complex way, the generations theme also turns on the biographical link between the universal applicability of the theory and his personal and cultural circumstances within which it was conceived as a response to real conditions. In plainer terms, in the thought of Marías we find the theory of generations spinning off an intense intellectual preoccupation with the topic in Spanish culture, while in his life we remain aware of the actual and identifiable generations that are not a theory but a personal experience. In a later chapter, we shall attempt to identify by profile these generations through an application of the theory.

But from any angle, the generations theme must be approached with considerable caution. Until recently, the very notion of generations veered more toward genealogy than theory, and this has allowed many arbitrary ideas and misleading notions to become attached to the term. For ages, people have written and talked about generations but with only the vaguest understanding of what they are. If we think about it, it is astonishing that we have known so little about an acknowledged human phenomenon mentioned so frequently but carelessly in otherwise serious writings. For example, how long does a generation last, twenty-five, thirty, or thirty-three years, or is it simply equivalent to the uncertain duration of a human life? Is it a biological or genealogical process, or a social component, or both? How are generations articulated? *Ecclesiastes* records that "One generation passeth away, and another generation cometh . . . ," which is obviously true, but what are the mechanisms, human and social, that regulate this rhythm of disappearance and replacement? And how do they work? Do the generational sequences or phases of men and women coincide?

In contemporary Spain, probably more has more been said and more so-called "generations" identified than anywhere else. With important forerunners in the "Romantic Generations" of the nineteenth century (which Marías has studied at some length), the celebrated "Generation of 1898" led off what has been a lengthy and often confusing generational parade through twentieth-century Spanish culture. There are the poetic generations of 1927 and 1936 (both somewhat arbitrary groupings), the post-Civil War generation, the abortive generation of the fifties, and others of limited or dubious status whose claims are still in debate.

Ironically, the seminal work by Ortega early in this century and the more recent revisions and applications of the theory by Marías with a view to bringing the popular generations theme under intellectual control may have helped contribute to that very popularization. For while the notion caught on even more strongly than before, the rigor they brought to the concept has been largely ignored.[7] As for Ortega's ideas on the generations theme, Marías notes that "The great presupposition—and as such never formulated—was this: 'If Ortega can say these things [about generations] then think how much more must be known about them in Germany!'"[8] In truth, a lot was said but apparently less was known in Germany, as Marías has shown convincingly in his study *Generations: A Historical Method.*

As for Spain, early in the twentieth century, Gabriel Maura, Pío Baroja, and Unamuno alluded to various generational configurations of Spanish society, and Azorín is usually credited with coining the phrase "Generation of 1898" in 1912 (although Maura first used the expression in 1908). Pedro Salinas treated the topic in his *El concepto de generación literaria aplicado a la del 98* [The Concept of Literary Generation Applied to the Generation of 1898] (1935). He failed to make use of Ortega's writings, preferring instead the less polished theories of Julius Petersen (*Die literarischen Generationen* [The Literary Generations] (1930). José Gaos dealt tangentially with the generations theme in his "Sobre sociedad e historia," *Filosofía de la filosofía e historia de la filosofía* [Philosophy of Philosophy and History of Philosophy] (1947). Gaos follows the Ortegan theory in his explanations, unlike Adolfo Salazar, who in his *El siglo romántico* [The Romantic Century] (1935) reverted to the genealogical understanding of generations. María Luisa Caturla expounded a more carefully crafted template of generations in her *Arte de épocas inciertas* [The Art of Uncertain Eras] (1944), relying more or less on Ortega but without the philosophical implications of his theory. Alonso Zamora makes passing references to the Ortegan concepts in his *Sobre Petrarquismo* [On Petrarchism] (1945).

The works of Francisco Ayala and Pedro Laín Entralgo on the generations theme are based on the Ortegan template. In his *Tratado de Sociología,* Vol. 2 of *Sistema de la Sociología* [Treatise on Sociology, System of Sociology] (1947), Ayala attempts to apply Ortega's theory to European society. For his part, in his *Las generaciones en la historia* [Generations in History] (1945), Laín Entralgo follows the Ortegan model of generations, although he also criticizes Ortega for excessive "biologism" and, like Ayala, generally avoids the broader philosophic postulates of the theory.

This aversion or indifference to the philosophic underpinnings and rigorous applications of the generations theory in Ortega and Marías has resulted in a restricted and superficial understanding. In general, the tendency in Spain has been to think in terms of "literary" or "artistic" generations, with occasional political or scientific adjuncts. In other words, the view has been that generations consist of certain writers, artists, and a limited number of "famous names," and that the majority of people stand excluded from these elitist circles.

Yet the popular distortions of the generations theme on the one hand, and the certainty on the part of Ortega and Marías that generations were real historical phenomena on the other, converged and became a genuine philosophic problem in need of clarification. These are the parameters within which they developed the theme. In order for us to retrace the process, we must begin at this same reference point.

The Generations Theory

Generational awareness begins with the most obvious human experience. Starting with a birthday, our life is defined at an elementary level by a numerical reckoning of years duly recorded in recent centuries on certificates, documents, and, eventually, tombs. Consequently, we are inescapably "age-conscious"; not only persons but things in general seem to be susceptible to temporal stratifications. We classify people immediately according to age grouping—baby, child, teenager, young adult, middle-aged, senior, elderly, etc.—generally corresponding to what used to be called the "ages of man."⁹

It is tempting to speculate on the depth and degree to which this elementary and non-mystical "numerology" regulates our life, beginning with the simple fact that we *know* how old we are and can count our years and measure our life according to inherited norms, taboos, and expectations. Imagine how radically this separates us from the animal world. We have a clue to its importance in the radical disorientation experienced by those who, because of imprisonment, impairment, or isolation, "lose track of time." Generally, as Marías has pointed out in his *The Structure of Society,* we understand human acts to be age-related, something that becomes readily apparent when people refuse to "act their age" and—from the customary point of view—insolently or hilariously do things out of time and season. But what happens when this traditional scheme of expectations no longer applies, or does not do so in the same sequence? Marías has noticed that in quite recent times it seems that not only life expectancy but also what could be called "age expectancy," for lack of a term to describe the phenomenon, have diverged radically, causing or affecting a series of conditions ranging from the social and personal to the metaphysical. (Later, we shall see how certain aspects apply to the generational paradigm.) Some of these concerns could fall within the scientific provinces of anthropology expanded to fit its own definition, were it not for the fact that as things now stand, the biased preference of anthropologists for primitive cultures renders it curiously indifferent to modern peoples.

Nevertheless, the fact remains that at any specific date most people are not living in the same time, nor at the same level, except in a grossly generic or biological sense. For a child of four, a mature person of fifty, and another of ninety, "today" represents very different "nows." (Naturally there are similar differences when they speak of the "past" or the "future.") When the elderly speak of "my day" everyone understands that they do not mean today. It seems that our life passes through a certain temporal zone that we sense—though often only later in life—is peculiarly "ours," whereas other times do not really belong to us, because we do not belong to them. Children live time as a threshold; they have little to recall but almost everything to anticipate. On the other hand, the mature man or woman is aware of being well advanced in life. They know they have come a certain distance and that a definite though undefined stretch of life remains. Unappealable decisions have been made; much can never be done again because they have done it already. Life begins to assume its definitive contour and tempo modulated from a still speculative but definite point called death. As the Ancients put it, *Mors certa, hora incerta* (certain death at an uncertain hour).

Meanwhile, the nonagenarian lives amidst finalities. In every sense, he is in the last phase of this life, without the future expectations that marked all his prior ages. This gives extreme old age a uniqueness that many find mysterious and troubling. For life is a futuristic drama and the elderly appear to have no significant future. Because of our essential imperfection, our existential indigence and neediness, we have to move from one situation into another not in simple eventful succession but in sequential anticipation of ourselves. As Marías observes, "Paradoxically, man can possess himself throughout life and be himself because he does not possess himself fully in any moment of life."[10]

This feature makes possible—and necessary—the narrative understanding of human life. The authentic novelist—a Dickens, or Flaubert, or Galdós—cannot simply *define* character and personality beforehand, and if they try to do so, their preliminary descriptions do not necessarily correspond to the image that eventually emerges from the narrative (witness Dostoevski). The lives they deal with must *unfold* in the narrative, for life is defined by its motives, projects, and passions—the true "plot" of the story—which become real, that is realized, only in being acted out. For this reason, human life is a reality that happens not once and for all but circumstantially *over time*. In order to understand and take possession of it we must take the time and have the patience to reconstruct as best we can its plot and setting. This is another way of saying that human life has *depth* in a way that other realities do not. This same intuition will reappear in a different form, as we shall see later, in the Marías memoirs.

Commonly, we say that time passes, but not completely it seems; in a mysterious way, it also appears to accumulate in human life, else how could we reckon age as a "personal" quality? "Old and full of days" is a revealing biblical description of life's final stage, when men seem to stagger and collapse under the immense temporal weight they bear. Perhaps this is why in the Bible longevity is often equated to physical strength. But we do not stop there; using this personal calculation as a measure, we impute age and years to inanimate realities. This may be a primary way of "personalizing" circumstance and converting it into "my" world. It is curious that science considers this imputed numerical and temporal dimension of things, which is thoroughly subjective at bottom, to be one of the most unquestionably objective and impersonal standards by which to measure reality. The ancient adage that man is the measure of all things may be much more than a humanistic truism. Most likely, Marías would argue that it is another instance of how ultimately so-called "pure reason" turns out to be a species of vital reason.

But there is a further paradox: as life gathers time it also runs short of it. In extreme old age life exhausts its temporal reserves and seems to lose its futuristic dimension. Unlike all other ages, it is final (leaving aside in this context the mystery of the next life). What then? One response is to disqualify it, to view it as meaningless and lamentable, and to look on the elderly as survivors instead of living persons. Whereas we think of ourselves as simply living, we are apt to remark with surprise that these elderly survivors are "still living." (This is the obverse and contradictory side of the modern notion that death is always attributable to accidental breakdown and that in theory—and certainly in our own case—it should go on indefinitely with the right drugs, doctors, medical technology, etc.) The etymology of "survivor" sheds some light here, for it means literally one who "lives over," that is, over or beyond what is normally allotted or expected.

Human Life as Metaphysics

We come to this point: life goes on in the ways we have touched on, but it does so as overlapping human time zones, or ages. In short, life occurs generationally. But because the reference to generations is of a certain order and precision quite unrelated to traditional notions or definitions, we must see it emerging from its philosophical context, that is, from a metaphysics, if we are to understand and make use of it.

This is less formidable than it sounds. Marías's introduction to the theme will serve us here: "Any metaphysics is a certain idea of reality, and each metaphysical system is distinguished from others by its discovering and exploring a new reality, or by its considering reality from a new perspective and thereby revealing hitherto unknown dimensions."[11]

Ortegan metaphysics, developed by both Ortega and Marías, begins with the fundamental personal—and phenomenological—discovery that I find myself with things, doing something with them, more, obliged to do something with them, in order to go on living. This is not primarily a rational dis-covery which may be "suspended" in standard phenomenological procedure or intellectually manipulated in some convenient fashion; at this level, it is not a theory of existence at all, but a matter of acknowledging the condition in which "I"—and other "I's," by theoretical implication—find myself living.

Shorn of theories and taken in its absolute immediacy, living is what I do with things and what happens to me as I do. This means that in some ini-tially undetermined manner, life is given to me (for I do not give it to myself), but it is not given to me ready-made. At the same time, I find in myself an image or calling to complete my life in a certain way, which for reasons that may include the prospect of happiness, for example, seems justifiable or sensi-ble to me. To accept to live life is to assume an unavoidable but "reasonable" task; we could say paradoxically that I have no choice but to choose to com-plete my life with the things or resources I find around me that I refer to as my circumstances, keeping in mind that these are everything around me, includ-ing not only the somatic and psychological person that I am but also the di-mensions of materiality, the "artificial" human world of history, art, and technology, the moral and social repertory of beliefs, codes, interpretations, obligations, rights, prohibitions, and customs, and a plane of ideal latencies, transcendencies, speculations, and outright impossibilities.

In short, I do things for a reason, and the reason is life, and therefore *life is reason*. In order to live, I must make some sort of total sense of things (even if I conclude that everything is nonsense) from my circumstance and perspec-tive and in keeping with my intention, my calling, to live in a certain way. Life, says Marías, ". . . apprehends reality in its connectedness."[12] No wonder then that this is the same definition he gives reason. This is why Ortega could reply to Unamuno that life is reason in process, that is, the holistic process of living.

In order to reveal this normally covert "life reason," which primarily functions only as we live, it is necessary to retrace life personally (in one's memoirs or autobiography) or vicariously by reconstructing its plot, which makes the progression of situations visible and sensible. For we understand life when we see one situation leading to, or arising from, another. As we do so, we come to realize that this "life" or "vital" reason functions at two related levels: first, it apprehends reality in its connectedness, meaning that to live is to understand things in a certain total way that includes not only process and sequence but justification as well. In other words, we are called to respond reasonably to things. Life is therefore a responsible endeavor and hence in-escapably moral (which is why it is also susceptible to immorality).

Second, this vital reason is self-illuminating. As it allows us to under-stand circumstantial reality in the totality of its relationships (minus most of the detailed knowledge of their workings, of course), it also reveals its own functions and mechanisms. To use a perilous expression, within this process and context it is self-evident and self-explanatory in much the same way that a story reveals its techniques in the telling.

In two fundamental ways, life appears to me as the "radical" reality. To begin with, it is "where" I encounter all other realities, regardless of their nature and location. They are my circumstance, constituting my possibilities and conforming to or resisting my vocation, my calling, to be the person I must be. And to the degree that I realize or abandon the projects implied in my calling, I allow my circumstance to be realized—or not. This is another way of saying that circumstance and I are engaged in a reciprocally responsible dependency. We need each other in order to be. Again, the Ortegan formula applies: I am I and my circumstance. (The copulative "and" follows the second "I," not the first; it is not simply "I and my circumstance," as in the older theories of environmental influence—meaning, among other things, that I cannot be I apart from circumstance. Or to put it in simpler terms, I live circumstantially.)

Thus, all realities appear circumstantially in my life in a relationship that Ortega and Marías refer to as "radical" and "radicated." This circumstantiality implies in the most fundamental and inescapable way that situation and chronology are involved in my relationship with realities. I move dramatically over time, entering and leaving one situation after another. From these situations reality appears to me only from a perspective. And since I am always circumstantially situated and localized, I am unavoidably susceptible to and dependent on perspectivistic reality. Thus, perspective is inseparable from reality and must be acknowledged as one of its components. Without perspective, for example, the primary temporal categories of "past," "present," and "future" would have no meaning. In this sense, time depends on a personal point of view in order to be humanly understandable.

A Metaphysical Turning Point

We have reached what Marías calls a significant "inflection" or turning point of philosophy. To say that life is not a thing, but in one sense the "alveolus" or "area" in which things appear in a "radicated" relationship to it, is to take the first step toward transcending both idealism and realism.[13] As Marías describes it, "Realism and idealism, strictly speaking, spring from a common idea of reality, and come into opposition with each other only in regard to the priority of certain realities over others. To be reality for one and the other is *to be a thing,* whether the primary reality is what we call "things" or *res extensa,* or whether it is that thing we call "I" *(res cogitans).*"[14]

The second "radicality" of life lies in its implicit transcendence of modern rationalism and its alter ego, irrationalism. If, instead of forcing rationality or irrationality on life, we allow life to speak for itself, to tell its own story and thus give its own reasons, we see that it is neither rational nor irrational but more than both: at a level that includes and surpasses these assumptions, *life is reasonable and therefore intelligible.* It makes sense. And this sense is, of course, effusive: it radiates over reality and allows us to see it perspectivistically in its structural connectedness. In this way, which in the most general sense describes living, we take intellectual and moral possession of this circumstantial reality, allowing certain of its latent potentialities to manifest themselves as "my" world. In one sense—an enormous one—living is transforming the world into personal reality. The process is not an inflexible determinism, nor should we be misled by the words "intellectual" and "moral." For it is not primarily a question of verbal definitions and congruences but decisions about living, and these may include what we see, or others see, as senseless, immoral, and unintelligent aspects of such decisions. But we do so from a certain clarifying point of reference. In other words, the senseless or the immoral presuppose a standpoint that is not merely senseless or immoral, else we could not render the judgment in the first place. To pronounce the world insane, for instance, is to say at a deeper level that we have a way of knowing what constitutes sanity and insanity.

Modern thought has not prepared us for the "reasonableness" of life and the "well-made world" it implies. Instead, in many instances it has coalesced around the suspicion—for it remains empirically unproven—that at its core the cosmos is meaningless if not insane and in any case, as Arnold says, ". . . without help for pain." Since Kierkegaard and the irrationalists, whole areas of Western thought no longer seem to be philosophies but therapics for our metaphysical neurosis. Kierkegaard's title *Fear and Trembling* could be the motto of this age. Not that this therapeutic approach offers much comfort; shorn of its bluster and bluff, it comes to rest on the disturbing assumption that ultimate truth and darkest dread are the same. As Father Bueno says in Unamuno's novel *San Manuel Bueno, mártir*, "Truth . . . may be something terrible . . ."

However, such speculation pales before the more immediate truth implied by it: the need for meaning and understanding is inherent in human life, for living forces us willy-nilly to make—or discover—the sense of things. In the boldest terms permitted by the context, we could say that life is created in the image of truth, conceding for the moment and perhaps forever that we know not how this happens. This is why falsehood, initially undetectable as such, registers differently from truth in our experience. On the other hand, the world, through life, proves "responsible" to this need, for it responds to us by appearing understandable. We shall not pursue these themes further, except to say that at the very least this provisional paradigm calls into question the heuristic and virtual assumption of atheism in modern thought. Marías's concise *aperçu* regarding this discoverable sense of reality is worth pondering: ". . . if the world has been created by God, it makes sense *that it would be un-*

derstandable."[15] It also makes sense that the problem of God would appear here, provided it is a real problem, that is, a human problem and not simply speculation that ends in a theological construct.

Social Reality and Generations

From these metaphysical considerations, we again pick up the generations theme. My life, which is mine alone, is not alone. The very term "alone," which appears to exclude any reference to others, does precisely the opposite. Through their absence others define my solitude. I could not know I was alone if I did not also know that others live in the world. They are, therefore, paradoxically conspicuous by their absence. Or as the Spanish say, *Brillan por su ausencia,* "they shine by their absence."

Usually, however, they are fully present. We are born into a society. Among the first realities I discover in my life are other people. I become aware of "my" life and "my" possessions by the presence of other "you's," and more remotely, "he's," "she's," and "they's." What is more, these others tell me who I am, beginning with the mysterious act of giving me my name. If I were truly alone, my life would simply be absolute and not "mine" at all, for there would be no "you" or "yours" to give me this awareness.

But Marías cautions against thinking of these "others" as simply "elements" or "entities" in my circumstance. To do so would be to consign them to nature. As he points out, "The decisive thing is that these men function as centers of other lives, of whose circumstances I am a part; that is to say, I find within my circumstance at once and from the first other men who also encounter me and who take me into account, as I do with them. Therefore, I take them into account in a peculiar way that includes their taking me into account. This is why our reciprocal behavior is very different from what happens in my conduct with things. For even though I am in things, they are not, strictly speaking, with me . . ."[16]

Other persons exhibit a "nearness" to me that things do not have. This is why people but not things can be "neighbors," that is, the one who lives "nigh." This quality allows us to live together *(convivir).* But we are still within the ambit of individual life, for this "living together" is not an addendum to "my" life but its primary mode of realization.

The next step for traditional sociology (Tarde, Durkheim, Freyer, Simmel, Weber) was to make the tempting but simplistic leap from the individual to the social, usually via the family unit, and to conclude that as soon as others appear or associate, society begins or is implicit. For Marías (and Ortega) this is an erroneous assumption. The association and interaction of individuals as such, say for example two lovers, is not an act of society but simply two persons carrying on what Ortega calls an "interindividual" relationship. What then is society?

Social *Vigencias*

Marías begins with this tentative definition: "A society is defined by a system of common prevailing modes, or *vigencias*—usages, beliefs, ideas, values, and aims. Therefore, it is not enough simply to group men in a certain way in order to form a society; if different systems of *vigencias* operate within a certain grouping, then more than one society is present."[17]

This definition is barely an introduction to the complex social analysis carried out by Marías in several books, particularly *The Structure of Society* (1955). Yet in the present context it serves the useful purpose of introducing the dynamics we find in generational articulation. When we speak of *vigencias* as a social system, we find an immediate link to history. Prevailing beliefs, ideas, values, language, usages, etc., all of which may be summed in the splendid but untranslatable term *vigencia* (from the Latin *vigere,* to be vigorous or lively), are historical. Essentially, we inherit rather than invent them.

This does not mean that our life is merely subject to history, or that it is in history, but rather that the ingredients, the content of our *vigencias,* with which we shape our life, are historical in nature. The very fact that things are primarily "nominal," that they appear with names, means they bear a prior interpretation. Indeed, the universal catchall category of reality we call "things," which functions as our primary metaphysical system, is itself an inherited historical interpretation.

My vocation, my calling to be a certain person and live a certain life, while mine alone, is also historically conditioned. I cannot aspire to be an emperor of the Ming dynasty or a medieval knight, because those options are historically precluded in my life. Therefore, not only circumstance and my perspective of it but also the "I" that I am are rooted in history at a very precise level. I am, in short, a historical person, or to put it another way, to be a person is first of all to be inescapably historical.

But this must not be taken to mean that I am the "subject" of history. If only I lived in the world there would be no history, for there would be no *vigencias,* prior interpretations, prevailing modes, language, numbers, or beliefs to serve as both its channels and content. In short, there would be no society, and consequently I would not understand myself as a person. My plight would be chilling and infrahuman—but only if seen from a social and human point of view. Ignorant of the primary metaphysical category of "things," I could not deal humanly, that is, reasonably and responsibly, with the bewildering complexity and atomization of reality. Experience would remain linear and untransferable, meaning that every new trifle would be an enigma and a possible peril for me. Most of all, without a personal name I would not really be "I." Mute and dumb without identity and language, my humanity would dissolve into mere nature, and I would be a human animal.

But if I am not the subject of history, then what is that subject? To work our way toward an answer to the question, we pick up again the fact that human life exhibits a temporal stratification. As we saw earlier in the case of a child, a mature person, and a nonagenarian, "today" has a variety of age-related meanings. We could say that all living people are contemporaneous but not necessarily coetaneous; they live at different age levels.

Approaching the same concept from the social and historical perspective, Marías writes: "History affects men insofar as they form a plurality that is at once coexistent and successive; historical life is therefore historical coexistence."[18] This means, in short, that society is the subject of history, but even as we say this we must remember that the social world is something I discover from the radical reality of my life, which is also historical. The circularity of these references can become vicious if we fail to remember this distinction: my life is not the subject of history but the area where I discover historical reality, including the historical conditions of my own life.

Elsewhere, we saw how human life is situational.[19] Because life is a dramatic and protean task, it moves, socially and individually, and this means going from one situation to another. Marías thus disagrees with the Comtian notion that society is a static reality sporadically spurred into movement by history. But if life moves it is because it has somewhere to go, and this means that it has an aim and vision of what it will or would be. Thus it is both real and anticipatory, conservative and innovative. Not that these features are mere hostile antipodes, as revolutionaries of all persuasions have erroneously preached. On the contrary, what Marías would probably call "vectorial" tensions describe the actual "plot" of history. In this regard also, the anticipatory dimension of life is also a function of its historical reality. History does not oppose innovation, is not the enemy of the future, but makes it possible in the first place. This is why true revolution, which turns cannibalistically on the past, always conceals a risk of barbarism and regression.

Social reality, as Aristotle understood, implies a certain temporal endurance. The situations we enter into last for an identifiable time. They are therefore *successive*. But it would be a mistake to think that time is the only situational criterion. In reality, situations are primarily qualitative rather than chronological. Each situation represents a certain human level, and since each level corresponds to an aim or aspiration, then we can say that historical change is always innovation, that is, change within a prior order. Interpreted by historical reason, this succession becomes understandable, for it allows us to see *why* situations emerge from or give way to others. But at the same time this means that a single situation, a single slice or moment of history, is unintelligible. Each must be seen as both a result of what went before and a preparation to what followed. Once again, and from another angle, we see that the understanding of human reality requires a narrative approach.

This brings up the question of the articulation of historical situations and the generations themselves. To begin with, we need to remind ourselves again that the historical situations are not simply a matter of time. At any moment, different age groupings coexist and constitute a plurality of levels. Upon examination these age groupings turn out to be generational and as such serve a dual function. Marías explains: ". . . they are at once the 'acts' and 'actors,' the 'who's' and the 'steps' of history. Historical movement is not continuous, like that of a moving vehicle or an airplane, but is rather discontinuous, like that of a quadruped or a man. In other words, it proceeds gradually, by grades, or steps, or better still, by numbered steps. These steps, which take approximately fifteen years, constitute the elemental historical *present*. A generation is a period of time during which a certain view of the world remains relatively stable."[20]

Consider Ortega's most succinct description of generations: "A generation is a time zone of fifteen years during which a certain way of life was predominant. The generation would be, therefore, the basic unit of authentic historical chronology; or, in other words, history marches and proceeds by generations."[21] This means, to put it in the simpler terms, that if society can be defined as a system of prevailing modes *(vigencias)*, then these modes are expressed generationally in discontinuous sequence.

The Structure of Generations

We saw that at any given moment a plurality of "nows" exist. Ortega spoke of three, but in reality there is a "now" corresponding to each generation. The following outline based on a similar model found in Marías's *Generations: A Historical Method,* summarizes the generational process:

1. The first fifteen years of life: *childhood.* The child has no historical participation or power, which means that the world of children in any period of history experiences fewer changes than other age groupings.
2. Fifteen to thirty: *youth.* The young absorb and learn about the inherited world they did not create, nor do they control.
3. Thirty to forty-five: *initiation.* Men (the case of women is treated later) begin to act and to impose their views on the inherited society. They struggle against the generation in power and attempt to supplant it.
4. Forty-five to sixty: *dominance:* Men come to power, imposing their views, while preparing themselves to defend their world view against the younger generations.
5. Sixty to seventy-five: *old age.* Men become survivors, surrendering power and dominance to the generation behind them. Death thins their ranks and they pass from the scene.[22]

To some extent, this convenient outline loses in detail what it offers in clarity. It tells us very little, for example, of the mechanisms by which power and dominance migrate generationally, nor does it describe the range of relationships possible between adjacent generations.[23] Ortega spoke, for example, of "cumulative" and "polemic" generations. By the former, he meant those generations (like his own) that adhered more or less to the legacy left them by their elders, whereas the latter signify ruptures and beginnings, revolts, revolutions, and the recent American experience of "generation gaps."

This points to what Marías calls a "minimal historical period." The fact that each generation is somewhat "polemic," and that alterations of *vigencias* are inevitable, does not mean a certain social profile may not continue over several generational successions. This is another way of indicating that several generations may also prove to be "cumulative." For example, successive generations may modify the political *vigencias* but without destroying them; in the end it will be the same system enhanced or weakened to a greater or lesser degree. In his examination of several historical periods, including the Romantic period of nineteenth century Spain, Marías concludes that four generations are needed to constitute the "minimal period" in question. But in order to understand the period historically, that is, situationally, two "flanking" generations must be added, making a total of six.

Marías warns against a mechanical application of the generational method. Everything we have said about generations so far is merely theoretical, which has almost nothing to do with their actual existence. Nor is there any arithmetical magic in the number fifteen or the dividing lines between generations. In every case, argues Marías, the abstract theory must remain susceptible to modification by field data.

In addition to his concept of a "minimal historical period," Marías has modified the Ortegan theory in at least two other significant ways in order to accommodate not only more recent historical changes but also those recalcitrant periods of uncertain profile. The first of these modifications has to do with identifying the generational series itself, that is, clearly establishing the sequence by locating a starting point. Ortega's procedure was to discover what he referred to as a "decisive" or "critical" generation, identifying its "eponym" (Descartes, for example), and taking the thirtieth year of this figure as the gravitational center of a generation.

The problem for Marías was that many uncertain periods of history do not have such an eponymous individual. The solution proposed by Marías was to take representative figures born fifteen years apart and clearly belonging to different generations. If we continue to add the names of those born in succeeding years, eventually at a certain year anomalies will appear. These anomalies, verifiable through comparisons with neighboring generations, indicate the year of generational change.[24]

Although he had noticed the phenomenon as early as 1949 in his first work on the generations theory, Marías published a short essay in 1974 entitled "Generaciones: Augustos y Césares," in which he addressed increased longevity and its effect on the generations. He notes: "This schema [of generations] has ceased to be valid. Men past sixty and fully active are legion today."[25] Either the fifteen-year generational cycle no longer holds, he tells us, or the generational paradigm must be modified to include an additional active generation. After studying the matter for nearly twenty-five years, Marías concludes that the generational period remains essentially the same but the generation of "survivors" (those sixty and above) now retains its numbers and vigor on an unprecedented scale. By keeping power beyond its traditonal limit, this older generation becomes "Augustan," whereas what was once the generation of unquestioned predominance must be content with a "Caesarean" status as ruler-designate.

Perhaps the most significant contribution by Marías to the generations theory, especially insofar as it constitutes a method of historical inquiry, has been made somewhat indirectly in his studies on the social status of women. As early as 1947, in his *Introducción a la Filosofía,* he wrote on the "changes in the situation and status of Western woman." This interest has never waned. He identified, for example, a special subcategory of *vigencias,* which he called *solencias* [the contrary of "insolent," constituting what could be called a "negative *vigencia"*], that apply primarily to women.[26] These are the "things one does not do." At the other end of the feminine spectrum, he has dealt extensively with the theme of women's "liberation" or emancipation (real and phony) in such works as *La mujer en el siglo XX, La mujer y su sombra, La felicidad humana,* and *La educación sentimental.* He has noted also the precociousness of women, which traditionally has caused them to be associated with older masculine generations. This has led him to consider a wide range of intersexual relationships with an especial emphasis on the feminine varieties of vital reason, friendship, love, and social life.[27]

The extraordinary attention given the generations theory and related themes in contemporary Spain would not have been possible without an elaborate philosophical, sociological, and metaphysical foundation. Marías describes it this way: "For such a theory [of generations] to be possible, philosophy had to take certain decisive steps toward establishing the basic postulates, and it has only been in the present century that these steps have been taken. But almost as soon as the theory was a possibility, it was indeed formulated—possibly without so much as a year's delay."[28]

But this account would be incomplete if we were to omit one final detail: if the seminal work of Ortega converted the theory of generations and metaphysics of life into philosophical resources, the advances made by Marías allowed them to become a usable method. This is apparent in the application and methodology we find in such works as *España inteligible,* and *Ortega: Las trayectorias,* to name but two examples. What is less apparent but supremely significant in understanding Marías is that, far from signaling a departure from philosophical theory, his strategy represents the very embodiment and inherent fulfillment of that theory. He is still advancing along lines established or plotted half a century ago, only now he is doing so "executively." I mean that instead of remaining at the abstract and theoretical levels of philosophy, he is applying its methods to concrete history, society, and human relations. I said earlier that the problems of philosophy are the problems of real life. And as Marías sees it, when philosophy enters this arena it also comes authentically into its own. In our day we speak of "doing" philosophy, but for the most part we have an abstract exercise in mind when we say so. In this context, to do philosophy means to deal not with the shadow but the substance and categories of real human experience.

4

THE GENERATIONS OF MARÍAS

Is there an implicit error in the chapter title? How is it possible to speak of the "generations of Marías," when in the previous chapter we have gone to some length to show that human historicity finds its concrete expression and modality in a specific generation, in his case the generation of 1916?[1] And as Ortega declares, "Each [generation] brings to the world a different sense of life; it lives inexorably enclosed within the confines of a cordial horizon that sets it apart from the preceding and subsequent generations."[2]

Yet in no way does the following commentary gainsay these assertions. To assign Marías to the generation of 1916 according to his own generational paradigm does not exclude a proximity and relationship to adjacent generations, just as the fact that one belongs to a certain nuclear family does not rule out remoter kinships within an extended family. If, therefore, the generation of 1916 could be thought of in this sense as nuclear, then the adjacent generations are its nearest relatives. Unamuno once referred to the generation born around 1901 as the "grandsons" of his generation.

However, instead of a family, this cluster, or constellation, of generations constitutes what Marías would call a "minimal historical period," to which he ascribes a span of at least sixty years, or four generations. Therefore, we may define this period as a way of life and thought that prevailed in Spain during the first decades of the twentieth century, that is, from the advent of the Generation of 1898 in 1900 or 1901 until a temporal dividing line that remains undetermined for the moment but which we would expect to be around 1960 or 1961. Although from our point of view this historical period is in one sense a past reality, it does not mean that it has ceased to exist. In any consideration of twentieth-century Spain we immediately encounter its imprint and presence. And to speak of presence means, naturally, that in some way it is still present, even though perhaps no longer predominate.

It helps to keep in mind that this "present" is more than just the present moment. Contrary to what Bertrand Russell argued, the present is not an unreal geometric or temporal marker lacking real time. When we speak of the "present time" in the ordinary sense, the sense in which we live and understand things in their everyday depth and structure, we mean a time that began in a more or less recent past and extends a certain distance into the future. This "living time" has no precise abstract boundaries that I know of; instead, it exhibits a vital consistency, what could be called "living space," that fluctuates somewhat in Bergsonian fashion with the expansions and contractions of historical life.

Thus, when we say "now" or "nowadays" we can mean several things. To begin with, the temporal boundaries of "now" may extend laterally, as it were, beyond one's lifetime, to include significant portions of the past and the future. In such times, we sense that we belong to an established and coherent age that seems destined to last indefinitely. Naturally, there is still our personal "now," always necessarily centered on the usual local urgencies and daily routines. But over against this limited zone of personal time, the broader secondary setting functions as a superior order of coherence to which local perplexities may be finally appealed.

Whenever this broad context is firmly fixed, the temporal quality itself appears to change. Not only does the contextual "now" extend historically and futuristically beyond our personal lifetime, but time itself seems to deepen and slow like a river flowing in an expanded channel. These are the ages of plenitude, of vital fullness and human richness. We like to call them "golden," but ages seem golden only from a distance and in retrospect, after their imperfections have been smoothed over or forgotten. In any case, this temporal alteration has little to do with the ideal perfection we sometimes attribute to eras too remote and too alien for realistic scrutiny. At the personal level, it is likely that the number of aggravations in the world remains more or less constant. The decisive difference is whether the world itself is perceived as being rightly or wrongly constituted. If we think the world is structured essentially as it ought to be, then we can accommodate a multitude of discomforts and wrongs. Contrary to common opinion, these "golden" ages tolerate many more irritants than, say, ours, which thinks of itself as being deeply wounded and hyperesthetically feels each new wrong as an intensification of its hurt. Its aversion to pain and concomitant emphasis on security and comfort offers a notable contrast with the toughmindedness, high spirits, and tolerance of discomfort common to "golden-age" societies.

At the other extreme of temporal plenitude, we may focus on the merest moment of time. We hear the argument that if the present is not all there is, it is all that matters. The argument is that by concentrating on the present moment, we allow it to linger indefinitely, thus extracting from it every possible pleasure and meaning. Yet to live life just for the moment, to find "eternity in an hour," as Blake said, is really to revert to Russell's unreal arithmetical point that lacks not only historical substance but, paradoxically, time itself. If the present is all we have, then we have next to nothing, for under these constraints time flies and nothing exhibits abiding virtuality, charm, or moral significance. Perhaps this is why this age-old philosophy, which has resurfaced in our day in the guise of the "now" generation, always contains a note of haste and a hint of panic.

As Marías sees it, such an era of temporal and historical deepening began around 1900 with the Generation of 1898 (1871).[3] Writing in 1971, he notes: *"Our time* begins with them and has continued for at least three more generations: those of 1886, 1901, and 1916. And what about succeeding generations? It may have seemed that they had turned to other things, but this is not certain."[4]

This means that before the advent of this new sensitivity there existed a different modal temper that Marías could not call "ours," except perhaps in a latent sense. He shares with the generations of Unamuno and Ortega the conviction that the Restoration era was the culmination of a long period of national disorientation lasting throughout the nineteenth century. During this time, Spain was inferior in manifold ways not only to the rest of Europe but also to its own possibilities. The overarching mission of the Generation of 1898 and its successors was to cancel—and in certain ways to transcend—this burdensome anomaly of Spanish life.

According to Marías, modern Spain began with the rise to power of the first Romantic generation born around 1766 and predominate from the years 1810–1812. Its attitudes were incorporated in the Constitution of 1812, which Marías describes as a prototypical Romantic document.[5] Although the Romantic era in Spain constituted a fully developed "minimal historical period" that lasted four generations (born respectively around 1766, 1781, 1796, and 1811), it exhibited a peculiar *décalage* insofar as its literary manifestations were concerned. Romanticism was already well established socially and politically before it appeared in literature. In fact, the most celebrated Romantic writers (Zorrilla, Espronceda, Duque de Rivas) were born in the last Romantic generation (1811), when Romanticism as a way of life was in its waning phases.

Marías attributes this anomaly to the twenty-five year period between the French invasion in 1808 and the death of Fernando VII in 1833. It was a time when nothing could be done and indeed very little was done: culture, education, industry, and statesmanship languished. "The result was a difference in level between Spain and Europe, of such magnitude that it seemed absolutely impossible to overcome."[6]

For Marías and his older contemporaries, the impression of irresponsibility in nineteenth-century Spanish society was as deplorable as it was undeniable. Menéndez Pelayo had described the shameful state of Spanish universities in 1845: "Nobody thought of studying; the chairs were unoccupied. . . . Teaching was pure farce, a tacit agreement between pupils and masters, founded on mutual ignorance, indifference, and almost criminal abandon."[7]

Nor had things improved very much by the turn of the century. Speaking through Andrés Hurtado in *El árbol de la ciencia* (1911), novelist Pío Baroja excoriates the pedagogical sham he finds in the University: "During the first days of class Andrés Hurtado could not get over his astonishment. It was all too absurd. He would have wished for a discipline at once strict and affectionate; what he found was a grotesque class in which the students poked fun at the professor. His preparation for science could not have been more unfortunate."[8]

During the second phase of the modern period, comprised of the generations of 1826, 1841, and 1856, the most representative figures of which were, respectively, Valera, Galdós, and Menéndez Pelayo, Spain continued to alternate between what Marías calls "stagnation and spasm." The last official vestiges of Romanticism were swept away in the *Gloriosa,* the Revolution of 1868, and following the short, half-hearted reign of Amadeus of Savoy and the abortive First Republic, from 1873 until the end of the century Restoration policies prevailed. Ortega called it a time of "illusion, appearance, fakery, phantasmagoria." After the disastrous war with the United States in 1898, Joaquín Costa remarked that "This nation which we thought cast in bronze has turned out to be a hollow reed."[9] As early as 1895, Unamuno had written a prescient article under the title "Sobre el marasmo actual de España" ["On the Present Stagnation in Spain"].

Although it was once common practice to attribute the formation of the Generation of 1898 to the calamitous war with the United States, Marías rejects the notion that any generation can be reduced to a singular event, regardless of its magnitude. Nevertheless, 1898 remains a significant date: "What the year 1898 signifies is the revelation of the emptiness of the basic assumptions of previous generations, the discovery of the falsehood on which Spanish life had been based, under a thin film of favorable appearances."[10]

This raises the broader but pertinent question of faithfulness to generational mission. Marías subscribes to the Ortegan view that each generation comes into the world with a purpose, a destiny, as it were, that it alone can fulfill or frustrate, not in isolation but in concert or disagreement with others that precede and follow it. But this also implies that it may choose not to remain faithful to its destiny. And since the fulfillment of this mission represents for a given generation its most fundamental relationship to truth, this means that to turn its back on its primary purpose is to renounce destiny and live in general opposition to truth.

In such cases of generational desertion the truth does not disappear; it becomes instead adversarial, unpleasant, and disturbing. When this happens, a general preference for the false replaces the tropism toward truth characteristic of generations faithful to their calling. Writing in 1947, with the Civil War and World War II in the recent past and the Cold War already looming ahead, Marías renders this verdict on the times he saw emerging: ". . . an extremely abnormal and paradoxical situation is possible, which is to live *against truth*. And this is—let us not deceive ourselves—the dominant [situation] of our time. Falsity for its own sake is knowingly and willingly affirmed. There is a willingness to enter into dialogue with it and accept it tactically, even though it may come from one's enemy, but *never with the truth*." [11]

Consequently, in such times all truths are at risk, Marías argues, for they relate to one another not in random juxtaposition but within a "truthful" structure or hierarchy of reciprocal dependency. Normally structured truths support and shed light on one another. On the other hand, whenever this structure ceases to function, or to function erratically, because the foundational truths that sustain it have been falsified, then the associated or derivative truths within the collapsed structure lose their obvious referential links and appear to be in random but general conflict with one another. Yeats warned that in such times "things fall apart," but this is poetic personification. What really happens is that without a coherent "truthful" system to guide us, we fall apart.

This "truthful" structure is both more and less than a rationally articulated philosophical system. It would be more accurate to say that rationality rests on the much vaster reasonable life system we discussed in a previous chapter. Indeed, in times of generational fidelity and plenitude it tends to function as a comprehensive (though not complete) subterranean system of beliefs and assumptions that by definition is seldom if ever articulated. As assumptions of truth, beliefs form a special class of implicit *vigencias*. As Marías understands it, beliefs are not what we "say" we believe but what we unquestioningly assume reality to be. Paradoxically, to "express" a belief is to reveal that it has come to the surface of reality and therefore is "superficial"; it has ceased in some sense to function as a belief and has mutated into an idea. In this regard, Marías notes: "The strongest, soundest, and most deeply rooted *vigencias* do not appear as such; they are neither announced nor stated . . ." [12] In other words, instead of expressing our beliefs, we live them in such a profound way that they remain more or less unconscious. They are normally too deep for words.

We have seen that "my" circumstance, that is, the circumstance of each person, is historical, meaning in the first instance that things appear to me not as abstract or absolute reality but as prior or historical interpretations. If I describe a certain object before me as an "old house," for instance, I rely more on my inherited assumptions and experience than its mere phenomenological presence. I cannot call something "new" or "old"—or for that matter even a "house"—without a tacit reference to learned criteria outside the object under observation. To describe something as "old" is necessarily to acknowledge in it also a prior state of "newness." Epistemologically we understand a house as an "old house" by seeing it not as a simple object before us but as a series of states of being embedded in time. Real vision, that is, vision that is also knowledge, never restricts itself to what is merely seen but immediately inserts it dialectically in life and time.[13] (No wonder, then, that *videre* the Latin verb "to see," from which "vision" derives, is related etymologically to the Sanskrit *veda*, "knowledge.") Thus, what appeared to be a simple observation of an old house is really a historical interpretation that transcends the visible object and our supposed objectivity. Seeing, therefore, is not simply the inert reception of images but the personal perception of relationships. Real sight is also insight. Humanly speaking, abstract phenomenology turns out to be as impossible as historical phenomenology is inescapable.

Thus, not mere objects but these historically understood nominal categories—stone, horse, man, automobile, etc.—function as our primary level of metaphysics and knowledge of the world. These categories include not only phonetic or written notations but also their connotations. Perhaps a rose by any other name would smell as sweet, as Shakespeare pleaded, but it might not mean the same. For names matter. The same "objective" or phenomenological reality alters its profile and transmits different levels of emotional charge according to terminology. Think of the chasm that separates medical descriptions of sexual anatomy from pornographic references to the same organs.

The generational antagonism toward truth we saw earlier not only creates a crisis in the hierarchy of express truths but also indicates a weakening of the superstructure of unexpressed and perhaps inexpressible beliefs. The result is that in critical circumstances our interpretations betray us. Cracks and fissures appear and spread in our universe; the familiar fails, and we are not sure what to make of things. And this means ultimately that we are not sure how to live, for as we saw earlier, living is having to make sense of things. Therefore, insofar as we cannot come up with the meaning of things, we can find no sense in our life. Cynicism and skepticism trace their common ancestry to this original human perplexity.

The First "Generation of 1898"

In many ways, what I have just written describes the situation encountered by the Generation of 1898 as it became historically active around 1901. But here we must repeat an earlier caution about the very meaning of generations. It begins with the trite observation that the Generation of 1898 was a *generation*. I mean that it involved not just the famous names of literature, politics, and science, but numberless people born within a certain "zone of dates." An incident in Azorín's *Antonio Azorín* may illustrate the point. A stranger approaches Azorín and tells him: "I know who you are . . . and I want to have the pleasure of greeting you. You are one of the men of the future."[14] This hints of an intuitive bond, a common generational understanding, between the writer-protagonist and this anonymous stranger. Had the "Generation" of 1898 been merely a handful of brilliant writers or eccentric intellectuals, it would have been impossible to carry out the transformation they accomplished. To resort to language reminiscent of Ortegan sociology, the initiatives and leadership of the generational leaders presupposed the intuitive acceptance and response of the masses. To what purpose? To put into effect a certain all-encompassing vision of life that corresponded to their understanding of truth and personal authenticity. In short, the Generation of 1898 amounted to a "program" or "style" of life, or better, a style for living, and the masses understood it as such.

Naturally, it is easy enough to lose sight of the generational nature of the "Generation" of 1898. The extraordinary personalities of such figures as Unamuno, Valle-Inclán, and Baroja may cause us to concentrate on their eccentricities at the expense of their shared generational qualities. Nor can we rely on their help to get at this linkage; after all, by imitating the examples of Nietzsche, Shaw, and the Romantics, they had come to assume that being meant being personally different from everybody else. It was an age that commonly confused originality with eccentricity. Not until Ortega's tutelage and praise did writers like Azorín and Baroja begin to understand how intellectual life could be lived and thought of as a normal activity instead of existential rebellion. Provincially aloof but preeminent, Unamuno seems never to have gotten this message.

Since Ortega's early writings on Azorín and Baroja, there have been many attempts to define the Generation of 1898. Ortega referred to the "catastrophic mentality" of his elder contemporaries. Donald Shaw identifies three criteria for "membership" in the Generation of 1898: ". . . participation in a personal quest for renewed ideals and beliefs; interpretation of the problem of Spain in related terms, i.e., as a problem of mentality, rather than as political or economic and social; and acceptance of the role of creative writing primarily as an instrument for the examination of these problems."[15] For his part, Laín Entralgo believes that the Generation of 1898 was defined by a common "dream" [*ensueño*]: the land, the people, and the past and future all mutually articulated and codetermined within the radical unity of a dreamed-of Spain. Out of this dream, three historical "myths" emerge to form the spiritual structure of the Generation: the myth of Castile, the third sally of Don Quixote, and the myth of a future Spain in which its peculiar history and intrahistory will richly blend with the "demands of present-day reality."[16]

Marías believes that the Generation of 1898 represented a unique "acceptance" of Spanish reality. This was accomplished first of all by taking visual possession of Castile and through it the rest of Spain. Curiously enough, none of the prominent writers of the "first" Generation of 1898 was Castilian, which meant that they discovered Castile by creating a "literary Castilian landscape." This involved a great deal of travel and observation. But it was a labor of love. "What a delight, to roam the backroads of Castile!" The words are Ortega's but they echo the sentiments of his elder companions as well.

Perhaps the Generation of 1898 has been defined too much by what its members said and not enough by what they presupposed. From a more or less common set of assumptions about Spanish deficiencies and a similarity of vital needs, the egregious figures of the Generation of 1898 moved along highly personal trajectories to the most disparate conclusions and forms of expressions. There is no way the modest splendor of Azorín's style can be mistaken for Baroja's blunt honesty, Unamuno's existential agonies, or Antonio Machado's lovely but understated moral and aesthetic insights. Like Don Quixote, the leaders of the Generation of 1898 had a good idea of who they were and what they were about, but their assurance does not always address our perplexity in trying to understand them. From our world view, for instance, it is hard to assimilate the fact that they seemed undaunted by the prospect of failure. Yet failure on a national scale was their starting point and the stimulus that moved them.

This is why their acceptance of Spanish reality did not mean conformity to it. Paradoxically, as Marías has pointed out, the Generation of 1898 accepted an unacceptable Spain. In other words, their historical reality could only serve as a starting point toward another destination, or better, another destiny, because they could not remain where they were and under the circumstances could not be fully who they knew they were meant to be. Though some, like Azorín, were modest men, they could not afford any sort of self-indulgent timidity in the face of their destiny. Marías describes their situation as *naufragio,* shipwreck. Their creative efforts grew out of a courageous urgency to save themselves and their generation. They were forced to create not only new literary styles but also new metaphors of life and new existential modes so as to begin the transformation and renewal of their cultural ethos. This is why to limit their general endeavor to literary categories and aesthetic innovations alone is to overlook the transcendency of their task and their genius, to say nothing of their personal courage. They exhibited a radical sincerity, or as Ortega said in the case of Baroja, a *fondo insobornable* [incorruptible depths] that rendered them essentially impervious to the common enticements of fad and fame just as it left them curiously indifferent to failure. The Generation of 1898 did not merely choose to do literature, art, history, and science. Given their perception of Spanish reality, their creative initiatives were not a matter of choice but of necessity. They believed their only genuine option was to create from the deepest levels of their life. This is why, as Marías notes, "No external reason—economic advantage, social prestige, political opportunities, automatism of institutions—led them to the intellectual life. It welled up from inside them, from the profoundest depths of their authenticity, because they needed it *to be themselves in the Spanish reality which they have accepted.*" [17]

This posture led to direct and often contemptuous antagonism toward the urbane Restoration skeptics, who thought it was more important to respect the conventions of art, science, and politics than to go to the core of the problems themselves. Writers of the Restoration era—Galdós, Alas ["Clarín"], Valera, Picón, Pardo Bazán, and even Pereda—were fashionable and correct in their writings. They made the most of current techniques and trendy European ideologies. But in general they lacked what Marías calls "page quality," which, he claims, ". . . can exist only when the author is present in every written line." [18]

What does this mean? Much of what the Restoration writers wrote was an impersonal transmutation of socially predominant clichés. This is why their literature offers few surprises and despite examples of genius—witness Clarín or Galdós—falls into a certain pattern of humdrum predictability. From our historical vantage point we can see with some clarity that beneath the hubris of their ideological themes and social controversies (often imported and learned rather than heated by native conviction), a bourgeois contentment with life took the edge off their art and held them to a leisurely existential pace. The grimmest themes of *Misericordia* or *Fortunata y Jacinta* cannot quite wipe away Galdós's indulgent bonhomie, nor does the naturalistic human decay of *Los pazos de Ulloa* and *La madre naturaleza* alter the pace of Pardo Bazán's comparatively placid discourse. And by today's standards, Pereda's elegant criticism of modernity would seem a peevish and snobbish defense of privilege. Only "Clarín"—and only on occasion—strikes a note in *La Regenta* pitched to contemporary tastes and expectations.

Little wonder, then, that Larra's acerbic criticism and romantic morbidity were much more attractive to the Generation of 1898 than the bourgeois positivism and urbane cosmopolitanism of the Restoration. Of course, by 1900 Romanticism had long since vanished as an all-encompassing way of life, but as we noted earlier, the most celebrated members of the Generation were provincials. [19] They came from the outlying areas and small cities where an antiquated Romanticism had lingered on in manners, music, and mothers. It is likely that this background accounts in part for the archaizing tendencies of the Generation of 1898, just as it gives clues as to why they more or less ignored Galdosian realism and the "science" of Menéndez Pelayo. Unlike the Restoration, Romanticism was too remote historically to be in direct conflict with the Generation of 1898. To use a human analogy, the new generation conformed to the frequent pattern of quarrelling with its Restoration parents by allying itself with its Romantic grandparents.

By rejecting the general Restoration style and tone the writers, artists, and scientists of the initial Generation of 1898 had no choice but to be personally and profoundly original. Their radical commitment to the truth, their brave acceptance of their unacceptable historical condition, meant that they could no longer count on the societal commonplaces to serve as the foundation of their creative endeavors, much less as a standard by which to live. Unlike Galdós, whose novels were in large measure fictionalized versions of things everybody knew and recognized as public topics, or Valera, who with a certain ironic and classic *hauteur* conformed to the codes of a genteel status quo, the writers of the Generation of 1898 abrogated this unspoken pact with prevailing bourgeois norms and initiated an era of intensely "personal" and neo-Romantic literature. Instead of simply completing works already tacitly half-written by society itself before they started, these writers and intellectuals had to create from a much deeper personal level. As Marías is moved to comment, ". . . those writers have been there, on the page, moment after moment, thinking, inventing, singing, recounting, and never letting 'people' speak for them. And this is why, when we read that isolated page, it seems as though we have felt for a moment the warmth of their hand between our own two hands."[20]

Yet literature alone, even the great literature produced by the Generation of 1898, was not enough to bring about the Spanish renaissance. But to make this assertion is to be obliged to admit in the same context that what Marías calls the "literary temper" of this generation was the indispensable instrumentality of that rebirth. From 1900 to about 1970, extremely high literary standards prevailed not only in such conventional literary genres as poetry and the novel but also in philosophy, history, theory, and science. Seldom have aesthetic expectations and intellectual rigor blended so efficaciously or come so close to the classic ideal of form and substance. It is a tribute to the rare spiritual expansiveness of that era that among the many master writers the one many acknowledged as the most dramatic—and likely the most elegant—was not a novelist or poet at all but the philosopher Ortega y Gasset.

The Generation of 1915–16

By his own definition, Ortega's generation is "cumulative." It was in accord—though not always in harmony—with its predecessor. There was once much debate over whether Ortega was himself a member of the Generation of 1898, i.e., the one born around 1871. By his own calculations and birthday (1883) and the generational paradigms set up by Marías there can be no doubt that he belongs to the generation of 1885–86. This is the generation of Morente, Marañón, Juan Ramón Jiménez, Picasso, Miró, Gómez de la Serna, Américo Castro, Eugenio d'Ors, Onís, and, we remind ourselves again, the numberless, unnamed, but real men and women who constitute the actual human substance of each and every generation.

The Generation of 1898 had posed the problem of Spain from a lofty literary and scientific perspective. Yet despite the rigorous and meticulous work by such scholars as Menéndez Pidal or Asín Palacios, it was hampered by the lack of comprehensive theory. In fact, several of its leaders were intellectually predisposed to take an anti-theoretical posture. Ganivet and Unamuno, for instance, the two intellectuals most capable of developing this theoretical base, both failed to do so. Ganivet died at thirty-three before his work had fully matured, while the irrational philosophy of Unamuno consisted of opposing rational theoretical constructs. Baroja tosses ideas at his readers, but for the most part they convey his various indignations and remain essentially extraneous to both the story and structure of his novels.

While admiring and continuing the "literary temper" of the Generation of 1898, Ortega's generation added its own propensity to theory, which Marías has described as a "philosophical temper." This led to a remarkable intellectual symbiosis between the two generations. Critic Inman Fox has noted, for instance, that while Ortega believed Azorín's work to be lacking in vitality, he also found in his older contemporary a superior intuition of life and history that corresponded to and corroborated his own metaphysics of radical reality.[21] In contrast to the Hegelian and Darwinian-inspired systems of the nineteenth century that interpreted human life as the evolution of colossal abstractions (biology, psychology, economics, progress, humanity, democracy, etc.), both Azorín and Baroja, each in a radically different way, describe the real dynamics of human life in a humble, often sordid, but always historical world. In time, this intuition was universalized by Ortega as the overarching *cogito* of his philosophy: I am I and my circumstance.

According to Luis Jiménez Moreno, this Ortegan affinity for the concreteness of the novel, as well as his mundane concern for the styles, fashions, and topics of his day, transcends personal whim or fetish. Instead, it points to the abiding Spanish predisposition to esteem human life with all its accidents and vicissitudes over abstract notions. From Gracián and Cadalso to Ortega and Marías, Spanish thought has always tended to center itself on human life and, consequently, to direct its greatest energies and enthusiasms to life as *praxis* and practicality.[22]

With few exceptions, Spanish thinkers have always tended intuitively to reject the fragmentation of human life. Elsewhere Marías has described the "bonus" of reality that Spaniards usually have. More than an isolated note or single voice, Unamuno's insistence on the whole person of "flesh and blood" appears to be a Spanish chorus echoing over the ages. As Marías explains it, "For Spain, man has always been a *person;* its relationship with the "Other" (Moors and Jews in the Middle Ages, the American Indian in a later time) has been personal. It has understood that life *is mission,* and for this reason it has placed it at the service of a transpersonal enterprise. It has shunned, perhaps excessively so, the utilitarianism that usually leads to a view of man as a thing."[23] The cited examples could be multiplied by the dozens.

No doubt this propensity has much to do with the celebrated affinity of Spanish thought for art and literature, for there it finds not only the distilled essence of human experience but an intuitive analogue of the dramatic and narrative dialectic it seeks. Taking the work of Unamuno as his starting point and Ortegan methodology as his guide, Marías has written at length on "the novel as knowledge."[24] But to all this we must add that while in the Spanish context almost everyone appears to share the intuition of human priority, very few have understood the mechanisms and philosophical implications of the radical methodological innovation it has led to in Ortega and Marías.

As we saw earlier, the manifold task assumed by Ortega's generation was to give theoretical expression to the cultural and literary intuition of human integrity and priority. It is important to understand that neither the Generation of 1898 nor its successors thought of this revival primarily as a function of governmental programs and institutional reforms. Although many notable intellectuals (Azorín, Ortega, Unamuno, Maura, Maeztu, etc.) were to varying degrees politically active and caused political repercussions, the Restoration image was still too recent for them to entrust human reform to the bureaucratic machinery of the State. And their reluctance was justified. Even the few political contacts they attempted turned out to be disappointments. Juan López-Morillas observes: "As to these political experiments the intellectuals of 1898 reached the same conclusion: the urgent need to seek in areas of thought and activity outside of politics the means of rescuing Spain from its progressive catalepsy."[25]

Most of the more prominent members of both generations eventually drifted away from politics and political thought altogether, which is probably an indication that they were never permanently called to politics to start with.

Like the initial Generation of 1898, or better, along with it, Ortega's generation, which for lack of an better term we shall refer to as the "second generation of 1898," placed the "problem" of Spain beyond politics. Like its predecessor, this generation was highly innovative but minimally revolutionary, if we take the latter term in its conventional meaning. But it went a step farther than its predecessor by suggesting a possible solution, or at least a more systematic understanding of the problem, in a superior phenomenology in which circumstantial human reality was the metaphysical base or radical reality and historical reason the method.

Even though Unamuno referred to post-World War I writers as "grand-sons" of 1898, the truth is that his generation exerted only minimal influence on these younger intellectuals. As Torrente Ballester points out, "The second generation [of 1898] . . . appeared in historical life and literary life at a time when the men of 98 were not yet in a position to "father" anyone. Its cultural preparation, which is one of its decisive characteristics, was not due to the men of 98 whose influence at that time was almost nil."[26] Though profound and highly innovative—and perhaps for these very reasons—the "first" Generation of 1898 was not especially precocious. Ortega rose to prominence at almost the same time as Azorín, Baroja, Valle-Inclán, and Machado, and although Unamuno was already known he did not become preeminent until the second generation of 1898 was already established. By 1920, when the older Generation of 1898 had become unquestionably predominant in letters and learning, it had to share prestige with its younger contemporaries: d'Ors, Ortega, Marañón, Pérez de Ayala, Juan Ramón Jiménez, etc. Could this be one explanation for Unamuno's short-tempered outbursts against Ortega and the other *papanatas* (simpletons), as he derisively called them, of the second generation?

Baroja's comments about the backwardness of Spanish universities in his youth point to a significant difference in the preparation of the two genera-tions. The Generation of 1898 was largely self-taught, and its university expe-rience seems to be decidedly secondary and often negative. Unamuno's long service as president and professor of the University of Salamanca may seem to contradict this statement, but it must be remembered that he wrote almost nothing in the areas of his formal duties and teaching responsibilities, but con-centrated instead on themes that reflected enormous personal readings and meditations away from the classroom and the presidency.

In contrast to the autodidactic character of the first Generation of 1898, the second was at once more imbued with European cosmopolitanism and uni-versity culture. Eugenio d'Ors moved easily from cosmopolitan Barcelona to the artistic milieus of France and Italy, while the personal circumstances of Pérez de Ayala and Ortega y Gasset, including travel and study abroad, brought them into lasting communication with the rest of Europe. No wonder Ortega with his Germanic experience was able to teach Azorín and Baroja several fine lessons about the intellectual life in the European mode. Com-menting on this relationship Torrente Ballester wonders: "How many of their qualities have the [members] of 1898 been made aware of thanks precisely to Ortega?"[27]

The "cumulative" nature of this second generation of 1898 was more a matter of concord than agreement with its predecessor. As for Ortega's own relationship with the older generation, Marías observes: "There was no agree-ment between them, but there was *concord,* above and beyond which differences, disagreements, and even controversies took shape. And this concord was based, if I am not mistaken, on the fact that both sides felt that they were participants in the same *undertaking.*" [28]

Thus, the two generations participated in the common Spanish revival from very different psychic and philosophical levels. If Baroja thought of his protagonist Andrés Hurtado as a "precursor" to some unnamed age to come and Azorín similarly described Antonio Azorín as "a man of the future," Ortega believed that many factors, not the least of them his own philosophic innovations—the discovery of radical reality, historical reason, a metaphorical heuristics, the reform of philosophic style and genre, etc.—heralded the end of modernity and the advent of a new era. If the Generation of 1898 sensed the approaching future, Ortega's "second" generation believed it had already begun. This is why he described himself and his generation as being "not at all modern and very much twentieth-century."

We should not overlook another seemingly external factor that at once links and separates the two generations: their simultaneous historical emergence and disappearance. Because of the relative precociousness of Ortega's generation and the exceptional mean longevity of the Generation of 1898, they flourished and vanished during approximately the same decades. The first Generation of 1898 gets most of the credit, but the truth is that Spain's "second Golden Age" was launched by two extraordinary generations working in tandem and tension in a shared ideal. Later, as death and emigration thinned these egregious ranks, the loss was doubly felt.

We have pointed to the "theoretical" propensity of this "second" generation, and elsewhere, to the general tendency of Spanish thought to initiate its quest for theory within historical reality. Both dimensions converge in this second generation in a new species of Spanish theory. But this requires in turn additional explanation.

As Marías has pointed out, for Ortega's generation to have insisted on theory as such and stopped there would have meant simply turning to European theory, for there was no "Spanish" theory of Spain. Indeed, many Ortegan scholars (Orringer, Benavides Lucas, Morón-Arroyo, Molinuevo, Cerezo Galán, and others) have assumed that this is precisely what Ortega did after his studies in Germany between 1907 and 1911. Elsewhere, I have disagreed sharply with this view, and it would be a distraction to resume the debate in this context.[29] But one feature of that polemic has a bearing on our present purposes. Because Ortega approached the problem of Spain from a theoretical level, he had no choice but to develop a philosophy that was more rigorous and more attuned to circumstantiality than anything he had found in the German universities.

This quest began with an implied question: how could Spaniards live within a Spanish setting and at the same time be at the level of the times, that is, in full possession of the techniques, problems, and possibilities of the modern world? The search for an answer led immediately to a set of givens: the quest must begin within the Spanish circumstance, as the Generation of 1898 had shown, but it could not end xenophobically on this note, as the older writers sometimes concluded. For Spain and its circumstances were also in Europe. What may appear to be a vicious dialectical circle turns out to be the most obvious given of all: for the "second" generation, a Spaniard must be European in order to be a Spaniard.

Probably no other intuition so clearly separates the two generations. Unamuno insisted that to be truly Spanish one must stand in opposition to what he derisively called European *Kultura*. For his generation, the choices seemed to be either the Quixotic exaltation of everything Spanish at the expense of the European or the embarrassing admission that Spanish culture was basically flawed and that the only reasonable recourse was servile acquiescence to the European model. The first Generation of 1898 had misgivings about both choices, which may account for the acerbity of their self-centered criticism as well as the grudging admiration for European thought one senses even in their bitterest anti-European tirades.

In the beginning, the second generation reduced its strategy to somewhat pat formulas. Spain was the problem and Europe was the solution. But there was another corollary: to resolve the problem was to convert Spain into a European plenitude. It was not only that Spain needed European thought, science, and philosophy, but whether it knew it or not, Spain was, or so Ortega argued, a European possibility *for Europe*. Was the young Ortega prophetic in his early vision? Perhaps, but we do not have to prove the case to make an obvious point: the second generation was able to transcend the timid or reproachful parochialism of its elders and to see Spain from a European point of view. But we must qualify this assertion by adding that this was not the usual "European" viewpoint one would associate with, say, French or German intellectualism. Even though it was European it was an altogether new and different intellectual species: a Spanish Europeanism, a cultural mode that until the second generation of 1898 had not existed for centuries, if indeed it ever had. Probably it was the most profound innovation of the era under discussion, a creation so rich in possibilities and so radical in scope that it is still to be understood and even further from being fully exploited.[30]

It could be argued, as Menéndez Pelayo claimed, that over the centuries Spain had produced many intellectuals fully versed and competent in European Science and learning. Father Feijóo, Jovellanos, Balmes, and Menéndez Pelayo himself come to mind. But there is an enormous difference between an erudite knowledge of European intellectualism and a creative posture within it. In an earlier time intellectuals like Feijóo and Jovellanos followed a pattern that was to become traditional in Spain: they accepted European thought and *reacted* to it, often in admirable ways but also in a dependent or subordinate manner.[31] Not until Ortega did Spanish intellectuals cease to be simply admiring spectators of the European mind and begin to *act* like Europeans themselves. From this perspective, we can say that Ortega's *La rebelión de las masas* was the first message by European Spain to the rest of Europe.

Much has been written about the celebrated polemic between the *hispanizantes* and *europeizantes* over the future of Spain but, relatively speaking, very little has been said about the resolution of the controversy. From our historical perspective it is now possible to say that the future belonged neither to the jingoistic *hispanizantes* ["Hispanizers"] nor to the imitative *europeizantes* ["Europeanizers"], for both these terms betrayed a deficient understanding of Spain's creative potentiality as a European society. With considerable simplification of what really happened, we could say that the Spanish Europeanism achieved by the four generations of 1898 obeyed this mandate: to restore Spain to itself by revealing its historical European destiny.

The Generation of 1930–31

Resuming our generational narrative, we find that unlike its two predecessors, the third generation of this epoch (1900–01 [1930–31]) lived under the unquestioned predominance of the new ethos. What had served as future ideal to the first two generations was now, to a significant degree, historical reality to the third. Thus, as Marías explains, the third generation ". . . is the first . . . to have Spanish teachers in a double sense: creative university professors with a mastery of the latest methods and valid literary models that were fully up to date and toward which they did not feel themselves to be in a posture of discord and estrangement."[32]

In the beginning, the way was easier for them. Thanks to the efforts of their elders, the general profile and social prestige associated with the intellectual life were by now defined and fixed, which meant that instead of having to create an image for themselves, as the earlier generations were obliged to do, the artists, writers, and intellectuals born around 1900 or 1901 had the much easier task of assuming an established role.

But if this feature was more convenient in comparison to the previous generations, it may also have been more confining. Perhaps the first impression one has of this "third" generation is that it was somewhat removed from the hubris of the times. Torrente Ballester describes this trait as a generic shortcoming: "The fundamental defect of the generation is its remoteness from life and reality."[33] It proved adept at what it did and was comfortable in its role, so much so in fact that it felt no need to wander beyond its allotted spheres. Consequently, its dimensions, ambitions, and idealisms are more human in scale. If Unamuno and Ortega strode a bit larger than life across their respective eras, the generation born around 1900 cast a more modest shadow. Although the "we" he uses is intended to be editorial, perhaps Laín Entralgo, born in 1908 on the "cusp," as it were, was speaking for this generation when he said: "Let us confess it without reservation: our spirit is unbearably learned and pedantic."[34] And Xavier Zubiri, a member of the third generation, used to shudder at Ortega's enthusiasm for the Escorial. Its gigantic dimensions and surging grandeur seemed overwhelming to his more modest sense of proportion and order.

Besides those already mentioned, a listing of its exceptional members would include Dámaso Alonso, Gerardo Diego, Federico García Lorca, Rof Carballo, José Gaos, María Zambrano, Lafuente Ferrari, Pedro Laín Entralgo, Salvador Dalí, José M. Pemán, Rafael Alberti, Vicente Aleixandre, Juan Antonio de Zunzunegui, Alejando Casona, and Luis Buñuel. Helio Carpintero says of them: "The aims of their predecessors were, therefore, radicalized. . . . The new men will bring the same attitude to politics as they do to science or art. . . . Pure reason in science, in politics, and I would almost venture to say rational and irrational purity in poetry . . ."[35]

It was not that circumstances, or circumstances alone, determined their elitist or minority status. Rather, as Torrente Ballester points out, "This generation begins by proclaiming itself to be a *minority;* it admits from the start the existence of popular forms of art, which it rejects as common and unworthy."[36] The severest critics have called this attitude bloodless and anti-feeling, with obvious links to Ortega's dehumanization of art and his claim that poetry can be thought of as an algebra of feelings. But neither Ortega nor this generation, which for a time followed his teachings, denied feeling as such; they merely rejected its crude and inelegant manifestations.

Unlike its predecessors, the third generation had never known intellectual and artistic mediocrity. During their lifetime, the achievements and the genius of what we may now call the "generations of 1898" were fully established and consolidated. On the one hand, this constituted an enormous advantage: the third generation of the epoch began already standing on the shoulders of giants. If the absence of genius was the rule that governed the Restoration era, its abundance appeared to be the norm of the new age.

But this genius was perhaps as daunting as it was dazzling. Precisely in order not to be inferior to the legacy of 1898, the new generation confronted the formidable task of assimilating a vast repertory of techniques, ideals, philosophies, and styles. No doubt this is one reason for its pedantic, elitist, and retiring tendencies.

This general program was of course serious business, but it did not mean that things always had to be taken seriously. As a part of his break with the heavy-handed ideologies of the nineteenth century, Ortega had proclaimed the intranscendence of modern art. It could save itself *as art* only by eschewing the melodramatic notion of saving the world. The third generation of 1898 took this message to heart and, for a time at least, followed Ortega's teaching. But it reacted to his teaching in its own characteristic way. Dalí's humorous caricatures and Buñuel's cinematographic satires of "real" life as the nineteenth-century bourgeois mind had understood it could be held up as prototypes of the new art and, in an oblique way, as a credo of their generation.

Marías emphasizes the friendship among the intellectual leaders of this generation. This was especially true of its poets, perhaps the most conspicuous members of the generation, who despite the divisive political antagonisms of the Civil War, for the most part remained personally loyal to one another. Alberti's eventual infatuation with Marxist proletarianism, for instance, did not diminish the personal bond and loyalty of his contemporaries. Nor did it lessen the public perplexity over his work. He was as misunderstood as a proletarian spokesman as he had been as an elitist poet.

Alberti's case illustrates another feature of this generation. Though public figures, they were not primarily public-minded. They seemed to prefer to write for one another and took intertextual pleasure in caricaturizing the publicly cherished commonplaces of art. No wonder, then, they excelled in lyric poetry and painting, the genres that most lend themselves to experimentation and snobbery.

Perhaps because it came to maturity in a world saturated with genius and replete with techniques, it seemed a relatively easy matter for this generation to turn everything it touched into artistic gold. If its writers could not boast the towering accomplishments of an Ortega or Unamuno, neither did they, as a rule, display the plodding style of a Baroja or the timid uncertainties of an Azorín. It was a generation elegantly at ease with its life and lot. Perhaps a bit nostalgically and with an oblique reference to his own situation, Marías observes: "This generation, in comparison with the others of our time, displays a predominance of facilities over difficulties." And he adds: "The protective fates have been in the habit of faithfully accompanying the generational team of 1901."[37]

Yet of the four generations the third seems to be the one least committed to their common historical endeavor. Marías notes: ". . . this solidarity becomes a bit frayed in the generation of 1901, which is very much 'wrapped up in itself' and a little less tied to the older and younger generations . . ."[38] Superbly endowed with talent and heir to a rich historical legacy, the third generation of the series seemed to hesitate before a multitude of choices. "They were too well endowed, had too many talents and gifts—think of Lorca—; too many roads beckoned to them; they had before and about them so many stimulating examples of their friends, so many facilities. In general they felt no urgency; they could wait, try, test, sample, and postpone any final affiliation."[39]

On the other hand, this generation was to endure intense ideological pressure. Unlike the nineteenth-century ideologies that made their appeal through intellectual and civil channels and for the most part dealt with abstract notions—evolution, psychologism, determinism, economics, etc.—modern propaganda flowed through the mass media as emotional messages often culminating in appeals not for mere intellectual allegiance but personal commitment and direct action. Thus, the elitist and erudite tendencies of this generation must be balanced against the lure of solidarity, brotherhood, and internationalism rendered melodramatic and gripping through civil and world wars. Not surprisingly some were, temporarily or permanently, swept off their feet emotionally.

The End of an Era?: The Generation of 1945–46

As for Marías's prominent contemporaries grouped around 1915–1916 a partial list would include these writers: José Ferrater Mora, Antonio Maravall, Enrique Tierno Galván, Camilo José Cela, Gonzalo Torrente Ballester, Miguel Hernández, Dionisio Ridruejo, Luis Rosales, Germán Bleiberg, Blas de Otero, Carmen Laforet, José Gironella, Elena Quiroga, Buero Vallejo, Víctor Ruiz Iriarte, and Miguel Delibes. In comparison to its immediate predecessor, this generation faced fewer but more drastic choices. To begin with, the new sensitivity initiated by the Generation of 1898 was the pervasive reality of its formative years. The illustrious names, works, and concepts of the preceding generations were now the household items of a rich cultural patrimony. If, chronologically speaking, only a few decades separated them from the Restoration era, in historical terms the distance was enormous. In that relatively short interval, Spain had gone from intellectual stagnation to renaissance.

But even though the temporal distance was short, it was sufficient for this fourth generation to look at its history with a certain detachment. This posture took the form of a critical choice: either they must reaffirm the new ethos or break away from it. Much more than their immediate predecessors, the members of this generation were confronted with the freedom of choice about their past. The decision whether or not to remain faithful to the prevailing ethos was understood not so much as a generational mandate as a self-conscious personal decision. To this fact must be added, and to a greater degree perhaps, the same ideological pressures that affected their generational predecessors. Hence the frequent "conversions," reaffirmations, transitions, and changes of direction characteristic of this generation. Consider in this light Marías's own repeated statements of loyalty to Ortegan philosophy or Blas de Otero's *redoble de conciencia* [drumroll of conscience], and remember that Ferrater Mora and Tierno Galván eventually abandoned the Spanish tradition altogether in favor of Anglo-American and Marxist thought, respectively. And there were defections and acts of treachery.

In an earlier chapter, we commented on the traumatic effect the Civil War had on Marías himself. And always allowing for individual circumstances, much the same could be said for the entire generation of 1916. Many, perhaps the majority, of its intellectual leaders were in their formative university years when the war broke out. As the existing order broke down and they saw institutions crumble and values called into question, they were obliged at an early age to make hard, life-altering choices. Some, like Marías, pledged their life and fate to saving what was lovely and true in the world they had known. Others chose to impose by force of arms communist, republican, or traditionalist systems. Practically all saw their lives and plans disrupted. This is why, as Helio Carpintero observes, "For them, even more than for those of the preceding generation, the war was to be a prevalent reality that would affect their very life to the core and would facilitate or threaten their future."[40]

Marías's choice to defend the ideals of this twentieth-century Spanish renaissance and his loyalty to the generations of Unamuno and Ortega are too well documented to need further corroboration here. But he is no less enthusiastic about the third generation of the series: "Our solidarity with these *three* preceding generations has been radical, unavoidable, and immune to reservations and dissatisfactions. We have felt that it involved the future life of Spain and the salvation of everything we held to be worthy, admirable, original, and essential in a millennium of Spanish life and in half a millennium of universal creativity beyond Spain."[41]

There is no known law that limits a historical era to four generations, nor any prior assurance that they must last even that long. If it is generally true that the guiding ideas of a historical epoch run their course in sixty years, it is also possible for ideas to be stunted earlier, or to be reborn, recharged, and to begin a second cycle, perhaps under a different sign and order. If the ideological paradigms of Romanticism and Marxism, to name but two historical examples, have obeyed the four-generation pattern of rise, predominance, and decline, others like democracy have enjoyed several reincarnations. In an altogether different order of magnitude and significance, think of the periodic revival of Christianity, which for two millennia has remained the same faith because it has not stayed the same.

A Legacy at Risk

With the advent of what Marías calls a "flanking" generation (1930–31 [1960–61]), the preeminence of the 1898 epoch falters and transitional symptoms appear. In his *Reivindicación del conde don Julián* and *Juan sin tierra*, for instance, novelist Juan Goytisolo disparages the "myths" on which modern

Spain supposedly rests. But probably nowhere is the melancholy decline shown more unflatteringly than in Martín Santos's uncharitable verbal portrait of Ortega publicly philosophizing in his later years. It deserves to be cited at length: ". . . solemn, hieratic, self-aware, disposed to lower himself to the necessary level, wrapped in the highest grace, with eighty years of European idealism behind him, gifted with an original metaphysic, gifted with friendships in the great world, possessed of a great head, lover of life, rhetorician, inventor of a new style of metaphor, taster of history, revered in provincial German universities, oracle, journalist, essayist, talker, he-who-said-all-already-before-Heidegger began to speak, doing so more or less in this fashion: 'Ladies (pause), Gentlemen (pause), this (pause) which I have in my hand (pause) is an apple (long pause).'"[42]

Despite the assaults, direct or implicit, mounted by writers like Martín Santos, Goytisolo, and Juan Benet *(Volverás a región* [1969]) against what they consider to be the vacuous myths and superannuated style of 1898, the older standards have proven much easier to attack than to topple. One reason for this has been the extraordinary longevity and productivity of certain members of the third and fourth generations of the series. Laín, Cela, and Marías are notable cases in point. Generally speaking, since these efforts began to occur with some consistency in the decade 1960–70, they have exhibited certain predominantly negative traits which we may partially summarize under the following rubrics: the prestige of cryptic textuality; the resurgence of archaic intranscendentalism; and the "marginalization" of intellectual life. Consider each briefly.

Prestige of cryptic textuality. If, as Ortega claimed, authorial clarity is courtesy to the reader, then cryptic textuality would be a form of literary rudeness. This should not be confused, as it often is, with the textual *difficulties* found in the philosophy of Heidegger or Wittgenstein, the narrative of Proust or Joyce, or the esoteric science of Einstein or Bohr. Yet the prestige of such towering figures seems to have persuaded generations of lesser writers that authorial prestige is directly proportional to labyrinthine complexity. Convolution for its own sake has become the sign of the time. Yet the present culmination has a considerable history. As early as the nineteenth century the idea arose—probably traceable to the image of the German *Gelehrtenkreise*—that the deep and the opaque were synonymous and therefore style, like medicine, to be effective had to be distasteful. Furthermore, to this earlier tendency must be added the recent blurring of the lines between art and academe. Under the guise of subventions, professorships, and monied support, creativity has been subverted by academic criticism and self-conscious theory. ("The Revolt of the Critics" might well be the title of a book on this anomalous cultural phenomenon of our time.)

No wonder, then, that late modernity, or postmodernity as some have

called it, has been characterized by pedestrian truths and unreadable philosophies. For in our day it is thought too much to expect that things beautifully
said can have the added virtue of being true. Thus, the first expectation of intelligence is that it be unintelligible. It has become a central irony of contemporary philosophy that what may be Heidegger's most obvious weakness—his
style—should become his most imitated feature.

Despite writers like Marías and Laín Entralgo who continue in the Ortegan mode of clarity, this deliberate textual obfuscation has become a feature
of much of contemporary Spanish philosophy. To this infatuation with the
cryptic—evident in philosophers such as Gustavo Bueno *(El animal divino*
[1985]) and Javier Muguerza *(Desde la perplejidad* [1990])—must be added
the influences of Anglo-American linguistic thought under Quine and his disciples, as well as the lure of the deconstructionist school featuring Derrida and
Foucault, for example, but filtered through American and British professors.
These analytical methods differ in many ways but seem to converge at several
key points: (1) a hostility to anything resembling the "grand narrative" commonly believed to rest on dehumanizing political, economic, racial, and patri-
archial myths; (2) a generalized assumption that reality is beyond reach,
which in turn means that all metaphysics and religious truths are either frauds
or products of the naive mind; (3) the primacy of criticism as an ironic and
self-conscious mediating activity between the limits of art and life; and (4) a
suspicious attitude toward language, especially unrehearsed discourse, arising
from the assumption that speech is a set of coded signs and symbols which because of metaphorical contamination never says what it means (nor means
what it says) or, most likely, has no final meaning at all.

The resurgence of archaic intranscendentalism. The antimetaphysical
bias of contemporary analytical philosophy is not really new, even though it
claims to be the latest word. What Marías calls the "eliminatory" antimeta-
physics of the late twentieth century differs in no essential way from its counterparts of a century ago (Comte, Marx, Freud, Darwin, Bernard, or Zola).
Both so-called "scientific" approaches coincide in denying *a priori* several
possibilities, for instance, God, immortality, and happiness. Don Alvaro
Mesía, a character in Clarín's *La Regenta* (1884–85) seems completely modern in this regard. The author says that he ". . . did not believe in happiness, a
metaphysical concept, according to him; he believed in pleasure . . ." And
consider Unamuno's moving meditations on the meaning of death and immortality in the light of Paul de Man's claim that death ". . . is the displaced name
of a linguistic predicament."

But what is "archaic" about such an attitude, especially if it continues to
be the prevailing belief of countless people? It is precisely because of that
continued presence. The archaic is not what happened and survives as the real

past but what continues unjustifiably as an unreal present. If there were no other choice, then such a continuation would be justifiable and not at all archaic. But following the antimetaphysical period of nineteenth-century philosophy, a period of splendid advancements took place with the Generations of 1898. Marías makes this telling point: ". . . our situation is not comparable to that of a century ago. It is defined by the existence of a philosophy extant and full of creative possibilities, by an archaic phenomenon, the replacement of the beginning of the present time by something clearly out of date, and, finally, by the abandonment of the philosophical perspective and the very questions that constitute the core of this millennial task . . ."[43] No wonder he views the current trend as a retreat into the failed intranscendentalism of the nineteenth century.

The "marginalization" of intellectual life. In an earlier chapter, we saw how the vocational substitutions that occurred under and as a function of the repressive conditions of post-Civil War Spain removed many promising thinkers from direct involvement with philosophy. Psychology in particular seemed to be the alternative for many who were called to philosophy but, finding official doors closed to them, had to look elsewhere for an intellectual career.

But there are other kinds of "marginalization" as well. We have heard Marías's description of "page quality." To repeat the essential idea, such quality naturally occurs if one truly creates the message, that is, if one is "present" on every page and in each line. On the other hand, when one merely parrots what is thought and understood socially—or, more likely in this case, internationally—when a writer is a conduit rather than a creator, then there is a corresponding decline in page quality. To put it bluntly, the decline of style characteristic of many contemporary writers and thinkers means simply that they are not thinking and writing for themselves. A telling clue to this condition is the swiftness with which such works fade from public consciousness. The truth they tell—if any—is not really their truth, and regardless of their novelty, their final message is insincerity.

There is yet another level of intellectual "marginalization." We have seen how the generations of 1898 were, with few exceptions, who they said they were. By this I mean something very simple but significant: they were unappealably novelists, poets, philosophers, historians, etc. They committed themselves wholly and wholeheartedly not merely to "doing" poetry or philosophy but to "being" poets and philosophers. For them, art was life, which meant that their life was also their art in uniquely personal and unrenounceable ways. On the other hand, in more recent times, probably as a result of greater affluence, philosophy, for example, has become a job one does, not necessarily a life one lives. Instead of being a philosopher, one is more likely to be a professor of philosophy. Philosophy, then, is something one works at for a time, not something one is forever. Hence the unlikely but revealing phenomenon of "retirement." The very fact that at a given time and with the requisite number of working years one suddenly stops being a professor, or poet, or scientist gives us reason to suspect that no unappealable personal commitment was ever made to begin with.

Here this "marginalization" must be understood at yet another level. The lack of a truly personal philosophical vocation implies an ultimate indifference to philosophy itself and an unnatural tolerance of ideologies that violate its very spirit. And since the spirit of philosophy, i.e., the unavoidable human need to know how to be guided in a problematic world, is the antithesis of such indifference, hostility toward real philosophy arises as a result. Critical deconstructionism, or as Heidegger prophetically anticipated it under its truer name of philosophic *Destruktion,* is the logical, if lamentable, anti-climax of an anti-philosophic age.

Marías stands in firm and active opposition to these erosive forces. Of all the thinkers of his time and circumstance he is the most solidly entrenched in the classic tradition he has helped to shape. But it would be an error to suppose that this attitude rests on dogma and fixed answers. More than the answers, Marías insists on the questions. The threat of the so-called "postmodern" era lies more in the poverty of its inquiry than in the attractiveness of its ideas. As Marías notes, "Do not lose sight of the fact that at stake is, above all, the elimination of the *questions* which man, and beginning at a certain moment, philosophy, have posed because of a deep need."[44]

Conclusion

In a now-lengthening watch over his world and time, Marías has done his best to see that the fundamental questions are asked, not as abstract notions but in response to genuine human needs and aspirations. Nor do these questions simply remain with us like curious relics forged by ancient intellectual craft. Rather, they arise anew as new urgencies whenever people seek to live authentically.

Yet we are not indifferent to the past, for it informs all the words and deeds that consitute our present life. Therefore, philosophy has a history not because it is history but because it must account for the past if it is to be responsible for the present.

Our trials are grave, our resolutions ever problematic or often impossible, but the questions they respond to are always real, defining, and enlightening, provided they arise in good faith from real and earnest life.

Not that this interrogative posture is ever enough to quiet our uncertainties. Indeed, it is for this primal reason that authentic philosphy, like the human life it reflects, can never be considered finished. Life goes on, and the moral, empirical, and philosophic human watch over our mortality is never over, though the guard and the post must change, the thinking never done once and for all. Yet even though we have no choice but to accept this protean necessity—this privilege—as a personal and vital imperative, its generational sequencing also frees us from impossible expectations and excessive burdens. For contrary to what the utopians of all persuasions have always taught, life does not require of us that we solve its problems for all men and for all time, only that we give them our best effort in the time and place, in the personal and historical world, that it has been our gracious lot to live. This being the gist of our condition, I will advance the opinion that in this demanding and rewarding effort Marías has lived up to his personal motto: he is doing his part.

PART II

METAPHYSICAL ANTHROPOLOGY

5

THE DISCOVERY OF BODILY LIFE

In 1957, Marías began to write what he called a "huge book" on Ortega, which was published in 1960 under the title *Ortega 1: Circunstancia y vocación* [José Ortega y Gasset: Circumstance and Vocation]. At one level the book was evidence of Marías's abiding loyalty to Ortega. Hear how he describes the task: "For me, the chief reason I am writing this book is that Ortega counted on it, and perhaps this gave him a certain sense of tranquility about the hazards of life and history. I think that probably his generosity made him too confident, and this fear both restrains and incites me. If I did not write it, I would feel that I had defrauded him, had denied him what he deserved . . ."[1]

But at another level we find in this work and in others by Marías a passionate but disciplined determination, not unlike a patriotic duty, to "save" the broader legacy of the 1898 epoch. Yet it is important to understand that for Marías this effort transcended formal erudition or study. In several cases, including Ortega, it meant going beyond what the writers had said to what the implications of their work signified, or could signify. (Witness also his work on Unamuno.) Orteganism was larger than Ortega himself and to confine it to Ortegan circumstances would have been to rob it of its transcendence and, ultimately, to reduce it to an inert scholasticism. The only way to save the past, as Marías understood it, consisted—in a dual sense—of a "surpassing" effort to transcend it.

For Marías, this effort began a score of years earlier. His *History of Philosophy* (1940) justified and summarized the philosophic past and brought him up to date. From this level, he launched into an exploration of philosophy as a general theory of human life in *Reason and Life: The Introduction to Philosophy* (1947) and *Idea of Metaphysics* (1954). In *A Biography of Philosophy* (1954), he shows how authentic philosophy responds and corresponds biographically, i.e., narratively, to dynamic human necessities in historical time and society. From there, it was necessary to describe life in its social concreteness, in *The Structure of Society* (1955). In his *Ortega,* Marías closes the vast circle by returning to his own philosophic origins. The first march around Jericho is finished.[2] And he does not return empty-handed but rather armed with a polished metaphysical method and an energetic sense of purpose that would

soon serve him in other areas which Ortega himself had not treated and perhaps had not seen.

Therefore, if his *Ortega* was a work conceived out of loyalty to his
friend and mentor, it was executed independently as a factor or component of
a personal trajectory that differed significantly from Ortega's. A disciple or
student of Ortega could have done a another formal and even valuable "study"
of his philosophy, of the type that abounds in bibliographies.[3] But far from
being merely a "study," Marías's *Ortega* is written *from the Ortegan level,*
something only a friendly peer could have achieved. And this means that instead of being merely a disciple of Ortega, as Marías is usually described, the
internal evidence of the book (to say nothing here of later works) tells us that
Marías addresses Ortega on the same plane and face to face, as it were. Thus,
while we are tempted to paraphrase Ortega's catchy title of a work on Goethe
and call this effort an Ortega *desde dentro* [from within], it seems more accurate to say that it is really from "alongside," which is the posture we would expect from a friend.

The Empirical Imperative

During his long foray into philosophy as a biographical metaphysics,
Marías became aware that a whole dimension of human reality was missing
from the general analytical or "intrinsic" theory of human life in both Ortegan
and Heideggerian thought. He saw it as early as 1947 and made formal references to it in 1952 ("La vida humana y su estructura empírica" [Human Life
and its Empirical Structure], *Obras,* IV, pp. 341–347), but more than twenty
years would pass before he was ready to attack the problem frontally. For
although the ideas were formulated, the style required for their expression
was not.

Meanwhile, if he could not do what he preferred, he did what he could.
His travels continued. Among other countries, he visited the United States,
India, and Israel, and wrote books about his impressions and experiences: *Imagen de la India* [Image of India] (1961), *Análisis de los Estados Unidos*
[Analysis of the United States] (1968), and *Israel: Una resurrección* [Israel: A
Resurrection] (1968). And there were other books on Spain: *Meditaciones
sobre la sociedad española* [Meditations on Spanish Society] (1966), *Consideración de Cataluña* [Consideration of Catalonia] (1966), and *Nuestra Andalucía* [Our Andalusia] (1966).

By the end of decade, Marías at last felt ready to challenge the theme
that for so many years had been taking shape in his thought. And so it was that
during an intense and unbroken span of sixteen months beginning in December 1968, he wrote his way into this unexplored area of human reality, in a
book he called *Metaphysical Anthropology: The Empirical Structure of*

Human Life. The wisdom of his long wait was evident: not only does this book reveal a new way of thinking about human life but also a new way of writing about it. Therefore, far from being an adornment, the style of *Metaphysical Anthropology* is the first evidence of radical innovation and dialectical sufficiency.

In effect, at this point Marías's thinking really "takes off." There is a noticeable acceleration in his work, marked stylistically by a greater frequency of *aperçus,* an increased boldness in drawing conclusions, and less reliance on what could be called in other circles "professorial documentation." *Metaphysical Anthropology* supplied the long-sought capstone of his philosophy. And once in place, instead of pausing to savor the achievement, his thought unfolds at a faster pace. As he puts it, ". . . instead of inviting me to remain in the work accomplished and perhaps enjoy it, it caused me to push on." And he adds: "It is not by chance that since this moment, and despite factors of extreme gravity that would have seemed to prevent it, my intellectual output has been much greater than during any other time."[4]

With *Metaphysical Anthropology,* we advance to another level of philosophy. Yet we must add that once there we find ourselves not in some esoteric or abstract realm but in that zone of life known by heart but obscured by familiarity. In this work, in which economy of language is more than matched by inventiveness of terminology, Marías develops the first comprehensive philosophy of physical life as we really live it, that is, in a body as a man or woman.

If this is the oldest of human experiences, it is probably the newest in philosophy, which has traditionally reduced the physical dimension of life to an anecdotal level. And this change of perspective requires that we also make certain *stylistic* modifications at this point. First of all, we must accelerate our pace to keep up with the greater outpouring of ideas; and second, we must always be alert to double back, as it were, to see how this "empirical theory" enlivens, justifies, complements, and completes the "intrinsic" theory that predates it by decades.

It is worth pointing out that in this endeavor we imitate the classic philosophic method; for the earliest image of *methodos,* "method," was that of traveling to and fro along a road, to a given reality and back again so as to keep it under alert vigil. Heraclitus called it "the road up and the road down." (Ortega's "Jericho method" is a different version of the same process.) But to be more exact, we must say that rather than *having* a method, real philosophy *is* a method. And this means that dramatic movement is inherent in all authentic philosophy. To claim that it can be what used to be called *philosophia perennis,* or "perennial philosophy," that is, an essentially passive disposition of the mind directed to an unchanging fund of problems, is a perennial misunderstanding of what philosophy really is.

For we must not overlook the fact that within this philosophic circularity our thought not only leans on and illuminates retroactively its earlier levels and components but also its future elements and planes. In other words, this to and fro motion reveals both the necessity and the evidence of a philosophy, its "why" and "wherefore." Here we gain a preliminary insight: the plenary understanding of a philosophy does not come merely from studying it. Instead, it requires that we retrace its internal movement and in a sense relive it and rethink its progressive stages or steps, so as to uncover the biographical forces that brought it into existence. In this way, we "see" and comprehend its internal necessity and structure. Naturally, we must be alert to its problems and dangers. For any solution comes flanked by deceitful alternatives; from any pathway we may always turn aside to possible pitfalls. The basis of intelligence, at least etymologically speaking, is the ability to elect or select and, consequently, to reject. Furthermore, in this etymological sense intelligence is also related to elegance. The elegant life is marked, and perhaps defined, by an alert and timely sense of when to say "yes" and "no."

In a strict sense, to philosophize is to consider things elegantly and selectively not as an exercise in dilettantism, but as a matter of urgency and responsibility. (Ortega understood this better than anyone of his generation, and for that same reason his philosophic elegance was widely misunderstood.) As for Marías, he defines philosophy as "responsible vision" and insists that it is incompatible with passivity. It does not accommodate drowsiness and indifference. And we could add that the bewilderment we often experience with contemporary philosophy is almost always a sign that it lacks internal dramatic coherence and structure, that is, biographically driven reasons for being in the first place. We cannot move within it because it goes nowhere, and in the deepest possible sense its passivity is alien to our life. Such philosophy fails to accommodate us because it was never a matter of personal conviction, or need, or passion, to begin with.

Whenever this philosophic or life motion stops, reality shrinks to the opaque hues of paradox and dilemma and philosophy ceases, even though its title and legend may persist. Not that darkness is the rule or reality out of reach as the neo-obscurantists repeat; rather, reality is a moving target that requires a keen aim on our part. Ortega once described it as a "dialectical faun." Philosophy is not for the fainthearted and the slothful. For as Marías puts it: "Philosophy is present only if man believes that he can progress from the patent to the latent, to uncover it and account for it . . ."[5]

Even as we emphasize the alertness and audacity characteristic of authentic philosophy (strangely akin to the attitude of a hunter, as Ortega had pointed out), we must also acknowledge the intellectual inertia that perennially untracks and paralyzes it. If such inertia may be defined simply as our persistence in old assumptions despite the evidence of common sense, then we could argue in this context that nowhere is this more clearly demonstrated than in our understanding of human life.

Consequently, our understandings often turn out to be our misunderstandings. We have persisted in thinking of life as a thing long after the evidence cries otherwise. We may be inclined to attribute this to comfortable mental habits, until we stop to think that our situation has been anything but comfortable. Because reality, especially personal reality, always rebels against the false, the various attempts to "reify" or "thingify" human life were never permanent or satisfactory. A parade of expressions—I, subject, self, consciousness, existence, *Dasein,* subjectivity, *pour-soi,* etc.—marched by in Western thought like soldiers in the long war to subdue life and convert it into another docile province in the realm of things. Marías concedes that all these expressions aim at life, but they do so from certain prior—and inertial—assumptions and thus do not mean the same reality. At best they capture certain aspects of life.

This occurs, Marías argues, because the starting point is a generic notion or theory of life within which disparate beings (men, plants, animals, God, etc.) must be accommodated. This means that from the first an abstract quality is introduced into our understanding of life. Life is replaced *a priori* with a theory, which true or not is still a theory (for example, the "biological" theory of life) and not life itself.

What, then, is the remedy for these persistent oversights? Marías urges us to reverse the procedure: "We must proceed in the opposite direction: the only life which is directly accessible to me, directly patent to me, is my own. Starting off from it, adding and taking away, I can perhaps come to understand in some manner what 'life' means when we speak of vegetable life, animal life, angelic life, or divine life."[6]

But this does not mean that we can simply replace generic life with "man." "Man is a reality which I encounter *in my life* (even the man I am); *I* am the one who finds himself in life; my subjectivity is simply one of its traits. The primary meaning of life is not biological, but—as Ortega always taught—biographical."[7]

Here, another possible error looms. If we take life to mean its chosen trajectory, then we overlook the fact that its reality also includes all the choices that were possible at any moment of life. To insist on this "real" life at the expense of possible alternatives is once again to give undue advantage to a part over the whole.

Life is primarily *my* life, what Ortega and Marías call "radical reality." My life is what I do and what happens to me; I with things, doing something with them, a doing we call *living.* Life is characterized by its dramatic "ongoingness." The commonplace that "life goes on" is truer than we know. For life is not a deed but a doing, not a fact but a gerund. And this means that life cannot be reduced to "psychic" or "psychological" states, as generations of modern novelists believed; my life happens outside of me on the stage called circumstance. This is why it is drama and why it can be told in the first place. Thus, Marías reasons, "The 'I' is not a thing at all, but a project or program, and that circumstance is a circumstance because it is *mine. I,* taken executively and in its full reality, far from reducing me to any kind of subjectivity, co-implicates or 'complicates' every other reality which I encounter in any form, and I consist in exercising an anticipatory and future-oriented pressure on that circumstance."[8]

Therefore, my life is the real organization of reality inasmuch as everything appears circumstantially within it—including the man or woman that "I" am. This means, among other meanings, that life cannot be reduced to a thing, for it is precisely the "where" or "wherein" of things. And life cannot be both the arena where things are encountered and one of their number as well. With life, we are not facing yet another "real thing," as Western thought has claimed for ages, but another meaning or plane of "reality" (and, of course, another meaning of "life"). Therefore, to speak of the things of life does not mean that we can reverse the terms and say that life is a thing.

But by no means have we escaped from theory. At most, we have progressed to the Ortegan theory that Marías describes as "intrinsic." But what does it mean to say that human life is a theory only not like other theories? To begin with, "my" life is where I start; it means absolute singularity and irreducibility. On the other hand, "human life" appears as an implicit proposition in the course of living.

In my life I find others. Life occurs primarily as a "living-with." Adam, says Marías, is a daring theory, philosophically speaking, and unimaginable in the worldhood we know. For life appears disjunctively as "my life," "your life," "his life," etc. In this sense, we can speak of the "life of each one," thus giving life a social reference at the most basic level. But unless I understand my own life intrinsically, unless it is in some sense understandable and transparent to me, then I cannot imagine or understand or communicate with other lives. And all these processes are necessary because my life does not come complete and ready-made. I have to create my life with the sum of realities that transcend me as circumstance. Because life is unfinished, I have to fulfill it—or at least try to do so—in the only direction open to me: the future. From yet another angle we see again that dramatic movement is inherent and inescapable in life. And this means, further, that I must prelive future things, consistencies, and connections. Imagination, projection, and prophetic foresight are grounded in the demands of everyday life. From this standpoint, even the sublime hopes of spiritual faith and the absolutely transcendent world on which it focuses its vision have anthropological correspondences in the here and now, though to acknowledge this link is not to subscribe to the age-old skeptical fallacy of reducing the spiritual to a figment of earthly imagination. Indeed, the reverse makes a stronger argument.

In this world I need to be able to count on things, to know their consistency and expected behavior. In other words, I have no recourse but to reason about things and explain them *in some fashion*. With this in mind, Marías has defined reason in his *Reason and Life* as "the apprehension of reality in its connectedness." If the phrase "I live" means that I apprehend or understand reality in its true connectedness, then I am by definition "reasonable" in the most basic, necessary, and urgent way. Marías can say, therefore, that life is the concrete form of reason and, further, that life is possible only through reason. This, in brief, is what has been called *razon vital,* "vital reason," since the early days of Orteganism.[9]

Hear Marías's summary of the matter: ". . . the only real life is individual, *mine* (the "mine" of each man); it is singular, temporal, circumstantial, and its expression is a *telling* of it; but I cannot understand, narrate, or tell *my* life except from the structure of life per se, which does not have reality. This structure is obtained by analysis of *my* life, and consists in the repertory of its necessary requisites, of its conditions *sine quibus non.*"[10]

Of course, only in the Adamic world could this primary analysis be possible as a solitary experience. Reality as I find it is already interpreted and appears to me generationally as social beliefs, customs, practices, etc., all pointing to and presupposing an idea of human life. The most reclusive hermit, the most desolate Robinson Crusoe, carries with him into solitude a social world along with its language and technology. As we noted earlier, I alone live my life; yet I do not live it alone but primarily with others.

But where do we situate life as such after we have conceded its social condition? According to the cliché, mankind exists within the cosmos, and we are embarrassed by our puniness. But if we take seriously what was said earlier, namely, that the man or woman I am appears to me within my life along with all other realities, then it appears that my life is not in the cosmos, but rather that the cosmos is something I encounter in my life. On the other hand, it may be true that man is also in the cosmos, but my life is not reducible to that cosmos, just as it is not reducible to biology, organic life, psychology, etc. All these are valid dimensions of life. The error comes from claiming that any one of them exhausts reality.

Where does this leave us? If we interpret man in all the dimensions mentioned or possible from the standpoint of life, we find that life occurs, prior to all interpretations, in the specific form of man. From this Marías draws a momentous conclusion: "Man, then, is not a thing, nor an organism, nor an animal, but previous to all that he is something much more profound: he is a *structure of human life.*"[11]

But an understanding of this structure requires something more than an abstract and lengthy analysis. I have already pointed to a change of pace. In addition, we must change our perspective and begin from a narrative stance.

Again the Narrative

Using the Jericho method, the only one that really suffices for philosophy, we reprise from another level and viewpoint Ortega's brief narrative account of Soledad as reported to Ortega by her lover, known to us only as A. The story is almost barren of details, yet this very feature will serve our purposes in an obverse and perhaps unexpected way to clarify Marías's theory. (The Ortegan reference is more than casual; in a general way, Marías himself often revisits Ortegan premises and, with other aims in mind, extracts from them their unexpected or latent consequences. We will make a similar, though naturally more modest, effort.)

In the reported narrative we learn that Soledad has left Madrid for several days.[12] In her absence, the city assumes a mournful and anemic hue. Things still appear before A in what may be, and likely is, their accustomed "real" process and order, but he realizes that his entire world, from nearest to farthest plane, has lost a splendor apparent only in her presence. He understands now that the geometry of the city is fully real only with this missing enchanted dimension. For without it there is no center or periphery. In her absence, then, things continue to appear before his eyes and ears but without arousing his interest.

How different his experience of reality when he expected to see Soledad! Then, unlike the abstract and objective measurements of space, the longest road to her was the shortest distance, but the shortest path was impossibly long if at the end he had no hope of seeing her dusky beauty.

Other people assume importance or sink in prestige according to their relationship to her. Some seem endowed with privilege because they live on her street and have spoken with her. This person vacations in the same resort; that woman has a similar hat. From behind, another woman resembles her, and his heart races until he sees her face and learns the disappointing truth. All who enter her life emerge sheathed in magic, and A looks on them as anointed beings. As Ortega puts it, Soledad seems to walk on a divine cloud formed by his emotional emanations.

Waxing more introspective, A realizes that she was his center of gravity, which ordered and attracted all the things of his world. And in a way that transcended the cardinal points of the compass, he was guided by a personal reference to her whereabouts. As he walked the streets, his real location was a function of how near or far she was.

The modest "narrative" ends with the admission that the city where she is staying surges from its abstract remoteness and takes on living significance for A. "It is a pillar of salt that becomes flesh again. Everything, finally, appears to alter its order and to become articulated in the meaning and under the influence of the new geometric center of sentimental attraction . . ."[13]

Implied and Implicated Structures

In our first consideration of the narrative, we were interested in what Marías variously refers to as the "intrinsic," "general," or "analytical" theory of human life, or in other words, the Ortegan metaphysics or radical reality, including, among other features, circumstantiality, historicity, phenomenological perspectiveness, the real "embeddedness" or radicality of realities that appear in "my" life, the implication of sociality, and, as the elucidating instrumentality that coaxes all this to clarity and shows it in its connectedness: vital or historical reason.[14]

Now we move beyond the first plane of "my" life, beyond the conditions that appear analytically as the necessary components of life at the foundational level, to life in its personal forms, which Marías calls empirical, because such knowledge is rooted in our experience examined from yet another analytical plane.

Consider the most obvious facts in the narrative: Soledad is a woman and A is a man. Furthermore, they are in love (or at least A loves Soledad). Yet the analytical theory has nothing to say about love (even though Ortega himself wrote a lengthy essay on the topic), nor does it recognize the primary human categories man and woman. Yet we know from experience—hence empirically and verifiably—that to be a man or woman is to be susceptible to the other sex in a series of special relationships that may culminate in love.

We read also that Soledad has talked with certain privileged persons known to A. From this we presuppose not only that she is capable of language but specifically that both she and A speak the same language, in this case Spanish, and therefore belong to the Spanish culture. From this assumption we readily admit others: the sharing of historical facts, enthusiasms, prohibitions, embarrassments, interpretations, beliefs, and credible absolutes of that culture. We reasonably assume that they have a common knowledge of certain cultural manifestations: foods, entertainments, fashions, public events, and an overarching code of conduct for each sex with its permissive ranges and zones of infractions.

We are not surprised to learn that Soledad wears a hat, for not only do we take it for granted that she has a female anatomy that includes head, face, hands, body, etc., but also that she dresses in a certain feminine way that reflects her epoch and social station. We could say that an intricate network of norms and normalcies circumscribes her personal uniqueness. Indeed, a liberal dose of the normal must accompany the unique in order for it to be uniqueness in the first place and not monstrousness.

Nor do we hesitate to think of A in similar anatomical terms and with the appropriate gentlemanly garb of the era, even though not a word on these topics appears in the narrative.

Without being told so, we suppose that Soledad and A are mature adults but not old, and, what is more, that they are approximately the same age. We know from experience and despite clichés to the contrary that barring extreme or perverse exceptions, love does not occur beyond certain age limits. We hold this kind of love to be impossible between, say, an infant boy and an elderly woman. The apparent expansion of these boundaries in our day merely serves to draw attention to the absolute limits inherent in amorous relationships.

If we press the matter, we realize that we take a "mortal" view of Soledad and A. They were born, grew up, and now find themselves at a certain measured point on their personal road through life (even though that measure itself remains a mystery). We concede that someday they will die. Their life is thus circumscribed by a precise birthday and an inevitable but unknown "deathday." It is through this essential circumscription that time makes its first penetration of human life, shaping and defining it along a temporal plane and establishing a dramatic timeliness to their actions. "Had we but world enough, and time, this coyness, lady, were no crime," says Marvell, acknowledging the mortality that informs life with priorities and finalities.

None of these features is described in the analytical theory of human life. The general metaphysical theory ignores sexuality, age, corporeality, and mortality. It does not account for language or dress. We could say that even though the analytical theory concedes the narrative or dramatic character of life, it makes no real allowance for the story itself.

Thus, we see that if at one level the narrative about Soledad and A is a minimal story, at another it is laden or undergirded by countless assumptions, only a few of which are found here. Yet without them neither this story nor any other would make any sense whatsoever to us. These tacit assumptions constitute in large measure what Marías calls the "communicability of circumstances" that permit narration in the first place. The verbal plot of any story comes accompanied and served by a company of silent assumptions, like unnoticed servants who prepare the heralded entry of a dandy monarch.

We said earlier that while the empirical theory is philosophically new, the experience from which it arises is humanly ancient. Soledad and A are *persons* in the ordinary understanding of the term. Marías's innovation consists of acknowledging and organizing what have always been the silent assumptions of human discourse. Using Cervantes as a historical example, he describes the empirical theory in these terms: "To it belong all those determinations which, without being ingredients of analytical theory, are not chance, coincidental, or factual elements, and therefore previous to each concrete biography and with which we can count, elements which function as an assumption of that biography."[15]

In theory, human life could occur in other forms (a common theme of science fiction). The fact that it happens in this specific corporeal way means that even though its attributes are not a priori requirements of the general or analytical theory, they are verifiable or empirical structural elements of all known human life. As such, they constitute the area of possible human modification. Marías puts it this way: ". . . [This] empirical structure appears as the field of *possible human variation in history*. Analytical and necessary structure is in fact articulated into stable and lasting, but in principle variable, forms in which it is realized."[16]

This has implications for the general theory as well. Even though we say—and say correctly—that human life is essentially circumstantial and inconceivable without being so ("I am I and my circumstance"), we still remain at an abstract remove from real circumstance until we deal with it here and now in this world and in this specific form of corporality. If we lived on other worlds with other bodies perhaps, circumstance would still be an essential ingredient of "my" life, but no doubt it would be different from the one I know. Therefore, instead of limiting ourselves to an abstract and analytical consideration of circumstance, we must tighten the meaning by thinking of it in terms of the particularly embodied person I discover myself to be.

For in this specific sense both the world and the bodily person I am are susceptible to modification. The world grows larger or smaller, more complex or simple, menacing or compliant, in ways that have little to do with its physical dimensions. "World" seems always to have meant a network of human relationships and reference points first and an objective, physical dimension only secondarily and as a reflective afterthought of self-conscious civilizations.

In natural terms, our "worldliness" begins sensorially. We see, touch, and sense things in order to take a certain possession of them for our need and gratification. But technology has expanded our senses far beyond the old natural range, so that an average person living today has a vastly more elaborate sensorial structure than our ancestors knew in the remote past. This is an example of the "modification" referred to earlier.

While the dramatic nature of life suggests an indefinite future, the man or woman that I am is mortal; death [*mors*] is the primary defining element of bodily life. Yet at the same time, human experience has determined that despite the mortal threat there is a certain—and changeable—life expectancy.

These changes, among others, are what Marías has in mind when he states that the empirical structure of life—men and women in their bod-

ily life—is the arena of possible change. Man is not merely a "natural" creature, though he always has a precise and variable relationship with nature.
Nor is he historically unchanging. As Marías goes on to say, "There are no
'historical constants' but acquired historical determinations, though their duration, at limit, may take in the whole of history from Adam to the Last
Judgment."[17]

The Forms of Worldly "Installation"

Unlike English and most other Western languages, Spanish has two
verbs of being, *ser* and *estar. Ser* derives from the Latin *esse* and is therefore
related to "essential" and "essence." It indicates inherent, relatively enduring
states of being. *Estar* comes from *stare* and is related to the English "stand"
and "stance." It describes location (the -stance of "circumstance"), transitory
states of being, and imperfective verbal situations. We could say, therefore,
that *estar* is the verb of circumstantiality and as such the linguistic key to an
analysis of life at the intrinsic or radical level. It is a basic component in
Marías's concept of "installation."

What does it mean to say that Soledad and A, as examples, are "installed" in the world? At the most basic level, we are speaking, naturally, of
location *(estar)*. Etymologically and primordially, the two lovers assume a
certain "stance" in world and time, thereby giving immediate meaning to the
terms "here" and "there," "before" and "after." In other words, because of
their stance, or better, through it, they relate to everything else, and this makes
it possible to "relate" or tell their story.

Yet we are still at the general analytical level. The general theory attributes installation as such to life, and not until we proceed to the forms and consistencies of installation do we reach the empirical level. Here, we must be
careful to distinguish installation, a biographical concept, from spatial, physical, biological, psychological, or historical categories, which apply subsequently to certain features. It is one thing, for example, to say that we are
"installed" in a language and to acknowledge that we interpret the world and
its resources in a certain way through it, and quite another to point out that
language is subject to the claims of anatomy, physiology, linguistics, semantics, logic, and so on. In other words, I "live" in my language in a vital, biographical way that precedes all attempts to objectify it. Or to put it another
way, the "objective" study of its features becomes possible only after we "possess" it unitarily and biographically.

Other forms of installation include corporeality, the senses, worldhood,
the sexuate condition, age, race (as a cultural and historical precipitate), and
caste or social class. If we analyze A's view of Soledad, we see that for him
she is not merely "in the world," as Sartre or Heidegger would claim (and cor-

rectly so, it must be admitted), but "installed" in a series of specific ways that make up a structure. As Marías states formally, "Installation is the empirical form of radication in human life as radical reality."[18]

Vectorial Structure: Inclination and Slant

But even as we consider the suggestion of immobility in these images, we become aware of an equally compelling sense of movement in the forms of installation. Life is not only what happens to me, but also, and more exactly, what is always happening to me and what I am always doing. Installations have to do with the way I am living. Or as Marías puts it: "The forms of installation are, therefore, forms of happening; or, if you prefer, forms for happening, inseparable from happening, without which they would lack meaning and reality."[19]

Marías defines the dynamics of this "installed movement" in terms of *vectors* of varying intensity. Mathematically speaking, a vector is a directed magnitude, which biographically might be translated as importance and significance. There is virtually never a single vector in living. Living is a matter of choice, and in vectorial terms, of compromise, among many paths we could follow, among the many forms and levels of importance and significance. Not that they are equally appealing. Some options, like distant stars, exert almost no gravitational pull on us, while others fiercely contend for our preference. When several vectors act at once, the result is another vector that does not coincide precisely with any of them.

But even though the notion of vectors comes from mathematical mechanics, the motor that drives them is desire. Life is desiderative, and the angle of relationship between where we are and what we desire appears as a vector, that is, as an unreal but possible trajectory toward satisfaction.

From another viewpoint this desiderative relationship may be thought of as "slant" [*sesgo*] and "inclination." We are "inclined" in a certain biographical way, and this gives everything that comes into our life a certain "slant." As Marías explains, "'Slant' is the manner of being of things when they are realities lived from a vectorial structure." And he goes on to say metaphorically, "Things take a 'slant'—always a dramatic one—when they are struck by the vectorial arrows of biographical projects."[20]

Inclination and slant cannot be reduced to phenomenological perspectivism. We do not merely "see" things. The visual and spatial relationship they assume before me does not exhaust that relationship. They also have a dramatic "slant," not through any necessarily exceptional virtue of their own but because to a greater or lesser degree they are subject to my projects. Life has a "radiant" or "radiating" quality that conditions the dimensions of the empirical structure.

Worldhood

Perhaps the vaguest expression in the common philosophical lexicon, "worldhood" has a precise meaning in Marías's nomenclature. He begins by noting that "my" world is circumstantial, yet not passively so. I incline proactively to things and they respond by assuming a certain slant in relation to my biographical projects. World is earth and cosmos extending as the horizons, limits, and ideal ranges of my projective enterprise. As such, it is order and not chaos. Other forms of worldhood might be possible, other circumstantial realms could exist, but empirically and as far as I know, bodily human life takes place only within this earthly worldhood. Therefore, in a dual sense I am "earth-man," of the earth and of the dust or dirt of the earth ["human" from Latin *humus.* Compare the Hebrew *adam,* which denotes "earth"].

I am at once of the earth and in the world. These general parameters indicate in addition to a very precise range of vital relations a telling fact: the world is neither a thing nor a combination of things but the *where* or *wherein* of my life. As such, it belongs to the general or analytical theory of life. Naturally, the world is full of things, but my being in the world appears to be of a very different order precisely because of my bodily being. Because as a physical person I am not merely in the world but always *somewhere.* "Here" and "there" make sense because they refer to my location and the movement I can execute; things are present or absent, vanished or yet to be. In other words, things exist perspectivistically as circumstance, within a total, encompassing structure that we call worldhood. As such, it is the first or radical form of "installation" that conditions all the others.

Customarily we "reduce" the things of the world—and the very world itself—to natural or material components in the curious belief that the smaller is the truer. The various concepts of "nature" or theories of atomic particles are probably scientifically valid, but we must remind ourselves that such components and reduced entities are components or reductions of something previous, complete, and therefore with prior claim to our attention. What? Quite simply, my spontaneous and lived experience of things as they take on a certain angle or slant in response to my calling to become myself. All this is implied when we speak of circumstantial possibilities.

Modern reductionist phenonomenology would persuade us that all realities are merely present and then only as reduced components of apparent things. Thus, even the reality of our fellow humans would finally be seen as a handful of chemicals, and these in turn as atoms and molecules. Yet it is obvious that I experience another's presence in a way that differs absolutely from my encounter with insensible things. For whereas things appear to me, I am not "present" to them (or at least I assume as much). Unlike the inherently reciprocal relationships with persons we meet, our mutual stances of appreciation and judgment, as it were, nature forms no impression and guards no memory of us, nor yet aggresses against our innocent or wanton timidities but enters compliantly into subtle alliance with the intimate agenda of our dreams. Because it is vastly imperfect to our simple native needs, it awaits the glories and griefs of experience and the enrichment of imagination to lend it significance. This is why the same solitude that youth often finds intolerable becomes the solace of richer age. Therefore, while we may communicate tensely or cordially with people, we can only commune in unanswered silence with nature. Yet the judgments we pass on these muted natural things tell a story of our own life: the world is as rich or rudimentary as we are.

The human meaning of things (though not their definition) lies not in abstract reduction but in their inexhaustible wholeness. The world is always more than we know. And these possibilities correspond to my living as an open-ended enterprise toward the future. We noted earlier that to be corporally in the world is to be somewhere, a somewhere that becomes meaningful and understandable through what Marías calls the "sensorial structure of the world." But this local installation must not be understood as a passive state. For I am somewhere doing something specific with things in a gerundive process we call living. Exactly what I am doing and how I am doing it, that is, the kind and quality of life I lead, is my personal story. To put it another way, the narrative of my life is the account of my particular installation in the world.

Here we must return to an earlier point that both summarizes what we have seen and sets the stage for what will follow: our worldly installation occurs in the two general human modes, man and woman, or in our brief narrative, Soledad and A. By reconciling in *Metaphysical Anthropology* our common experience of "sexuate" and bodily life with the general Ortegan theory of life as the radical reality, Marías comes into full possession of his own doctrine and method. And as we shall see, this achievement has permitted him to write with singular intelligence, elegance, and sympathy about those relationships between men and women that, unhappily, have also attracted the attention of many others moved more often than not by the sheer intensity of bad faith.

6

Men and Women

Through Ortegan phenomenology, we come to realize that everything known and knowable, discovered and discoverable, appears embedded or rooted in a precise temporal and historical way in "my" life. Formally speaking, therefore, we could say that all epistemology begins as the general science of human life. But herein lies a momentous paradox and, so Marías believes, a historical turning point in classical metaphysics. Although those of Romantic eccentricity have always claimed otherwise, thinkers of cooler dispositions have customarily treated the world and the things of the world as though they stood apart from our life, indeed, as though the further they stood from us the more rationally and morally trustworthy they became.

This is why, it seems, Western metaphysics, stated or implicit, has devolved for ages on the notion of *objects*. This has principally been modulated as formulations of idealism and realism, and secondarily as subjectivism and objectivism, that is, objects as volitional or desiderative phenomena or, alternately, as things existing apart from mind, imminent and immanent within themselves yet sensorially perceptible to a more or less remote and detached observer.

We note a confrontational substratum of meaning hidden in the term *object*. For "objects" are, etymologically speaking, those things that are "thrown in our way" (*ob,* "before" or "against," + *ject* [*-jectum* from *jacere,* "to throw"]). In the primordial sense, then, objects are obstacles or impediments that stand in our way and must be dealt with in the first instance as puzzles or problems. Only then does the happier but secondary meaning of reality as facility come about.

But if we look at the whole phenomenological context, we realize also that objects alone cannot constitute a logically valid metaphysics, or for that matter, standing in isolation, cannot even be objects. For by definition they are objects and facilities *for me,* before me, in my presence, and as a phenomenon of "my way," that is, my life. Quite literally, they are "in my way," bearing in mind both the annoyance and possible opportunistic connotation this expression has in everyday language. My life, or better, my living allows the objective and facilitative qualities of things to manifest as circumstantial reality. We could say that the possibilities of things, even the possibility of becoming objects, remain latent without the advent of "my" life to activate them and let them become obstacular reality, just as the presence of "objects" allows me to transcend desiderative idealism and engage in real experience. Patency is the primordial state into which things emerge whenever my life touches them—and it is important to add—*in some fashion.* Thus, my relationship with things is not primarily "objective," not reclusive and distant but effusive and intimate. Living requires that I reach out indigently, fearfully, or perhaps generously to them. But my vital need, my fear, my generosity, becomes for them a chance for fulfillment. Living is the dynamic process by which the created, potential world becomes my real world, that is, the world manifested to me and thus the only real one I know.

Therefore, a truer phenomenological description of objects must include the person for whom they stand or function as objects and opportunities in the first place. What I really find, then, is I myself living with, among, and by means of things, always wary of their obstacular qualities but unavoidably avid for their facilitating help.

For centuries, this human presence was either taken for granted and consequently dismissed as an anecdotal detail of common life and common art or, later, deliberately removed, reduced, or discounted in the interest of so-called objective purity. To look at it another way, the various objective philosophies rested on the assumption that the objectivity of things was absolute and impenetrable rather than humanly relational and referential.

Ortega's new equation, in which human life is elevated to a metaphysical system, is a characteristic consequence of *aletheia,* that is, truth as vital function that sheds light on, and uncovers significance in, everything around it. In dramatic fashion, I suddenly become aware of what I had always unquestioningly assumed: the world becomes my world in the form of circumstance.

My relationship with reality tends toward a concentric, "circumstantial" configuration, without, however, losing its eccentric notes: the world is so astonishingly accommodating to my presence that anywhere I am becomes my circumstantial center of things. We could say that rather than being in a detached or objective relation to reality, human life is always central within it. Dwelling always at this movable center of creation, I am engaged in an "eventual," consequential, and hence dramatic series of acts and would-be acts that within limits can be and must be narrated in order to be reasonably understood. And the first person who needs to understand this life meaning is myself.[1]

We can say, therefore, that in the midst of life we discover that we make sense of reality with things instead of without them and, what is more, that we have always been making sense of it in this way in order to go on living. Life, it turns out, is inherently reasonable and *therefore* communicable to others of a similar reasonable disposition and responsibility. To our good fortune, life communicates with life.

We alone are responsible for our life, yet we are not alone. Because it is a communicative enterprise life is inherently social and humanly responsive, and all the eccentric exceptions to the contrary make the rule more apparent and normative.

Now a fact of singular importance emerges from this circumstantial cycle of reason and correspondence: once I wax bold enough to consider reality in a truly phenomenological way without preconditions and bias, I find myself to be an embodiment of life in a very specific sense. I am of course a person, but a certain kind of person we know as man, as another nearby is acknowledged as woman.

Called by Name

Despite its accuracy, what I have just stated remains patently inadequate. For unlike inanimate things and organic creatures, we are not merely acknowledged or described as men or women but called by a personal, proper name: "Soledad" or "A . . . ," or any of the other names that identify persons and set them apart from all others. It is almost impossible to imagine a person, human or divine, without a name. Even though we may speak of "nameless" people, we simply mean that we do not know or may not care how they are called. Alluding to its full and surprising etymological meaning, we could say that its vocative condition expressed as a proper name means that human life is a "proper" reality and as such not to be mistaken for "im-proper," unnamed things. From this perspective, we see that it is a gross "impropriety" to attribute generic captions to human life. In several senses of the word, including the religious, personal life responds only to a "calling." From the first human episodes in Eden, God chose to "call" man by name.

Life transcends the generic because it is unique. But it would amount to begging the question of uniqueness to attribute it merely to such name-calling. The human name acknowledges this uniqueness but does not create it. For Marías, perhaps the greatest error of modern thought has been its persistent assumption that human life is *derivative* and can be reduced to baser, lower, and cruder realities. The peripheral or contextual truth affecting this assumption makes it all the harder to resist. For instance, a child's physical body, those physical and genetic elements that correspond to the *what?* of its life, obviously derives from parents and ancestors. *But not the child itself, not the who? that by corresponding to a personal name distinguishes it from all others.*

It is the unique irreducibility of human life that gives meaning to and makes possible a whole range of relationships: love, friendship, etc. We love or loathe a person not because he or she is just anyone, any-body, but because that person cannot be just anyone or any-body. And cannot be called by just any name. (Modern attempts to model love and other human relationships on the supposed interchangeable human equivalencies, the "any-bodiness," as it were, of human life, have had predictably tragic results.)

For Marías, the uniqueness of human life, the irreducible "who" of persons that we vocatively acknowledge every day in our mundane relationships with them, appears phenomenologically as creation. As he explains it, ". . . creation becomes the only adequate manner of describing the origin of personal realities. The person as such is derived from the 'nothingness' of every other reality, for it cannot be reduced to any of them. If we do not regard it as 'created,' it becomes literally inexplicable to us, or appears as forcibly reduced to what it cannot be: a thing."[2]

This irreducibility means that a person must be named but that appellation does not constitute a definition. One's proper name points to life's internal propriety and opacity. Life is essentially modest. The name we call another is our primary acknowledgment of that person's inner mystery and uniqueness. In its superlative form this reticent internal life takes the form of intimacy, which in love and other relationships may be shared but not exhausted. For life is not simply given and revealed once and for all but is always being given, always being revealed, and always subject to levels of concealment. To varying degrees that reveal personal intensity, life is always a process of getting ready to live more. All prior living is a prelude to my expectation of a greater vital becoming.

But I cannot live more without the world's complicity in my surpassing effort. I need things and people in order to become more truly myself. This modest intimacy must therefore turn effusive and external if I am to intensify and extend my life. My inner life, modest and mysterious but also projective and futuristic, has no choice but the paradox of partially externalizing itself and its secret to others and the world. Human life is therefore a matter of *expression*.

The Human Face

How does this expression occur? Marías explains: ". . . the secret intimacy in which that arcane person consists rises to the surface in the face—which is the person as he is projected forward."[3] Here the word "face" becomes verbal: we face the world in a forward, futuristic manner, we look ahead and express our anxieties and anticipations in our eyes, our grimaces, and our words. Therefore, we can say that the face is the physical correlate of the forwardness of life and the personal metaphor of our unfolding life story.

This is why in order to know someone we must learn to "read" that person's face, and especially the eyes, which are "the mirror of the soul," that is, the reflection of mysterious personhood.

But just as the face expresses our intimate life it may also conceal it. It seems deeply meaningful that the face, the strictly personal part of our body that identifies us, is also linked to the *persona, or prosopon,* that is, the comic or tragic masks worn by Classical actors. In this aspect the face is also our "façade" or "role." And this puts us on the track of yet another aspect of personhood.

The persons we see and treat in the ordinary commerce of life, and certainly the person we are ourselves, are at any given moment only partially revealed. A person is never simply there before us in a state of completeness but is, instead, always coming into new being while preserving the resonance of other scenes of life left behind. As Shakespeare says, "All the world's a stage, and all the men and women merely players." Personal reality is dynamic and thus dramatic, and this means that it can be understood in something approaching—but never reaching—fullness only in the acting out and the telling of its plot. Life is a narrative, and because we must express ourselves with greater or lesser skill in order to go on living our premeditated life, ours is first of all an autobiographical tale. As Ortega once observed, we are novelists of ourselves.

Therefore, while we are always the same person throughout the changing scenes of our life, we are not the same as we were or will be. For human life incorporates and exhibits temporality; it has a history, that is, a story of its trajectory, and a future because at any given moment it has an unfulfilled need that responds only to a hereafter. Now then, this temporal incorporation occurs primarily in the human face. We study another's countenance so as to discover where that person is in time as well as the quality of the time already lived and the anticipation of time to come. We could say, in summary, that while things appear to be external to time, human life happens *over* time. (Perhaps from this point we could argue that time is a phenomenon peculiarly relevant to human life, and that it remains questionable whether it ought to be applied to inanimate realities at all—though by external *analogy* we infer that time also happens to animals. From our personal perspective, time would be relative to "me," that is, something that happens to me as I live and because I live. The eschatalogical and theological possibilities implied by this notion of time and the hereafter are fascinating but lie beyond our present scope.)

Sexuality and Sexuateness

Now we can say with deeper understanding that human life occurs in two forms, men and women. Genesis records that at the foundation of the Edenic paradise, God created the sexes: "Male and Female created He them."

This radical duality—in which no superiority or subservience was ordained or intended—is the most obvious phenomenological human fact of all. Marías describes this foundational relationship as "reciprocal" and understands it to mean that far from any sort of separate life with sporadic intervals of love, conflict, or cooperation, each sex is to be understood, defined, and fulfilled *in the other*. Life is therefore disjunctive and reciprocal, meaning that instead of being divisive, it is a disjunction that links men and women.

This reciprocal relationship includes the sexual nature but it is not confined to it, as modern psychological theories since Freud have routinely assumed. A part of the difficulty lies in the descriptive limitations of the terms "sex" and "sexual." Marías offers a more inclusive neologism: "sexuate" *(sexuado)*, and clarifies it use: "The sexuate condition, far from being a division or separation into two halves, which would split off half of humanity from the other half, *relates* each half to the other, makes life consist in the fact that each fraction of humanity has to 'work things out' with the other."[4]

What does this sexuate disjunction mean? In the most radical sense, we experience ourselves as men and women only within this disjunctive linking. To put it another way, without the other sex it would be logically impossible to think of ourselves as "man" or "woman," just as we could not know what "north" means if there were no "south" by which to define it disjunctively.

Naturally, this radical sexuateness, which is the primary form of human installation in life, is previous to sexuality as such. We are "sexually active" perhaps for a portion of our life but we are "sexuately installed" from birth to death. This means, further, that although our sexuateness takes biology as its marker, it unfolds as a function of our biography. In other words, our biological sexuality represents a component or resource of our biographical sexuate condition that absolutely supersedes it. As Marías explains it, ". . . blue or pink garments are prepared for the newborn baby. This means that its sexuate condition, starting with the genital data discovered by inspection at the moment of birth, is going to be interpreted socially. Since man is not Adam (or Eve), but the inheritor of a tradition, composed of historical and social substance, so is his body, and of course his sexuality."[5]

Masculine and Feminine Reason

If what we have said earlier is true, then it follows that the sexes are linked humanly and ontologically in a relationship that transcends the contemporary flashpoint notions of equality, inequality, or separateness. Life is dramatic; people do things, and the sum of their doing and what is done to them is a dynamic series of phenomena we call living. Nothing human stands still, and this means what we all know: human relationships are susceptible to change, better, they consist only of change, readjustment, plenitude, and decline. Men and women are endowed with purpose, will, energy, foresight, and regret. Each sex functions as both the other's indispensable biographical reference point and its possible fulfillment. This means that a dynamic balance necessarily holds between them.

But if this is so, then why at a mundane level has history nearly always been understood from the masculine point of view? If men and women share the earth in an essential parity, then why has it always been taken to be "a man's world"?

An introductory explanation leading to others beyond the limits of this writing may be that history does not have to be written to be real. As we saw earlier, history is not primarily what we find in books, chronicles, and museums but what men and women have done and what has happened to them as they did. Herodotus understood history as a method of saving notable events of the past from oblivion. But there is an unspoken assumption in this view that for everything saved much is lost. Although "official" history may incline preferentially to the deeds and purposes of men, "forgotten" history, the undocumented story of life in home, market, street, and temple— what philosopher Miguel de Unamuno called "intrahistory"—would give at least equal importance to women and quite possibly might favor them over men."[6]

This may sound condescending but whether it is or not, at least one thing seems certain: contemporary women are not pleased with these terms. If this is, or has been, a man's world, then it seems reasonable to assume that it is essentially unfair to women and that woman's life is unduly burdensome. To most feminists and their allies, this is an indisputable article of faith. For them, the whole human past stands as a vast record of injustice to their sex.

Without denying the arguments favoring this assumption, at the same time we need to be aware that many aspects of our modern world would probably seem unbearable to women of former times. How would a lady of the eighteenth or nineteenth century react if she were suddenly exposed to our congestion, noise, crime, pollution, haste, and assorted dangers? Would a woman of the Victorian era really believe that the uncouth codes and new vices of contemporary women represent an advance over her time and condition?

If we think about it, our way of life with its intricate rules and rampant crime, its tight schedules and wrenching tensions, would probably seem an inhuman and unhappy world to our ancestors, male and female, just as theirs appears so to us. We are all historically conditioned to live only in a particular world structure, which inevitably means that comparisons of historical eras turn out to be ontologically biased and therefore suspect. Unlike Spanish poet Jorge Manrique, who sang that any past time was better, modern men and women take it for granted that in any context the present time is best.

In any case, the dynamic balance between the sexes seems to be shifting, and this has intensified the traditional perplexity men experience in trying to understand women. (And for similar reasons the same is true of contemporary women, whose tragically mounting misjudgments of men render suspect the feminist assumption that men are an easily manipulated species of psychological simpletons.)

But this bewilderment must not be overstated for either sex. Although male perplexity over women is a legendary commonplace, it amounts mostly to exaggeration. Social convention *requires* men to say that they do not understand women, but an even stronger human need *obliges* them to understand them—without admitting it, of course. The socially adjusted man shows his understanding of women every day in his harmonious relationships with them. On the other hand, the man who really has a problem with women, who bores or frightens them, who cannot win their friendship or enjoy their company, who is truly baffled and rejected by them, is looked on by both sexes with pity and contempt as the failed man he really is.

Yet for all its conventional exaggeration, this male perplexity rests on a kernel of truth. And for good reason. To be a woman in a man's world means having to live by logical premises different from those of men. Montaigne was right when he observed: "Women are not altogether in the wrong when they refuse the rules of life prescribed to the World, for men only have established them and without their consent."[7]

Marías argues along similar lines: "In the whole history of the West woman has had to live in a world that has been fundamentally the world of man in which the majority of creations—at least the more visible ones having to do with 'things'—were masculine. Woman has had to live within this [masculine] world and shape for herself her own particular world within it."[8]

Here, we note certain benefits and advantages for woman in this masculine setting. In more restrictive eras, the perceived idiosyncrasies of feminine logic afforded her a measure of personal freedom, a small but necessary margin of mystery, as it were, within which to maneuver and pursue her own agenda without the excessive male scrutiny that prevailed in much of life. We could think of it as a modest social analogue or compensation for the legal rights she lacked. Modesty, coyness, reticence, demureness, excessive clothing that hinted of an impenetrable moral reserve, these were some of the means by which the mystery and mystique of women were enhanced.

Although contemporary feminists routinely interpret this peculiar role as proof of historical injustice toward women, it may also be seen in another light. Because of her existential condition woman had to understand the world of men, whereas it was neither necessary nor expected, indeed frowned upon, that men would become versed in things feminine.

Perhaps this explains why, as so many jokes tell us, woman is able to manipulate men, even those men who may be or think themselves to be intellectually superior to her. She has learned his way of thinking and anticipated his actions, as the hunter understands through keen observation the movements and reactions of his prey. This is why, as the Spanish saying goes, "when man is on the way, woman has already been there and back." Marías observes: ". . . woman has had to imagine man, to place herself in his viewpoint, to divine the structure of his reason, in order to lodge herself in his world and work out her own place in it."[9]

Therefore, whereas man proceeds in the name (at least) of reason and makes of it—or its parasitical ally, irrationality—the foundation of his philosophic vision of the world, he generally fails to grasp the peculiar rhythm of feminine rationality. When Professor Higgins in *My Fair Lady* wonders why women cannot—or will not—be like men, he repeats what men have reasoned *illogically* for ages. For if woman must live her life from very different premises, how could she be expected to reason in the same way men do? Nothing would be more unreasonable than to expect it.

Masculine Expressiveness

We start with a paradox: even though human life is expressive, normally we express ourselves facially and manually and conceal the rest of our body with clothing. Generally speaking, the human face and hands are uncovered, the body only exceptionally. But seen from another perspective and in a deeper sense, this corporeal concealment becomes an odd form of personal expression. For the clothed and concealed body is a visible though silent component of our "narrative." It constitutes a part of our "body language," which picks up where our words stop, continuing and even contradicting our verbal account of life.[10]

This facial expressiveness means that in order to acquire knowledge of a person we must "focus" on the human face in a way and to a degree unknown in our contacts with other life forms. We cannot say, for instance, that a woman is beautiful or a man handsome without reference to their face. But we do not normally think of animals, especially lower animals, as even having faces. The human body is strangely, even disturbingly impersonal—a torso— without its facial component. Human life is first of all a facial matter.

But what qualities do we see when we look into a man's face? We said earlier that life is indigent, mortal, incomplete, and limited in time and space. Yet in his disjunctive relationship to woman, man aims for strength, security, and knowledge. Hear Marías describe it: "Man is ignorant, he does not know what to hold to, he is weak, he is threatened, subject to constant insecurity, destined to failure, condemned to death. And yet, man's pretension . . . consists in the exact opposite: knowledge, strength, power, security."[11]

Does this mean, then, that man is simply an imposter, claiming to be what he is not? Modern psychology and certain feminist theories urge us to this conclusion, and men themselves may fuel these suspicions by their exaggerated bravado. But it is important to distinguish between claiming strength, knowledge, and power and aiming for these qualities. The sincere man knows that in an absolute sense he is not really strong, knowledgeable, or powerful, yet he also knows that *in order to be a man* he must try to be so. Therefore, his manhood is measurable not so much by what he is already but what he tries to become and struggles to remain. If he is not strong, he knows that he must tend toward strength; if he lacks knowledge and security, he must seek to achieve these qualities. The frontal nature of human life means here that man must face the future in an effort to become all the necessary things he is not and will never be absolutely in this world.

Naturally, like all human tasks, this manly "becoming" can be avoided or denied. To a certain noticeable degree, man can reject the disjunctive polarity with woman that makes it necessary to be strong, secure, and knowledgeable in the first place. Man may then choose to withdraw from woman, to indulge in so-called "manly" amusements, to become addicted to sports or drink, for example, or to attempt to persist indefinitely in pre-manhood adolescence. (In passing, we may note that the growing prevalence of these trends in our day most likely indicates an enormous crisis of manhood.)

For Marías, the sought-after qualities we have been describing may be summed up as *valor,* understood here not only as bravery in the face of danger but perhaps even more as steadfastness and virtue amid daily tedium and moral mediocrity. In this context, valor revives its etymological sense of "value" or "worth." For historically, the brave man has been considered to be valuable or worthy.

All these qualities, including their falsification, exaggeration, or denial, mark a man, and primarily so in his face. For the human face is the visible metaphor of life's frontal mission. We live in a forward, facial manner. We face the world, and our face reflects not only what we see there but our strategy for dealing with it. The pain and the disappointment, the harshness and the hope, the happiness and the labor register in man's countenance. Beyond his genetic format, his face reveals the contours of his personal destiny as a man.

How shall we, then, describe a man's face? First of all, it registers the seriousness of life. Behind his joviality, handsomeness or ugliness, his family or racial imprint, a man's face displays the burden of life. In it we see how he has come to grips and to terms with the responsibilities thrust on him. Or, alternately, we note how he has shirked his destiny; we read his failures and false resolve. We detect his courage or cruelty, his nobility or frivolity. Because the face may also be a "mask," a man may hide his motives and true feelings for a time and to a point, but eventually the "facial" record unmistakably reveals its coded message.

Beautiful Woman

Do we begin by excluding many women, perhaps the majority? Obviously not all women are beautiful, just as many men are not especially virile, strong, or knowledgeable. But just as man must aspire to these qualities so as to be a man, so woman must strive to be beautiful in order to be a woman. In other words, the ideal of beauty functions as an assumption of the feminine condition. This is why, as Marías states, "The woman who does not try to be beautiful does not function as a woman; she has withdrawn from her condition."[12] Nor it is enough for a woman simply to be beautiful in the eyes of others. Many women, beautiful to other people, deny their beauty, think themselves ugly, and resist all arguments to the contrary. In terms of a woman's femininity, therefore, beauty is not in the eye of the beholder but in her own mind.

Naturally, beauty as such is not the exclusive property of women. Men may also be harmoniously beautiful in form, voice, movement, and manners. But normally male beauty requires an effort on our part to abstract it from other qualities summarized earlier as *valor*. (The fact that usually we describe such a man as being "handsome" or "good looking" instead of "beautiful" alerts us to a different sort of aesthetic appreciation.)

On the other hand, beauty is primary in woman, that is, readily visible or missing when we first see her face. We notice immediately that her face is less massive and more graceful than man's. (Man often feels—and sometimes says—that woman is too good for him—or at least too good for the other man—too fine and beautiful to be in intimate union with his harsher and heavier features.) Her face suggests beauty without necessarily being beautiful. Grace in a woman is analogous to valor in a man. This is why men have a primary impulse—long since culturally domesticated in civilized men—to look first for this graceful beauty in a woman and to experience satisfaction if they find its hint or disappointment if it is missing. It is as though the woman who fails to project the effort at beauty has defrauded both sexes.

Woman is lighter of body and features than man and hints less of the cruder forces that harden man's life. (Perhaps this is why obesity and harshness in women usually seem more pathetic and grotesque than in men.) As *Genesis* tells us, she was created at a remove from Adam's coarser clay. This lightness combines with softness of her facial features to produce the elusive mystery that perplexes and provokes man. As Marías notes, "Woman is stimulating because her function is to set man in motion, to call him; this is why she can be pro-vocative (a word which would be inapplicable to the masculine kind of attractiveness)."[13]

Here, the dialectical differences between the sexes we noted earlier reemerge to enhance woman's provocative elusiveness. For if man presses for outright absolutes, woman is less direct but no less meaningful in her responses. To man's insistence on a definite "yes" or "no," to his impatient syllogistic rush to resolution and conclusion, woman prefers time, patience, and "maybes," and dislikes all forms of haste. She seems to understand far better than man the importance of process and prelude. For her actions respond to a very different vital logic.

Summary and Prelude

Woman always provokes in man a trace of ontological panic. He senses in her reticence a fugitive and elusive charm that promises to rapture him out of his heavy and somber fate. But it may also elude his clumsy grasp unless he acts quickly so as to claim it lovingly before it vanishes magically into thin air before him. In woman he glimpses the nymph that lures him with delightful beauty but dances artfully just out of his reach. This is why in man, love and desperation, courage and fear are never far apart.

Yet this fanciful view of man and woman is but one dimension of their reciprocal relationship. If woman eludes man initially, it is her invitation for him to pursue her—if he is truly interested and interesting. And if he is and if he starts the pursuit (in older language, becomes the "suitor"), then his incipient despair delights her. For she knows then that he is worth her response. For she is never so elusive that he cannot overtake her—if he really wishes and if he persists. Consequently she directs her indignation—and perhaps pity—not toward the awkward but sincere suitor but the half-hearted man who lets her get away.

Beyond the pursuit, both man and woman reveal very different, even paradoxical, forms of installation in their respective conditions. As Marías puts it, "The fugitive, evasive, elusive woman, who seems to be always in motion, who draws and incites man and takes him far away and higher up, *stays* somewhere in the end and puts down roots."[14]

For man, who lives with his feet solidly planted in materiality, who feels responsible for the world and who—like Atlas—bears its weight on his shoulders, has another side to his life also. He is at the same time pulled by an ontological wanderlust. Far horizons and distant possibilities beckon to him. Woman's abiding fear is that once man is in motion he may not stop when she does, that her charms cannot finally compete with man's adventuring spirit. Perhaps this is why she often dreads his greater ambitions and senses in them the nemesis of her own hopes.

In our day, we hear of the "war of the sexes," but if sexuate differences can be called a war, then it is more spectacular than real. Because each sex is defined, understood, and fulfilled in the other, then any essential hostility between them would not be war but something more akin to human genocide.

The truth is that the sexes *normally* are enthusiastically attracted to each other because of their dynamic reciprocity. The male pathway leads toward woman, and woman meets him halfway on her own life road to him. And most likely this prevailing normalcy is the reason why it goes largely unnoticed, while all the attention is concentrated on mere eccentricities, aberrations, and exceptions to this general condition.

On the other end of the sexual spectrum, an equally erroneous notion clouds our understanding of human life. For here we find the repulsively crude idea, in vogue since Freudianism, that all sexuate relations, including intersexual friendship and even family ties, may be reduced to a disguised or frustrated sexual impulse. Yet the facts of life tell a different story. Having acknowledged this initial reciprocal sexuate enthusiasm, which is altogether different from a sexual urge, we note at once that in the overwhelming percentage of cases it remains a fleeting impulse of no real consequence. Numberless people of the other sex stride through the distant corners of our life without leaving a noticeable trace or lasting impact.

As seems always the case, these erroneous notions do the most harm to the best that mortal life has to offer: the love that calls us to be truly ourselves. For Marías the human love story begins with the reciprocal sexuate need we have been examining periodically and at different levels since our first encounter with Ortegan metaphysics. But much of the tale is yet to be told. For as we follow its ideal narrative, we shall see it converge in Marías with those finalities of human life around which revolve the unsuppressable questions of authentic philosophy.

From another perspective we find reminders that the question of human love is also and probably equally a particularly personal concern for Marías. Here, the reference is not only to the remarkable and perhaps unmatched synergy of his private life and public doctrine but also to the difficulties, some of which were seen earlier, he experienced with Ortega's theories on love. Additionally, he felt obliged to refute and replace with sounder reasoning a series of widely acclaimed but dubious notions about human love and sexuality. He notes, for example, that it is a "dangerously stupid" notion to insist on a doctrine of equality between men and women (a notion possibly of political ancestry) while ignoring the *human* reality that consists of a dynamic balance between the sexes.

Why is this commonplace notion "dangerous" enough to provoke Marías? What difference does it make whether the sexes are dynamically balanced in their relationships or simply equal in some abstract or legal fashion? The summary answer is that these are matters of enormous importance because they affect in a fundamental way the chances for human happiness, that is, of *both* sexes.

In a further and more general sense, unchallenged these dangerous notions would trivialize human life, reduce it to the merest of mundane hopes, and rob it of its legendary enchantment. In the case of woman, this reductionist assault has been especially pernicious and persistent.

No wonder, then, that Marías has taken it upon himself to reject these teachings with all the doctrinal weapons and personal energy he can summon. Admirable sympathy and considerable indignation often surface in his writings on women, as though he were championing all those women—mother, wife, friends, and students—he has loved so deeply or admired so generously, and to whom, by admission, he owes so much, personally and philosophically.

We need not attempt the impossible task of formally separating the anthropological doctrine of the sexes in Marías from the ultimately mysterious human context and communication to which it implicitly speaks. For one thing, our allusions to this delicate setting are held in check by our friendly respect. But this corresponds to our method itself; for all along, we have been insisting on the biographical structure of the Marías doctrine and we have attempted to do so biographically, that is, with a constant but understated awareness of our limited range and perspective and the tendency—as inevitable and exhilarating as it is risky and enlightening—to meet these insights with our own interfacing biography.

Yet if much is necessarily excluded or distorted by this approach, much remains, for we proceed on the conviction that the philosophical and moral impact of a doctrine grows immeasurably greater and more efficacious once we move beyond its abstract shadow and glimpse it in action within and as a free consequence of its real human circumstances, both personal and transpersonal.

This removes any possible charge that we are simply being presumptuous in moving this close to the making of a philosophy. Marías himself invites this cordial closeness not only because of his hospitable character but also for doctrinal reasons. He has insisted many times that the profile of a human life is the key to understanding a way of thinking. And what is more, this cordiality is also an invitation to enter into a collaborative enterprise with the philosopher so that the doctrine ceases to be abstract and alien and becomes ours. Only one quality is necessary to begin this appropriation: the same generosity of spirit in accepting that was shown in offering it.

As we shall see in the next chapter, nowhere perhaps in Marías's cordial philosophy do analytical theory, empirical structure, and personal motives coincide more convincingly—or more beautifully—than in his masterful insights into human love. Deriving on the one hand from a metaphysical and anthropological doctrine elaborated earlier and, on the other, from personal life, his views of love converge in some of his most splendid writing on the human condition. Hear one summary of his efforts: "One would have to illuminate all the possible forms of love, particularly, all those that are *com-*

possible, biographically reconcilable, that may coexist on different planes and dimensions. If things are taken in this sense, in all their complexity and richness, then woman would turn out to be a mysterious continent the exploration of which could be a matter of a whole lifetime, and I hope, of the next one as well." [15]

LOVE AND HUMAN FINALITIES

Love

The amorous condition of our life derives, so Marias informs us, not from our feelings, psychic states, or psychological predispositions, not even from our enthusiasm for a person of the other sex, but from our structurally reciprocal sexuate need that "happens" or "befalls" plotlike, dramatically, and vectorially in our unitary life installation.

Here, we make first contact with one feature that later will deserve more commentary: the adventitious and extraordinary nature of love itself. Love is an archly personal experience, yet because we customarily live our lives amid and attentive to remote and impersonal things, we do not at first—if ever—know what to make of love. Suddenly we are illuminated by an experience that seems to come from the core of our being and yet at the same time from far beyond it. This astonishment seems to be etymologically embedded in the curious expression in English, "to *fall* in love," suggesting not only the unforseeable element of chance (as in "befall") but also our clumsiness in reacting to it.

Remember that in this context we are referring to an unusual meaning of "amorous," that is, to the permanent human predisposition to love, and not to its usual connotation of erotic moments or random susceptibility to a member of the other sex.

We could say that we are natively disposed to love or, in more formal terms, that human life reveals a fundamentally "lovely" predisposition, even though this condition may never culminate in erotic love itself, just as the human need for happiness does not necessarily mean that we shall ever be fully happy. Mankind, Marias tells us, is an "impossible," contradictory creation, for we must try to be what we cannot be.[1] This leads dialectically to the finalities to which we shall turn our attentions in the second part of this chapter.

Pessimists and determinists alike customarily mistake such frequent deficiencies for an obverse law of life and then appeal to it so as to justify a rejection of the ultimate questions. Yet Marías reminds us that what we strive for is more defining than what life is at any given moment. More to the point, he

adds that human reality is *primarily* a matter of striving.[2] Here, at the empirical level and thus in an another sense, we may repeat what we said earlier at
the analytical stage of our inquiry: the unreal and unrealized—and the unreal-
izable—appearing as imagination and desirable aim constitute a major and
probably decisive portion of human reality. That such finalities may transcend
our vision and possibilities does not render them any less necessary and unavoidable. Giving a different slant to Marías's insistence on striving toward
the unreal, we could say that we are formed in the image of the transcendent.
Perhaps modern thinkers would not feel compelled to reject transcendence if
life itself did not first direct them to it.

This is why—one reason why—we cannot render honest judgments on
the supposed futility of the transcendent unless we have first made an honest
effort to acknowledge and come to grips with it. Marías finds that without this
effort, even the supposedly "safe" questions of a reduced field of inquiry turn
out to be elusive, and he offers as proof the sterile conclusions of reductionis-
tic ideologies from determinism to deconstructionism. Of course, it is doubtful
whether certain problems have solutions, but of the problems themselves there
is no doubt whatsoever and therefore *no valid reason for pretending that they
do not exist.*[3]

Our fundamental "lovely" neediness, which we express as the projective
and transcendental task of living, means that our love story must also be our
life story. For as we have seen, love is not a thing, episode, or object we encounter in definitive fashion, not something we do with a lover, not an act and
thus not merely given and complete, but a state of being that consists of always coming to be, of be-coming. To use Marías's language, in the most fundamental way we are amorously "installed" in life. Or to put it another way,
the amorous or "lovely" condition is primary inasmuch as from it we grapple
with reality and project our life within it.

Consider an illustration to clarify certain implications of what I have
just said. In order to tell why I need food, I can point to my biological or physiological need for nourishment. But in order to explain why I need a person, I
must tell my intimate biography (or at least an important portion of it). On the
other hand, if I need that person for some purpose that is not strictly biographical but episodic or biological—physical skills, professional expertise, sex,
etc.—the need is still real and has personal features, but unless otherwise
countered, it tends toward the impersonal, with the corresponding degrees of
dehumanization never far behind.

On the other hand, my intimate need of another person is personal to the
second power. It arises from my ontological or biographical indigence, which
is always personal and necessarily permanent inasmuch as I am a person and
therefore always coming to be. But the person I need is also always needing to

be and always coming to be. Thus love and—at another level—friendship co-implicate two unitary life installations in biographical, i.e., vectorial fashion.

Therefore, this personal need for another person is very different from my need of things or impersonal contacts, even though both kinds of neediness correspond to ontological incompleteness or indigence. Things, objects, and facilities respond usually as givens, as things before me more or less susceptible to my need of them. But my biographical need for another person does not involve a given but a *giving* of the very special and superlative kind we know as self-giving, the giving of oneself. As Marías notes, "This 'something' may be *given* to me, or if you prefer, may simply *be there*. By Contrast, 'someone' can only be in state of 'giving himself' and, owing to the 'arriving' quality of the person, is not simply 'there' but *is arriving*."[4]

Here let us take note of Marías's prior caveat: ". . . far from taking as basic the abstract and undifferentiated need of one person for another, reality forces us to take the opposite path and to start off from the radical, inherent, and structural need of one sex for the other, in which human life consists."[5]

In an earlier chapter, we said that the sexuate condition causes men and women to project themselves with native enthusiasm and undeniable (though often denied) need toward the other sex, that in fact each sex is defined and understood disjunctively in terms of the other. We have said that love cannot be reduced to a series of acts. It is not subsumed in courtship, caresses, making love, or doing something, erotic or otherwise, with the person one loves, although all these may appear as subsets or consequential effects of love. Love is a form of life "installation" in the precise sense in which Marías uses the term as we saw it described earlier. Therefore, we can say once again but from another perspective that love is not something one has or does but a state in which one is installed and from which one lives. Hence its plotlike structure.

But before we go any further, let us suspend this line of reasoning for a moment and consider at this foundational level what appears to be a troubling rebuttal to Marías's premise. Experience tells us that even though nothing promises us more than love, nothing seems to break its promises more often. Therefore, from the beginning love seems to exhibit a capricious and unreasonable character that calls into question the supposed amorous condition of human life.

While we are at it, we may as well recall other unpleasant aspects of "this thing called love." It comes to us wrapped in myth but also laden with hucksterism. It is the stuff of fairy tales and folklore. The fond theories of classical philosophers adorn it, and in our day a whole publishing industry of popular psychology exploits its themes in a torrent of books, articles, and statistical studies. For if true love stands as one of the highest of earthly ideals, it is also the most democratic of calamities. It spares neither the simpleminded nor the sophisticated. Yet its repeated failure does not abash us for long. Newly seared and scarred by its flame, we are soon eager to scamper again into its fire. For as Dryden says:

> Pains of love be sweeter far
> Than all other pleasures are.

We commonly assume that love is the panacea for the world's evils, yet an immediate if more commonplace truth is that we get into trouble much more quickly over whom we love than whom we hate. In recent times people have been intrigued by the notion of "free love," and today perhaps most lovers would repeat the defiant cliché that their love is nobody else's business. But wiser people know better. Love is everybody's business for an archly compelling reason: life itself is born of love, and for this reason none can or should be truly indifferent to it. This is a principal reason why, despite current arguments to do away with them, love continues under considerable moral and legal shackles.

But which love are we talking about? To begin with, heterosexual, or better, "heterosexuate," love, that is, erotic love between a man and a woman. There are of course other loves: parental, brotherly, and filial love, religious love, and patriotism, for example. But it would be a mistake to reason—even though it is common to do so—that an understanding of love must begin with a generic approach that subsequently focuses on specific manifestations. As Marías declares, "I do not believe that this love [erotic love] is a 'species' of that 'genre' but rather that all the other forms of love spring from intersexuate love as the basic form of personal need."[6] Elsewhere, he observes: "This love between man and woman is the concrete nucleus of the very broad amorous condition. By this I mean that the latter orders itself entirely about the former. This not to say that all the other 'loves,' in the broadest use of the term, are modifications or transformations of this heterosexuate love but rather that their root is to be found there, that is, that within the empirical structure all love is rooted in that [amorous] structure which is precisely heterosexuate."[7]

Here, the Pauline description of divine love summarizes our condition. We live, and move, and have our being in love.[8] But we must be careful to point out that unlike religious love or love of mankind, heterosexuate love is preeminently selective. It exists only for one special person and renders the lover essentially indifferent to all others. Nor is there anything brotherly or sisterly, parental or filial, in true heterosexuate love, although this exclusivity does not preclude *filia, agape,* or other kinds of love *at subsequent stages and different levels.*

Thus, we live our life in "lovely" susceptibility. As we saw earlier, every sexuate encounter is slightly charged by this inclination, so as to be inchoately or potentially amorous or "lovely." Unlike our usual contact with things, sexuate encounters exhibit the normally slight but wonderful quality of ontological enhancement, depth, and promise.

But as we saw earlier, this promise seldom leads to anything. The slight amorous hint hardly ever means that we fall in love. Even though life is characterized by a "lovely neediness," love may well be statistically rare. Like gold, its very rarity enhances its worth and desirability.

The lover meets, or seems to meet, our expectations. Of what? Of being our most authentic self. Love is always an experience of coming into our own. From this it follows that ". . . authentic love presents itself as *unrenounceable*, and to this degree it is happiness. I mean that the lover, even the most unhappy of lovers, thinks that his love has been worthwhile; he would not accept its not existing, would not want the calm, tranquility, and pleasure which he could enjoy without it." And he adds the decisive reason: "He prefers his love, with all its consequences, no matter how troublesome or painful they may be, to its lack of existence; he says 'yes' to it unconditionally, because anything else would mean saying 'no' to himself."[9]

In our day, this unswerving determination is often taken to mean that love is quick to violate social conventions. This may happen, of course, but if so it usually means that love has been contaminated by extraneous causes and is in danger of being subverted to other and usually questionable ends. As Marías sees it, real love is not an act of public rebellion but of personal fulfillment. In love, our true self emerges, often to our own surprise as well as to the puzzlement or amusement of those who knew only our preliminary life. For love is the name we give to an intimate transformation; it is an inner ontological shift which, when viewed as a psychological process confronts and often shatters not the generic public mores but our private crystalizations and personal conventions. Like everything personally authentic, it is a brave, risky, but exhilarating endeavor, and this is probably why love nearly always comes accompanied by courage and daring as well as by a certain thrilling trepidation. In all but the most reckless souls there is a moment—at least—of vital hesitation before assenting to love's lovely fall. We know that we are staking our lives on a card dealt by fate, and we may lose the gamble. When this happens—and it does—our love may still transform our life, may continue to be unavoidable for this same reason, but now its promise and profile of fulfillment fade, and it becomes instead what Marías calls *lo doloroso irrenunciable*, "unrenounceable painfulness."[10]

On the other hand, as novel as reciprocated love is, as wonderful and unaccustomed as it may seem to us, this new "lovely" state of being is not repulsive or alien. Far from it; in this enormous "fall," this breathtaking "befalling" of love in our life, we find ourselves perhaps for the first time to be, or better, to be becoming, the person we were always destined to be.

Love is our deepest calling, our most basic vocation, and our original destiny. For surely, our first purpose, our prime endeavor, and our supreme hope in this world must be to become the man or woman we were meant to be. As Marías describes it, "Giving oneself over, freely and necessarily, to authentic being-in-love is the supreme form of acceptance of fate, and that is precisely what we call vocation."[11]

Earlier, we referred to the adventitious quality of love. Nothing we have experienced before can quite prepare us for love, yet everything that preceded it now appears as preparation. Hence the profound sense of gratitude that lovers often experience. For regardless of how hard their former life has been, all now appears to be justified and rendered worthy by their new state of being.

How shall we describe this state? In abstract terms, as an ontological intensification. But in the lyric tone that now prevails, we could say that the languid tune of our former life has become an infinitely glorious melody. In love we find meaning where before we saw only nonsense. We are fascinated with details that once tiptoed by scorned or unnoticed. Beauty now hovers around the most pedestrian realities, for ugliness has yielded its vast control over creation. We commune with whole sectors of the world that before knew only our indifference. Poetry and music claim a novel priority in our affairs, and radical harmonies filter through the drab fabric of our life.

The cynic would say that all this has happened a thousand times before in other lives. Perhaps so, but never to us, never personally. And the personal is always new because it is absolutely unique. Every lover knows that his love will never be duplicated. In this irreplaceability there is a hint of incomparable worthiness. Unamuno argued—with or without exaggeration—that each person is worth more than the entire universe.

Nevertheless, far from explaining the final enigmas, this experience of illumination and vital fullness reveals further mysteries, and primarily so in the beloved person. Love is personal, and therefore the prime task as well as the supreme joy of the lover is to come to know the beloved person. This is why lovers are so intensely curious to know everything about each other. Love may appear tyrannical in this insistence, but it is a benevolent tyranny that possesses by giving itself first in an altruistic outpouring of self. This is why true love and selfishness enter readily into conflict and do not rest until one of them is vanquished.

Hence the interminable conversations and fascination with the beloved's face and features. For each person is an intimate mystery whose primary modes of *expression* are, as we saw earlier, verbal and facial. For this reason, Marías is skeptical of so-called "silent" versions of love when such silence is simply a lack of anything to say. Love is the maximal attention we can pay another person. As Marías puts it, ". . . the supreme delight for man is to see how woman progressively shows herself, uncovering and revealing her intimate self until it envelops the male with his own personality within it."[12]

Not that his rapt attention is simply a matter of obsessive or prurient curiosity. For in discovering the intimate secret of the beloved, the lover also catches a glimpse of himself in her eyes. The poet Machado once said that a man is not a man until he has heard his name from the lips of a woman. Perhaps this helps explain the odd sensation of *recognition* lovers often experience in this facial and verbal encounter.

Yet here, in this enduring progression, love often fails. As Marías observes, "The problem is whether or not one reaches the personal core. When it happens, one experiences to the full the perception or, if you prefer, intuition of a person. It is an experience known only to a few."[13]

This may seem to be a particularly harsh judgment. After all, if love is our most authentic calling to happiness, then how can it end so often and so ingloriously? If lovers prefer their love, even their failed love, to anything else in life, then how can it slip from them?

Marías suggests several distinct but related causes of love's demise. First and perhaps most fundamental is the lack of imagination. Taking an example from fiction, where art often intensifies life, he points out that although Don Juan could provoke love in many women, he seemed to lack the capacity to sustain it. Crafty in devising seductive strategies, he was unable to nurture love past its initial eroticism. Yet like all personal realities, love is biographical, which is another way of saying that it must be projected, imagined, and renewed *over time*.

In the first instance, this projective character assumes the concrete form of imagining the *person* of the beloved. Ideally, it means exploring for a lifetime the inexhaustible mystery of the beloved person. Marías calls it "the progressive discovery" of the beloved. This is why the older terms "conquest" and "surrender," or their cruder counterparts of today, are grossly inadequate to describe the enduring love relationship. Shakespeare makes the point with marvelous poetic economy:

> Love's not Time's fool, though rosy lips and cheeks
> Within his bending sickle's compass come;
> Love alters not with his brief hours and weeks,
> But bears it out even to the edge of doom.

Writing in 1991, Marías noted that although, in some ways, never have conditions been more favorable for this lifelong "discovery," never have more opportunities been squandered. Love requires imagination, intimacy, personhood, and authenticity in generous and sustained amounts. But this goes against the modern grain of the world, which pushes us to ever-deeper entrapments in the generic and the impersonal. The packaged, noisy glamor of movies, stars, music, videos, and television creates a collective craving for the "good life." But there is an offsetting and devastating loss: the capacity to imagine, the wonderful human ability to commune with the unseen.

If the supreme intensity, intimacy, and projective imagination of human life culminates in love, then it stands to reason that to weaken the case for love is to jeopardize the very quality of life itself. This is why love does not favor those who live on borrowed dreams and vulgar enthusiasms. It shuns the empty and dreamless life. Those who take love to be another form of entertainment or a cure for boredom will not find it, or finding it, will soon lose it. Love is the antithesis of what Marías calls the "primitivism" of our time which he defines in this context as ". . . undifferentiated sexuality, multiple, passing, and *without importance.*"[15]

Thus, we should not be surprised to note that in the quarter-century since his achievement of an anthropological and empirical theory of love (*Metaphysical Anthropology,* 1970), Marías has revisited and amplified the theme in other writings (*La mujer en el siglo XX, La mujer y su sombra, La felicidad humana, Mapa del mundo personal,* among others). As he sees it, love is the best human life has to offer, but in our time the best is everywhere under assault. Whole portions of what we could call this newly discovered "anthropological continent" risk being eroded away by the backwash of reductionist philosophies retreating from higher aesthetic, moral, and intellectual forms. This retreat, says Marías, ". . . is the most profound form of decadence, because it is not economic, political or cultural but rather affects reality itself."[16] His unyielding and unapologetic insistence on human love in its fullest manifestations and final consequences may be seen as a major component of a wider commitment to save and transmit to more sensible future generations the general philosophy of the human person so painstakingly achieved during his age.

Human Finalities

Love, which above all savors the plenitude of the moment, also urges us to pay attention to the eternal. This seems paradoxical until we realize that we live to the full and toward the future only through imagination. Imagination cannot be satisfied by visible fact and handy reality but is by nature projective and plays out its purpose in communication with the unseen and even the improbable. Yet within this seemingly playful range of pure exuberance, imagination also fulfills an essential role: it allows us to anticipate life, to live already in the future and in another sense in eternity. And not just in a predetermined world as set by present conditions. We transcend determinism through pretense, that is, by pre-tending toward what is latent, possible, and alternative. To the degree that we can imagine the future, we place ourselves within it and experience ideally what we may never know, or even wish to know, in fact.

This projective, imaginative character of human life, far from being a mere aberration and a flight from reality, is a movement toward ourselves. The person I am, man or woman, cannot be reduced to any present or circumstantial reality. Ortega's old formula, "I am I and my circumstance," is not a reductionist recipe but rather a stated means of relating the unique reality of life to an indefinite and perhaps infinite series of structurally interrelated realities. But neither is the uniqueness of life confined to or exhausted in this serial relationship. What I said earlier is misleading if we stop there. The projectiveness is not simply another trait among the several that life exhibits. It would be more accurate to say that human reality consists precisely in this projectiveness, which elsewhere we have described as narrative, historical, and dynamic.

For this reason, the ancient question, what is man?, contains, as Marías sees it, a fundamental error: ". . . I am not something that I may encounter because *I am the one who does the encountering* of that something. Even when I encounter myself, the real 'personal I' is the one who does the finding, not the one who is found."[17]

Now, at the empirical level, that is, where bodily life becomes the dynamic articulation of a *who* and a *what,* we face an apparent paradox that was already implicit in our first encounter with Soledad and A. Ortega described A's anguish upon learning that Soledad had departed, but Marías raised the question of mortal separation: what are the implications when Soledad departs absolutely through death?

Living is the only viable response to the correct question of life and philosophy, who am I? But this means the correct response is eventful (and thus eventual), narrative, and temporal, for I live a scenic life. Because I am never wholly fulfilled, happy, defined, and complete at any given moment, because I stand in constant need to be more than I am, I must keep on the move, passing from scene to scene toward or unto death.

Consider again the ancient paradox: we move needfully toward fulfillment and come eventually unto death. We accumulate time and in doing so, exhaust the time we have. Our life consists of indefinite futuristic projection, but the physical person I am faces certain death in the process. Our only hope of fulfillment lies in the future, but there also death awaits possibly as the ultimate irony and annihilation of our final hope. We acknowledge the potential irony by describing ourselves as those beings who bear death inescapably within themselves. We are not only *mortals* but also *moriturus,* mortals who must die.

But we add a supreme irony of our own to this initial paradox: we are mortals who would go on living forever. Man is a closed mortal structure, but "my life" is futuristically and perhaps eternally "open." Hear Marías's description: "The human person appears as a creature, whose reality is received but new and irreducible, needy and indigent, condemned to a closed empirical structure and called to mortality, but consisting in incessant hope: a project which struggles with death. 'That which' I am is mortal, but 'who' I am consists in aspiring to be immortal and not being able to imagine myself as not immortal, because my life is *radical reality.*"[18]

Naturally, this indefinite biographical projectiveness affects love—and is affected by it—inasmuch as it is the culmination of the amorous or "lovely" condition in which we live and move toward the transcendent and the eternal. Having rejected the notions of "fusion" and "possession" as inadequate descriptions of the nature of loving, Marías quotes Saint John of the Cross who says that the pleasure we experience in love requires the persistence of *la presencia y la figura* ["presence and face"] of the beloved person. And since this continued communication can take place only in the future, no true lover will accept anything less than an eternal love even though death involves an evident physical separation. As Spenser says:

Love is life's end; an end but never ending.

Therefore, personal love stands as perhaps the most poignant and appealing evidence that almost nothing human can be understood without reference to the future. Our life is not primarily a matter of existence, essence, being, or definition but the biographical and dramatic story of our becoming, of our futuristic striving to become who we would be. Death stands in our way either as an obstacle and an end to our story or as an incentive to project our life and our story through unnumbered chapters in a limitless hereafter.

If we consider the matter of death from the empirical point of view, that is, from the perspective of bodily life, then evidently we come to a final stage of living beyond which there is no other. For man is indeed biologically mortal. But from the viewpoint of the "living I" [*yo viviente*] that I *also* am—this viewpoint is always personal—then I discover that my life is directed biographically and structurally not toward annihilation but rather to indefinite projection. It may be, of course, that personal death follows biological death, but this remains to be proven, and the burden of proof rests with those who deny life's open and enduring structure and not those who acknowledge it.

As Marías sees it, the assumption that my life in all its structures simply ceases at death without possibility of the eternal rests not on considered proof but on a poverty of imagination. To the classic but always personal questions, who am I? and what will become of me?, increasingly the modern tendency has been to respond not with an answer, not even with a lament, but with an intellectual shrug of the shoulders.

Yet the questions, the striving, and the transcendence reappear each time we become sufficiently responsible to require of life meaning and intelligibility. In the process, we also come to realize that mere indifference and passivity are at odds with life's native exuberance and earnestness and therefore constitute ethically false positions.

To strive for life in this world or the next, to imagine life in a potentially unlimited future, means that we have an ample and fundamental range of personal freedom. We would have no need to imagine a single, predetermined course; we would not need to strive if life were an inexorable singularity. As Marías puts it, "Man makes his life, to be sure with things, conditioned by his circumstance, which imposes what he is, but he has to imagine, choose, and decide who he would be, as Ortega saw from the beginning of this century."[19]

Where does this free striving take us? Certainly through so-called "real" portions of the world—materiality, facts, dates, and relationships—but also through exalted passions, unrealized dreams, and false moments. There are, or may be, unlovely stretches where we stray from the authentic and the true, and moments of reconciliation with the higher image of ourselves.

Through it all, we cannot responsibly avoid the need to find the meaning of things. For as we have seen earlier and subsequently at different stages, *living is making sense of reality.* The task is not easy though error is. Reality is modest and reticent, and this is why we must strive with it for its secrets. Yet it yields itself, if not totally at least sufficiently, to our persistence and situation. Perhaps we could say that its revelation is equal to our need, though normally not prematurely lavish. Generally speaking, reality seems to offer our efforts a general accommodation. Consequently, the world appears as great or small, as empty or exalted, as we are, and in manifold ways it takes on our image.

In living, therefore, we discover in creation personal correspondence and sense, at least to the degree that we can with some self-assurance declare things to be sane or insane. And this is exactly what we would expect to find in a world created by a personal God. With a sharp twist on his words, Marías says: ". . . if the world was created by God, then it is understandable *that it should be understandable.*[20] By this same logic, we would be hard-pressed to explain this correspondence and understanding if the universe were a random consequence of cosmic chance. Sense and truth, logic and structure, love and personhood, and the detectable similitudes between ourselves and the world, which we translate variously as aesthetics, science, and axiological systems, would stand as the most inexplicable of enigmas if we excluded the possibility, more, the likelihood, of Divine creation. Contrary to an ancient misconception, the burden of proof is always on the skeptic.

Thus, Marías finds in creation an abiding integrity that sustains our freedom to project and fashion our life. To the questions, who am I? and what will become of me?, the reasonable answer can only be: I will be who I have wanted to be. "To this we condemn ourselves: to be in truth and forever, what we have wanted." For everything truly desired will come to pass.

Here, Marías chooses not to venture further into what clearly begins to verge on religious and theological questions. His aims, he reminds us, remain the levels and structures of personal human life in this world. Nevertheless, these levels and structures point necessarily to questions of death and transcendence, not as adjuncts of simple curiosity but as necessary requirements of life here and now. Perhaps this allows us to suggest an additional turn to the words of Saint Paul: in the midst of life we are in death. Unamuno, for one, would probably have agreed.

Summary

Although much has been left unsaid, we now have outlined at least most of the major premises of Marías's philosophy. While this outline assumes a general chronological profile and brings us to mid-decade of the 1970s, we have also included other refinements, additions, and restatements from later works. In doing so, we violate no internal prohibitions of his way of thinking. On the contrary, we saw earlier how philosophy is a *method,* a road as it were, that leads to and fro, up and down, and which supposes a readiness to reexamine, correct, and restate in order to progress.

At any rate, the essential features of his method are now in place, which means, somewhat paradoxically, that his philosophy is further than ever from being over and finished. For as his method has grown to its mature formulations, becoming progressively more responsive and efficient, the problems and conditions to which he applies it have increased in urgency and complexity. The responsible vision of his early work has now broadened and extends to vast and sometimes uncharted areas of an increasingly irresponsible world. Marías has taken philosophy into regions where seldom if ever it had ventured before.

But the insecurity, here appearing as unforeseen chance, "which accompanies the philosopher as a shadow follows a body," was soon to subject his work and his life to severe trials in two very different ways and at very different levels. In the first case, a transpersonal one, this took the form of a possible redemption; in the other, an irretrivable personal loss.

Without forcing these events into a misleading arithmetical precision, for life has its own precision beyond the reach of abstract numbers, we could say that a lull occurred at this juncture of Marías's life and he paused for a lengthy personal reassessment. The temptation is too great, recalling egregious examples of thinkers from Plato to Ortega, not to call the eventual re-sumption of his philosophical tasks *along altered lines* a "second voyage" into philosophy.

But we need to understand that by "second voyage" we are by no means referring to any substitute philosophical system on his part. During the second phase, his writings become even more distinctly his own. For it was to be a journey characterized not by a departure but by an arrival. Now he truly comes into his own in a display of philosophical creativity that rightly deserves to be called astonishing.

Yet if most critics generally were unable, and often unwilling, to see beyond Ortega's hand in Marías's earlier works, they have also failed to see the remarkable innovations of his recent thought, to which we now turn.

PART III

THE SECOND VOYAGE

8

CHRISTIAN QUESTIONS

Shall philosophy always consist essentially of an exposition of hypo-
thetical conjectures and strategies, or shall it at some point outgrow its narcis-
sistic fascination with its own abstractions and in an altruistic gesture apply its
instrumentality to clamorous human needs? Does it willfully impose extraneous methods from without on reality or is it itself a method informed and disciplined by the structures of reality?

For Marías, such questions converge on the very nature and justification
of philosophy, assuming, as he does, that it must be a responsible vision of reality, that is, that it is to be morally and methodologically responsive to real
human problems and not, as we commonly suppose today, an esoteric and precious intellectualism unmoved by the accidents of life, history, and circumstance.

Probably no thinker of our time has responded more ethically and rigorously than Marías to such questions. Clear proof of this will stand forth in this
"second voyage," and as we examine his response, it will be seen that his way
of thinking assumes its most efficacious form not as theory only but theory on
trial with human concerns. In a Christian and Catholic context he speaks of
looking at the world with intelligence and love. It could be a general description of his philosophic stance.

It bears repeating that this philosophic step beyond abstract theory
was not a late addendum to his work. From the beginning of his intellectual career, Marías had displayed what he himself calls ". . . that bonus of
reality that we Spaniards usually have."[1] Witness his writings on literature,
women, patriotic and political matters, his insistence on the biographical foundation of history and philosophy, his "transpersonal" works on Spanish society and governance, his many *aperçus* on styles, customs, and national
idiosyncrasies, and, of specific interest to us here, his thoughts on religious
questions.

Earlier we saw how, even if he had been so inclined, circumstances precluded a cloistered life for him. This closeness to the throb of real life meant
that he was to be "present" in his writings, and not just stylistically or rhetori-
cally so but personally and often passionately. Marías has always written with

a sober enthusiasm and respect for what we may call the human integrity of his topics.

During the "second voyage" this presence was to become even more apparent. Commenting on the resumption in 1978–79 of his personal writings, he explains: ". . . the resolution grew in me to fill the time I had left with works that were 'mine,' because if I did not see them through it was likely that they would not get done."[2]

Let us restate an earlier allusion: during this new phase of his life and thought he did not abandon the analytical and empirical theoretical constructs fashioned over the previous four decades of philosophical labor. There was no break with the past. With the publication of *Metaphysical Anthropology* (1970), his theoretical method was essentially complete and functional and the general anthropological area of inquiry outlined. Naturally, there would be subsequent refinements, restatements, extensions and rejustifications. But now there was no primary need to concentrate on theory as an end in itself. Instead, from now on theory was to function as an internalized and assimilated means to other ends. If his philosophic construction could be likened to a ship, then theory could be compared to its superstructure, always presupposed and necessary but invisible in the sailing vessel.

Throughout the earlier trials of his life, Marías had kept his religious faith and it had sustained him. No wonder, then, that he would launch his "second voyage" with *Problemas del cristianismo*. His drastic personal loss in 1977 called for a "radicalism of faith," and he admits that he would have used such a term had it not been so often profaned. But in any case he began to write from the depths of his being without any other consideration except the "seriousness of life," adding that if we look closely at things, this is what religion really is. Reflecting on the matter years later, he writes: "It is not strange that my thoughts would be directed toward what had been the object of my reflexions for a long time: religion, and very specifically Christianity, its significance, its consistency, if such a term may be used, its historical achievements, and its risks."[3]

Yet as compelling and urgent as these personal motives were, they were not the only reason for writing *Problemas del cristianismo*. There were also questions about the direction of the Church—and christendom in general—following the death of Pope Paul VI. For example, what would become of the reconciling and liberating work begun by Pope John XXIII and the Second Vatican Council? In Spain, the Franco regime was replaced by a fledgling democracy, which signaled a significant modification—and perhaps more—of the unusual and often regressive symbiosis between segments of the Church and State. Furthermore, within and without Spain there were grave symptoms of a growing religious disaffection. To the disturbing "apostasy of the masses," long since generalized in modern Europe, was added the religious crisis, deceptively disguised as indifference, of the younger generations. Finally, Marías had long been insisting that 1976 would mark the beginning of a generational shift. Within a few years a great many of the current personalities and priorities would fade into oblivion. Marías interpreted this change to mean that new concepts and problems just beginning to appear on the historical horizon needed serious attention.

These were some of the concerns that converged with his personal situation to form the setting of *Problemas del cristianismo*.

The Heart of the Matter

"Christianity does not give solutions," Marías wrote in 1964, "it gives light by which to seek them."[4] Perhaps this could be seen as a rebuke to the pharisaical Christian legalists of every strain of Christianity, Catholic and Protestant but particularly the Thomists, or on the other hand as a censure of their Sadduccan counterparts who would enslave it to purely worldly concerns without hope of transcendence.

The moral wisdom inherent in the Christian faith at times displaces its irreplaceable message of *salvation*. When this happens, Christianity is in danger of being reduced to an ideology. A nominal belief in God and the hereafter may persist, but its expression is anemic and trivial. For the next world is no longer the real focus. As Marías puts it, "[Christianity] is taken as a 'point of departure' toward other things, which are the ones that really are of interest."[5]

It is easy enough to say that ideally Christianity speaks to both the mortal and eternal dimensions of life, even though throughout its history it has tended to swing between these extremes rather than to balance them. In any case, the theological and secular tendency to "start from God" in a preferential search for other things, such as metaphysics, social order, notions of power and authority, etc., contains a double error. To begin with, Marías points out that God is of interest for *His own sake* and not simply because we may think He serves as the backer of our schemes. Even Unamuno's vision of God as the guarantor of our immortality relegates God to a utilitarian role.

As Marías understands it, we do not start with God in order to reach Him, much less use Him as a convenient beginning point for going on to lesser things. Instead, we remain in Him. Our starting point, what used to be called our "itinerary" toward God, is the created world of things, especially insofar as we find in it its created nature, its standing as "creature."[6]

The second error, closely related to the first, consists of trivializing the divine mystery of God so as to hasten on to urgent but relatively secondary matters, *all in the name of God*. Elsewhere, he complains that in our day everything may be called "theology" provided it has nothing to say about God. For instance, there are "theologies" of work, war, feminism, and revolution. Similarly, men speak of a brotherhood of mankind, but without God the Father it remains utopian and unconvincing, probably doing more harm than good because it trivializes human relationships and leaves us with an empty terminology instead of an exalted status.

On the other hand, just as the trivialization of the belief in God tends to create an inoperative image of a remote and impersonal deity, it also encourages an insistence on the humanity of Jesus at the expense of the divine Christ. To put it another way, this reasoning separates Jesus and God by magnitude and essence and hints that for different reasons both are superfluous in the affairs of mankind.

These trivialized images of the first two Divine Persons and the omission or nominal mention of the Holy Spirit correspond to a vision of a Christianity without mystery, a Christianity easily domesticated and bullied by various naturalistic theories. The only thing wrong with this view is that it is wrong, for as Marías sees it, Christianity is essentially and necessarily mysterious. This is why even though it serves as an inexhaustible resource for humane theories, it can never be their servant.

The heart of the matter is this: ". . . the evaporation of religion as such, the projection of Christianity toward other planes, which may not be alien to it, indeed may be essential to it, but precisely as a religion and from a religious perspective. From this viewpoint the questions which concern men may justifiably reappear. Without it Christianity will appear powerless, bloodless, ineffective, and lacking in interest, the demonstration of which may have been the purpose all along."[7]

This Life and the Next

To prefer the rumors of this world to the "Good News" of Christianity is to misunderstand our possible relationship with God. These misconceptions appear in several theories of human reality. We are asked to believe ourselves to be variously either a little lower than angels or a bit higher than apes. Marías observes that we ignore death on the one hand and judge all life by it on the other. The most characteristically human traits—sexuateness, historicity, dramatic life, personality, bodily being—are the first sacrifices made on the altar of abstract thought.

Even the Christian understanding of freedom tends to be either poorly understood or itself reduced to a kind of divine determinism (predestination, for example). The notion of an impersonal and unapproachable God with a preference for mechanical manipulations of the world is the probable ancestor of most secular versions of determinism.

Ideally, the Christian believes that he serves and obeys God, praising Him for His graceful benevolence culminating in the redemptive sacrifice of

His Son. He is in God's hands but freely so. Far from the references to cosmic abandonment or loneliness that abound in existentially inclined writings, the Christian is alone *from* or *of* God, with both words relating him to God. For God is always with us, only absent and unseen if we insist in a material sense. We could say that God allows us to be alone from Him, but it is vigilant allowance that does not leave us alone, that does not abandon us. In summary, with Him I know myself to be free, while under His watchful care I find myself to be alone *from* Him.

My relationship to God is, therefore, personal. (Would we overstep propriety by describing it as "person to person"?) And this opens the door to a *personal* interpretation of human life, which in summary is precisely what Marías's philosophy is all about. This is not simply a passive compatibility of his faith and thought but a dramatic relationship enlivened by the deepest Christian truths and meaningful resonances. If his is not formally a Christian philosophy, then at least we can say that it is the next thing to it, or perhaps the next stage before it. For Marías has laid the groundwork and indicated the principal directions for a Christian philosophy.[8]

The cismundane tendency of modern Christianity is not in itself a problem. After all, Christianity was from the beginning a message directed to people in the here and now of their historical circumstances. The problem begins when this world is taken to be *the* world, that is, the only world. When this happens, the themes of this life naturally assume an aggressive priority; economics, sociology, politics, psychology, revolutionary reform, and the like push aside the divine and become both the proclaimed cause and final end of religion. To use theologian Dietrich Bonhoeffer's terminology, the claims of the penultimate overshadow the truths of the ultimate.

In Catholic cultures in particular, though not entirely, this problem is exacerbated by the susceptibility of priests to modern ideologies. Ironically, this condition was brought about by a desire to shield them from these very influences. Marías notes in several of his writings that the Church has skipped over three centuries of modern thought, and particularly its most characteristic advances in philosophy and science. Meanwhile, "Teaching in the seminaries has been reduced, with scattered exceptions, to stagnant forms of Scholasticism which had ceased to be creative by the middle of the fourteenth century."[9]

With this and similar statements, Marías rejects the Scholastic position, still the approved—though not always observed—philosophical-theological doctrine of Catholicism, that all philosophical roads must converge on Saint Thomas. But an equally unpardonable offense, as Anton Donoso has interpreted it, was that ". . . he had put Ortega in Aquinas's key position and claimed to be his mentor's heir."[10]

Because of Catholic hostility toward modernity, there has been little "inoculation" of its clergy against modern errors. At the same time, it has failed to assimilate useful and legitimate modern advances, especially in philosophy and science. The loss is particularly telling in the twentieth century in view of new ways of thinking that would have been capable of reviving and updating Christian theology.

Even though he does not expressly say so, it is almost certain that he has in mind here Orteganism and Unamunean thought as principal components, both of which are assimilated at different temperatures in his own philosophy. Ortega was hardly a Christian thinker in any formal sense, while Unamuno loudly claimed to be nothing else, and both were equally suspect to the Thomist orthodoxy of their day. Yet in both cases their potential compatibility with Catholic Christianity is remarkably evident in the way Marías has been able to accommodate both in his own Christian posture.

Three points need to be made here before we proceed. First, there is no question that Marías faithfully believes in the personhood, and specifically the fatherhood, of God and no less in the redemptive grace and efficacious work manifested through the Second and Third Persons of the Trinity. Second, he leaves no doubt that his beliefs accord harmoniously with Church authority and legitimacy in matters of faith. Third, his own philosophy calls for personal survival beyond mortality, especially the survival of those we love. From the Thomist viewpoint, the problem with his view of personal transcendence would likely be that it arises not through formal Aristotelian logic but through the instrumentality of "vital reason," through the reason that is life from within rather than a reasoning about life from without.[11]

In 1905, Unamuno could still write that the "only question" that really mattered in life was knowing what would happen to my consciousness, to yours, and to that of everybody else when we die. Marías mildly criticizes this typical Unamunean exaggeration by stating that instead of being the only thing that matters, it would be more precise to say that this is *one* among several important questions. But certainly he seems to be in much closer sympathy with Unamuno than with more recent thinkers. By the second half of this century, Marías wonders whether most people think this question matters at all, whether indeed it is still a question at all.

Perhaps the predominant idea of our time—indeed, so predominant that it seldom needs repeating—is that human life ends once and for all with biological death. Even where politely tolerated out of civility or respect for convention, belief in the hereafter is often regarded by unbelievers and nominal Christians alike as an antique embarrassment inherited from a credulous and superstitious age.

It follows, therefore, that if life ends completely in this world, then whether God is or not no longer matters. The existentialist skeptic may hold that this condition offers us a negative freedom: at long last we are free from hellish dreads and punishments. But it is a poor freedom after all, for it also robs mankind of the greatest of hopes: what Plato called the exhilarating possibility of immortality.

On several occasions, Marías comments on the indifference and apparent ease with which modern people surrender their belief in the hereafter. It is common for contemporary people to look back longingly but patronizingly at a simpler age of belief now thought outgrown, but Marías finds in this melancholy not a superior sophistication but a deficiency of imagination. Modern man cannot believe in an afterlife because he cannot imagine it.

At once the objection would be made that we are incapable of imagining life in the hereafter. To which Marías readily agrees, but with this explanatory observation: "No doubt it exceeds our possibilities, in the sense that of course it will not be as we imagine it. But this will be because we are not able to imagine it adequately and so fall short. Certainly it is not because we imagine something *superior* to [its] reality. Is it conceivable that man could reach where God does not?"[12]

Without this imaginative continuum even Christian understanding fails to establish the connection between this life and the next. The very "otherness" of the hereafter has caused us to overlook a very basic human and Christian truth: my life in the next world is *still mine* in some sense yet to be revealed. Far from being an alien imposition, my life will be the life I have chosen. Thus, according to the formula proposed by Marías, "We can imagine this life as the choice of the other life, the other as the realization of this life."[13] This means that the radical (in the Ortegan sense) link between the two worlds is their reciprocal reference to "me."

We saw earlier how the man I am, or empirical structure of life, is "closed" and leads to my mortality, my death. But "my death" is apprehended *from* my life, which is future-oriented and open perhaps to immortality. In other words, my "manly" death appears within "my" life, which structurally and in principle goes on forever.

The alternating tendencies of Christianity to focus either on this life or the next can now be seen as the errors, possibly the heresies, they really are. The exclusive emphasis on this world at the expense of the next ignores the very structure of human life, which *requires* a transcendent life well before any formal thought can be given to its possibility. This "half-life," as it were, presupposes an isolation—of ourselves and our problems—quite apart from eventual speculation as to whether the "other half" is possible or not. From the personal standpoint—the only one accessible to us—immortality is not merely a cosmic chance lying mysteriously beyond life but a requisite attribute of its structure in this world and time and avoidable only at the risk of extreme distortion and disorientation.

On the other hand, to dwell exclusively on the next life to the neglect of this one is to ignore this empirical world with its legitimate demands and plea-sures. This view contains the potential heresy of questioning God's reasons for putting us in this life to start with. If life in this world matters little or not at all, then God could have placed us directly in Paradise and avoided the whole dramatic skein of human history. At certain moments, Christians have rea-soned along similar lines and concluded that the sooner they end this life and get on with the next the better.

But as Marías argues, if God had not permitted this life, had not let us live in this world, then we would be altogether different beings. "Man is the being who, once created and placed in life, *makes himself.*"[14] And we should add, in this world. If the next life is the realization of this one, then it follows that we must initiate here and now that which is worthy of eternal realization. Thus, if we deny the worthiness of this life, then what shall we begin with in the next? For how can we raise to eternal dignity that which we have esteemed so little?

Neither of these postures is religious, Marías tells us, or at least not Christian. True religion must inform and dignify this life through its reference to the next, that is, to God and His will. In the Lord's Prayer we repeat, per-haps unthinkingly, the connection of this world to the heavenly realm by pray-ing that God's will be done, ". . . on earth as it is in heaven." On the other hand, while our concern for this life is fundamental, what counts for the Chris-tian is our total destiny appearing in two indivisible parts.

One of the causes of this shifting emphasis and resulting error, Marías tells us in conclusion, is that periodically we forget that certain ills are un-avoidable and therefore beyond the power of any human agency or govern-ment to correct, at least in the short run, which seems to be the only one of interest in our day. The true opiate of the people, he writes, ". . . consists of *creating a panacea and denying all the ills that it is incapable of curing.*"[15]

The reference to Marxism and its kindred deterministic doctrines is ob-vious.

Social Justice and Other Justices

The worldly concerns that often divert Christian attention from the next life may be summed up in the expression "social justice."[16] Yet Marías insists that ". . . *social* justice is only one particular form of justice, and beyond jus-tice there is a host of things that matter."[17] It makes no more sense to make God the mere custodian of our social justice than it does to ascribe to Him the exclusive role of guarantor of our immortality. Countless gifts come from God, among them perhaps social justice.

Nevertheless, for over two centuries social justice has been the prime imperative of Western societies. Some of its corollaries seem simplistically self-evident: political and civil equality of all races, sexes, and classes, economic betterment, universal education, etc. Yet according to Marías, other concepts are unclear. Perhaps because it was so easy to detect and treat obvious injustice in the old inequalities, it was too temptingly simplistic not to include *all* the ills of the world in the sweeping category we call social injustice.

This implicit premise is fallacious, for even though it would be absurd to define as social injustices those ills that arise as a matter of course from climate, illness, accidents, and age, empirically this is exactly how they have come to be treated. Thus, in modern times poverty has fallen under the jurisdiction of social justice, yet for thousands of years it was simply the real and unappealable condition of most of humanity. Uncertainty and insecurity are endemic to human life, which is given without guarantees. Yet in the name of social justice men ask for protection not only against death and disease but also the fear of them. The unprecedented drive for security may be the strongest motivation of modern people. More than fifty years ago, journalist Walter Lippmann made the startling observation that given a choice, most Americans would not hesitate to exchange even the most basic freedoms for personal security.

But if these ills are not necessarily or originally examples of social injustice, then what is? For Marías, the definition is clear: *"Social justice is that which corrects a social situation that involves a prior injustice which invalidates just forms of behavior, or individual acts of justice."*[18]

These pseudo-injustices pale in comparison to the much greater injustice of depriving mankind of eternal hope. Yet ironically, this commonly happens in the name of social justice. Witness the Marxist attempts to deny immortality by advocating an earthly paradise as its substitute. In our admittedly post-Christian age, probably many people no longer trust in personal immortality and yet do not appear to be excessively troubled by their skepticism. But Marías is: "To me this seems to be the worst, for besides losing the horizon they have lost the awareness of what it is to live, that is, to need to go on living forever, and, what is more, to need their loved ones to go on living forever, whose annihilation, if they really are beloved, turns out to be unbearable."[19]

This loss of hope degrades human life and lowers its personal temperature. By historical contrast, whether happy or wretched, fortunate or miserable, the Christian did not consider himself any less *personally real* because of his regrettable state or condition. He was never so economically or socially debased as to lose the dignity of his eternal spiritual life. Indeed, this dignity existed on a plane that transcended earthly power and privilege. Though he may have had few personal or civil rights as we understand them today, in his personhood he was fully real and unique *forever.* This why Marías believes that the gravest injustice is to deprive mankind of this inviolable eternal condition; it is a personal loss, or better, a loss of person that no worldly gain can compensate.

An internal contradiction attaches to the very notion of "justice" in deterministic doctrines. For if human life is "determined" willy-nilly by impersonal forces, if we are not really the authors of our own acts but rather the manipulable objects of forces beyond any human control, then it makes no sense to speak of "justice" and "injustice." Neither justice nor injustice would apply in a world where everything happens only as it must happen. In such a scheme, necessity replaces all notions of moral and immoral behavior. We cannot be responsible for our actions if we are not free to act on our own.

Yet this internal paradox has not stopped economic determinism from profoundly affecting contemporary Christianity. The argument is made that economics is important and that Christianity must address economic reality. And of course it must, for economics has to do with life's basic resources. But resources for what? To this Marías would answer, for the projects which we plan and of which life consists. This means that for all its importance, economics is secondary to our projects. In other words, our life allows it to become a resource. Far from defining life in terms of economics, as Marx did, we must think of economics as a subset of life, as Marías insists.

This inverted order of priorities is but one of many in the modern, post-Christian world. In the name of collective social justice everything from politics to race, from sociology to statism, tries to assume priority over personal life. To the Christian mind this is unacceptable, for it inclines more cordially toward Unamuno's claim that each person of flesh and blood is worth more than the whole abstract universe. Nor is there any easy hope of reconciling the two perspectives: "We see that we are in the midst of a gigantic operation that consists of *inverting* the order of things that a Christian perspective imposes. Now then, that inversion is intellectually a falsification, morally, a perversion."[20]

The Right Questions

The shadow of moral relativism falls across all post-Christian doctrines. To the traditional Christian claim that all moral postures are, or ought to be, absolute and therefore impervious to history, modern people, including many Christians, are apt to respond that values are relative to history.

Where does the truth lie? For Marías, the question must first be correctly posed, and for him this means from the standpoint of life's structures, which earlier we described as analytical and empirical. If my life exhibits a certain analytical structure without which it could not be called human life, it assumes concrete material form as an empirical structure. Within these structures the particular life I live as a man takes place, and together they constitute the theme of anthropology as Marías understands it.

Now Marías's insistence on posing the question in what initially seems to be a circuitous fashion begins to make sense. For rather than excluding history and circumstance, this structural approach requires them. To give an example, speech is a requirement of the general or analytical structure. Human life is verbal. But speech is an abstraction; what we find empirically when we begin to examine actual human life is language, and what is more, a specific language that involves physical means of expression. Furthermore, this specific language will be found within a certain historical and cultural continuum.

Likewise, morality is a requirement of the analytical theory, for man chooses his life and justifies the choices in some fashion. In other words, he lives responsibly and *therefore* by his own standards—if by no other—may also be irresponsible and immoral. But having established this general principle, we must then admit empirical historical variations into our reasoning. For instance, in our day it would be morally outrageous to formulate moral stipulations for the treatment of slaves, because historically we have taken the more drastic attitude that the very institution of slavery is morally reprehensible. Yet from the Apostolic Age of Christianity until modern times, the treatment of slaves was a pertinent moral question because slavery was an unquestioned—or at least essentially unchallenged—social phenomenon. Today we reason about such matters from our contemporary morality which condemns them *a priori*, but do we have the right to condemn earlier ages because they likewise reasoned from their world view? Even today's relativists turn absolutists in censuring those who do not or did not share their historically conditioned morality. They naively (or is it narrowmindedly?) believe that the unpardonable sin of past eras was not having twentieth-century thoughts.

The same general questions and reservations can be raised about poverty. By no stretch of the imagination could poverty be thought of as something immoral as long as it was the general condition of humanity, although no one ever denied that it was painful and awful to be poor. Yet to Christ's admonition that the poor would be with us always, today we are more likely to take such remarks to be hard-hearted. To us, poverty is morally intolerable because at a given historical moment we made the collective decision that it could be eradicated and therefore should not be tolerated. For this reason, to modern Christians it would be a sin to impose poverty on men.

The point to be drawn from these examples is that moral and ethical norms, along with everything human, are susceptible to historical modifications, and, further, must necessarily be so. I shall summarize the reasoning. As we saw in an earlier chapter, human life exhibits the analytical quality of being "installed" in multiple ways in the world. But once we begin to discover the real forms of installation as they appear empirically, we find that they assume what we could call a "variable specificity." Marías refers to this mutability as the "field of possible human variation in history." In other words, analytical or general installation appears *only,* and therefore necessarily, as historical human variation.

Because the analytical structure of life includes installation that is subsequently and necessarily subject to variation at the empirical level, we need not fall victims to the relativistic claim that everything, even what Marías calls "installation," is a function of historical time and place. The claim is far too sweeping and too far from the truth. Because man's historical life is understandable only through an appeal to these universal structures, it follows that the empirical variations come to light only through articulation of the historical and the universal.

This clarifying articulation cannot be reduced to simplistic formulaic statements. In each case, it would be a matter of determining the moral degree and dimension affected by historicity. In other words, we must proceed not by emptying life of its historical content so as to proceed with the relatively easy manipulation of abstract schemes, but by the opposite procedure of fleshing out each era in its full dramatic unfolding. In order to do this we must not scorn any of the multiple witnesses to the human condition. This is one reason why Marías often appeals preferentially to the testimony of poets, ". . . for theirs is a voice modulated by human circumstance, the expression of a sensitivity that is not only individual but the key to discovering the hidden heartbeat of time."[21]

In our day, this testimony tells us that Christians live in a world that is no longer Christian. Concern for this historic departure from Christianity surely constitutes one of the great debates of our time. Yet to see this cultural apostasy as the major calamity of Christianity itself is to misplace the proper emphasis. As Marías points out, what matters most is for individual persons to be Christian, for after all only they may be saved or condemned. Whether cultures and countries are, or may be, Christian is an altogether different matter, and in the final view, probably a secondary matter.

Even the assumption that Christianity has entered into irreversible decline is open to serious question. Marías warns against the "definitive" mindset characteristic of the nineteenth century and still very much with us because of the archaic mental habits of contemporary men. Human destiny is much less sealed and settled than we are led to believe. The fact that in our time society is not Christian does not preclude a Christian rebirth. Contrary to the deterministic proclivities of recent centuries, history continues to be a futuristic enterprise. It could not be otherwise, for so is individual human life.

At another level, Christianity displays an astonishing vitality. The most pressing problems of our day—abortion, divorce, sexual relations, marriage, and home—are squarely centered in a religious context in which politics, science, and art function as important subsets. The common assumption is that religion, and especially the Christian religion, has been all but abandoned. The truth seems to be exactly the contrary. If anything, it is society that has been abandoned or at least turned over to secondary forces and second-rate truths. Christianity itself is very much alive and surprisingly well despite the early reports of its demise.

The Cutting Edge of Christianity

Edward Sarmiento says of Marías: "It would be, I am quite sure, a mistake to attribute to Sr. Marías any real disconformity with the mind of the Catholic Church but—and he is not alone in this—he would prefer a new approach to the question of the use to be made of traditional philosophy."[22]

This is certainly true, and we have seen already how Marías himself has used his analytical-empirical levels of human life to good effect in understanding certain areas of Christian thought. But there is more to be said. In the first place, much of what Marías had hoped for in 1951, when Sarmiento wrote his article, began to unfold in Vatican II and in later years. Hence the enthusiasm with which he greeted the liberalizing spirit released during the papacy of Pope John XXIII.

Secondly, by establishing coherent intellectual concepts that can mediate between moral absolutes and historical variations, Marías has been able to suggest ways to sort out and deal with the enormous cultural residues that have accumulated around Christianity and which themselves have been invested with a kind of religiosity. But because they are the fossilized remains of what were once living realities, they are inherently resistant to the continuous modifications of life. Indeed, many of the most divisive controversies arise not from articles of faith but from what could be called "articles of social accretion."

It may be that the very accretions just mentioned and the unchanging style they encourage, which are commonly taken to be the richness of Christianity, are the most visible if paradoxical proof that we live in a post-Christian era, an era that is structurally—and perhaps morally as well—removed from Christianity. For if the contemporary social world were truly Christian, then it is reasonable to suppose that the peripheries of Christianity would be subject to constant modification so that this "change at the margin" would be the rule rather than the painful exception. The urgency of new realities would cause them to insinuate themselves into the Christian fabric; old things would fall away, allowing all Christian things, even unchanging things, to be renewed.

One cause of confusion and dispute in erstwhile "Christian" societies seems to be that today Christian beliefs tend to be *nothing but Christian*. This requires an explanation. In former times, an appeal to religious beliefs was at the same time a social appeal, for religious *vigencias,* or binding observances, were also social *vigencias* and therefore had a double strength. For this reason, it is likely that many so-called "articles" or tenets of faith depended less on their own evidence than on their prevailing social acceptance.

Today, however, the social dimension of these beliefs in most cases has declined or vanished altogether. We are left with the belief only in its religious dimension. Privately this may be enough, and millions would readily testify to undimensioned conviction of their faith. The social problem is that in a great many instances the case for these beliefs cannot be made publicly. To attempt to do so absent the public and overt proof is to fall into what Marías calls the "cynicism of faith."

How must the Christian proceed in this non-Christian setting? Obviously as a Christian, which means among other things that he must respect the situation of others and not proclaim as publicly evident and binding that for which incontrovertible evidence cannot be summoned to convince the non-Christian. Marías says of this: ". . . the Christian, regardless of how firm his personal certainty may be, must present as uncertain that which for many other men is uncertain, and insofar as it is possible he must justify his own certainty."[23]

This should not be taken to mean that the Christian is to be any less earnest in trying to bring others to the Christian faith. But he cannot do so by demanding that they conform automatically to a viewpoint they do not share and perhaps do not understand. Marías urges the Christian to ask himself these questions: if I were not a Christian, would I see this matter in the same way? And am I seeing it myself from a Christian perspective, bearing in mind what Christianity reveals?

Thus, sincerity and truthfulness require of the Christian an introspective self-checking which leads to an accord between his faith and his ideas and conduct. And it has a broader application: it establishes the integrity and the dialectical communication through which Christians and non-Christians alike may agree on what is sure and certain and susceptible to reasonable justification.

There are examples to illustrate this procedure. Take the matter of marriage and divorce. In Catholic Christianity, marriage is, or has been, indissoluble, whereas in secular society hardly anything is less binding and divorce everywhere abounds. On a personal and Christian level, Marías shows very little sympathy for divorce, although he notes that the Church permits the renunciation of priestly vows. The very possibility of divorce tends to insert a provisional and tentative note into marriage and to make real happiness in marriage more elusive.[24]

Opposition to divorce usually takes the form of legislation, passed or proposed, against it. A much more promising approach, or so Marías believes, would be to enhance the reasons—religious if possible but human surely—that justify indissoluble marriage, reasons usually much weakened among Christians. As far as Marías is concerned, it is not enough to erect legislative barriers to protect what religious and moral authority seems incapable of doing.

Stated in more positive terms, the first task of Christians is what Marías refers to as the *religious revival* of the contents of faith, not the coercive imposition of legislation that even Christians themselves may not really consider to be authentic.

In passing, and with a promise to write at length on the theme, Marías includes abortion as another problem that ought to be approached differently. To the Christian, abortion may be a sin or even a crime, but to the secular world neither of these objections is acceptable and must, therefore, be relegated to a secondary importance. Within *this* context, those who oppose abortion would have to do so on purely philosophic anthropological grounds.[25]

It may be that the world is no longer Christian, Marías tells us, because Christianity itself turned too worldly and became the enemy of its own commission. Obsessed with having a world organized according to Christian structures, it often lost interest in seeing to it that people were Christian in their personal lives. The clerical reaction to this manifold secularization has often been unenlightened. Those clergy, he argues, who take a perverse pleasure in the anti-Christian restructuring of the world, in the erroneous belief that it represents a cleansing of Christianity, fail to see that this simply adds to the social contamination.

In summary, Marías finds more saving possibilities in the liberating power of Christian truths than in the restrictive expression of unexamined orthodoxy. The effort to cling to the former and resolve the latter is certainly worth the effort. Marías never doubts that the Christian life is as rewarding as it is difficult, and neither rewards nor resolutions are possible without a living faith and a clear head. He cannot, therefore, take issue with Saint Thomas Aquinas, who argued that *stultitia est peccatum,* for surely by Christian definition stupidity is sin when it becomes willful and avoidable and harmful to the Christian faith.

9

UNDERSTANDING SPAIN

August 1984. The time had come for Marías to return to a topic—suspended since the period of his personal trauma—that most deeply characterized the historical epoch we have called the "Generations of 1898." Beyond this specific work, however, concern for Spain had always been one of his foremost themes. If Ortega could say that all his life and work had been in service to Spain, the same is true of Marías. Even during the period when his "personal" writings were suspended, his "transpersonal" service to Spain continued. Witness, for example, his service as senator and his best-selling three-volume work *La España real* [Real Spain], published between 1976 and 1978 and intended to help the nation during the difficult transition to democracy and constitutional monarchy.

As for *España inteligible* (translated as *Understanding Spain*), he tells us that he had known for twenty years what the title would be and for all that time the content of the work had been taking shape in his thoughts. Both *Los españoles* (1963) and *La España real* represented partial developments of the theme. But it is no exaggeration, though at first it may seem so because of the magnitude of effort involved, to say that a book like *España inteligible* (1985) had been implicit throughout most of the twentieth century, both as a categorical and transpersonal theme of the age it defined and as a personal obligation for Marías, whose life and work are so finely illustrative of that era.

As we have already seen, Marías utilized the generational method and historical reason, both instrumentalities of Orteganism which Ortega himself described but did not bring to full application, to illuminate the work of the Generations of 1898. Witness his study of Unamuno and his commentary on nearly all the major figures of the era. In "completing Ortega with himself," Marías subjects Ortega to the same process, or to put it another way, the Ortega we meet in the writings of Marías is an Ortega understood through his own implicit method.

But why call his method "implicit"? Quite simply because many of his works were either unfinished—*Meditaciones del Quixote* and *La rebelión de las masas* are examples—or in an odd way "pre-Ortegan." Marías points out that both Unamuno's *Ensayos sobre el casticismo* (1895) and Ortega's *España invertebrada* (1921) were written prior to most of the advances in historical analysis, especially "historical reason," which ". . . no one, not even [Ortega] himself, had applied to the investigation of Spain."[1]

As far as I know, neither has anyone acknowledged the contributions Marías himself made toward shaping historical reason into a usable historiographical method. These contributions include a more profound and extensive examination of social *vigencias,* refinement of the generations theory, the complexities of beliefs, ideas, and opinions, the configuration of collective aspiration and happiness, the structures of power, and their combined meaning for human relationships. In such works as *La estructura social* (1955) and *Antropología metafísica* (1970), among others, Marías described its theoretical application to history and personal human life.

Following this careful elaboration of the historical method, Marías decided to take advantage of these advances and attempt something no one had tried before, perhaps because no one, not even Ortega himself, had been in a position to do so. I will offer again the advance opinion that more than a book, *España inteligible: Razón histórica de las Españas* is in several senses a historical response to the so-called "problem of Spain," as well as a methodological advance in the treatment of this and similar questions. The earlier Generations of 1898 had sought both meaning and method in the perplexing unfolding of Spanish history. By discovering that meaning through the instrumentality of historical reason and building on the work of such predecessors as Menéndez Pidal, Ortega, Unamuno, Castro, Sánchez-Albornoz, among others, Marías not only summarizes the work of his own age but offers a coherent view of the civilization that Spain built.

The subtitle is important, for this is an elucidation not only of Spain proper but also of *las Españas,* a term, or really, a concept, lacking in English and other languages because it is missing from the experience of other European peoples. For this reason, we do it a certain stylistic violence by translating it as "the Spains."

If we read attentively, we hear Marías dialogue as perhaps in no other work with illustrious figures of recent and remote generations. There are moments of likemindedness and cordial agreement with mentors and predecessors and instances of irritation with unchallenged clichés and subversive agendas.

These latter, pernicious and persistent, Marías seeks with all the tools at his disposal to reveal and dispel. Until *España inteligible,* Spanish history in the main had amounted to interpretations based on a comparatist methodology that pointed not to Spain but to other nations as a standard. By freeing Spanish historiography of extra-historical clichés and imported templates, he allows us to see the world that Spain built on its own terms and in its own true light, the light of historical reason.

Dispelling the Myths

Marías begins his analysis with the general epistemological premise, variously stated throughout his works, that misunderstandings of the kind that distort Spanish history arise not so much from a lack of historical information as an excess of "deformation," or as we would more likely say in English, disinformation. For isolated historical facts do not explain history but rather themselves require explanation if they are to make sense. But to be more precise, we would say they require their *own* explanation and not an extraneous scheme bent on forcing the sum of their modest truths into a larger mosaic so that it becomes a summary mistruth.

The Generations of 1898 posed or better, suffered the "problem of Spain" with extraordinary passion and neo-Romantic feeling, but until the advent of historical reason, Spanish history had nearly always seemed to be an anomalous enigma characterized by special circumstances. For the most part, its history was written and understood as a spasmodic tale of excellent starts and inglorious stumblings. Despite its richly woven tapistry, the threads always seemed eventually to unravel, leaving no coherent pattern or satisfying summation save its individualistic folklore and the afterglow of sublime but failed ideals. Throughout most of the Modern Age the consensus within Spain and beyond was that it was simply too esoterically different to accommodate rationality. Its staunchest defenders and worst enemies agreed on the singular point of Spanish abnormality. And if that deviation earned it a "black legend" of hostility from its adversaries, among Spaniards it often took the form of a strange and stoic pride in what they understood to be their wayward and perhaps unredeemable character. Hence the ambivalent attitudes we find in the writers of the first Generation of 1898. Thus, it served as both proud badge and embarrassing explanation of Spain's travails in the modern age. Perhaps this is why Spanish historians and many of its writers and thinkers seem to dwell preferentially on historical idiosyncrasies rather than the obvious virtues of Spanish civilization. Consider as examples the views of Ortega and Américo Castro.

The presumption of abnormality as a national constant led Ortega to seek its remotest possible causes. In *España invertebrada,* he argued that the same factors that permitted Spain's sudden rise to preeminence in early modern times also led to her decline by the seventeenth century. Spain, says Ortega, lacked egregious minorities of the sort that Ortega identified in France, for example, and which he believed essential for the enduring vitality of nations.

This weakness, he assures us, dates from the age of Gothic rule in Iberia. The Goths, already enervated by contact with the decadent influences of a declining Roman civilization, arrived in Spain sapped of vitality. Unlike the Franks and the Saxons, who invested with barbaric vigor the collectivities of what would one day be France and England, the Iberian Goths were unequal to the task of nation building. Consequently, not only was the weak aristocracy they established barely able to survive the Moorish onslaught, but the feudalism they developed was not an adequate base on which to construct a modern nation. Therefore, far from being a modern phenomenon, this historical deficit or inherent decadence is apparent at any point one may choose to compare Spanish history to the European.[2] It followed, therefore, that Ortega considered the absence of able elites to be the key to Spain's supposed historic failure. Historically speaking, in Spanish dominions only those things were done that an energetic but undisciplined populace could do. Later he would include rebellious masses in his thesis, as the obverse complement to the concept of failed elites, and in *La rebelión de las masas* extend the paradigm to the whole of contemporary European society. But this difference is worth noting: whereas in the rest of Europe the possible cultural collapse brought on by what Ortega called the "desertion" of capable minorities was a recent phenomenon, in Spain it was a constant from the beginning of its history. By this reasoning, we would have to say that Spain was born decadent.

For his part, Américo Castro believed that Spain could be understood only as a tripartite civilization of Christians, Jews, and Moors.[3] In Castro's works, the splendors of the semitic civilizations, Islamic and Jewish, were sympathically contrasted to the supposedly backward European Christians, thus helping spread the notion that they constituted the civilizing elements of Spanish history. In this sense, Castro's work is a both a lament for aborted possibilities and an accusation against the surviving culture. The Christian Spain that emerged religiously and militarily triumphant seemed destined to stand forever inferior to the richer images of a Spain that ought to have been.[4]

The inherent decadence described by Ortega and the modern cultural mosaic minus its essential pieces propounded by Castro constitute two of the five "myths" that Marías believes must be exposed and disposed of before a truer understanding of Spain can emerge. Castro's sympathetic portrayal of Moorish influences has long since become a cliché which Marías acknowledges: "Now, the Moors have become affixed to the image of Spain to such a degree that there is a tendency to explain everything by their presence or absence."[5]

However, this image of Moorish Spain leaves out the Romanization of Iberia. Long before the advent of the Moors, Spain had been thoroughly Latinized. It boasted a network of roads, a superior system of agriculture, as well as juridical and ecclesiastical codes and writings. Probably a stronger case could be made for the Latinization of Islam than vice versa, beginning with the fact that in North Africa, where Latin and Christian civilization was totally replaced by Islamic culture, nothing comparable to Spain ever arose.

On the other hand, this same Islamic factor which supposedly gave rise to a superior civilization is often cited as the cause of Spain's congenital and perhaps ethnic inferiority. The old French quip that "Africa begins at the Pyrennees" has been taken for centuries within Spain and beyond as an irreparable cultural deficiency that explains the whole of Spanish history, especially its worst chapters.

Far from denying the importance of the Moorish presence in Spain, Marías argues that it must be openly acknowledged, which, he reminds us, is very different from simply presupposing that it is the cause of nearly everything good and bad.

Probably no feature of Spanish life has sunk deeper into the collective Western mind than the image of the Spanish Inquisition. Its very mention evokes images of gratuitous cruelty and religious persecution. Here, Marías himself indulges in a bit of historical comparativism by pointing out that the relatively few real abuses by the Inquisition pale before the incredible atrocities committed during the religious wars and witch hunts of Central and Northern Europe. He points out that even though the Inquisition is blamed for the nation's cultural backwardness, it actually coincided with Spain's Golden Age. Furthermore, the most notorious executions—Thomas More, Michael Servet, Giordano Bruno, Vanini—occurred outside of Spain. One does not have to deny the repulsive features of the Spanish Inquisition, and Marías has no intention of doing so, to remind us that the religious persecutions in the England of Henry VIII, to say nothing of France and Germany, claimed many more lives and were much bloodier and more ferocious than anything in Spain at that time.

With the writings of Bartolomé de Las Casas, especially *Brevíssima relación de la destruyción de las Indias* [A Very Brief Account of the Destruction of the Indies] (1552), another chapter was added to what has become known as Spain's "Black Legend." Both the motives and accuracy of Las Casas remain subject to serious doubts. But for Marías the most serious consequence of his accusations was the deleterious effect they had on Spanish history in general. Even though Spain has been the greatest builder since Rome, she has been looked on by her enemies and the ill-informed as a "destructive" country. But if this misperception distorts the history of Spain and the evident reality of Spanish America, it works a greater evil by perverting the future possibilities of these Spanish-language cultures. By thinking of themselves as the offspring of a destructive Spain, Spanish-speaking peoples find that a note of doubt and revulsion threatens to poison their historical possibilities. Marías suggests that this single factor may have been the greatest obstacle to the development of these countries since their independence.

What Is Spain?

By posing this venerable question anew after stripping away the five historical clichés outlined in the preceding section, Marías confronts Spanish history in its native phenomenological presence. But where does one go from here? Obviously, with the flow of the story itself, for historical reason shows that a society is understandable only in the light of its storyline, meaning in this case the real and verifiable collective aspiration of the society we call Spanish. But this statement turns out to be misleading if we aim no higher than mere storytelling because we do not know precisely "who" the subject of our story, our hi-story, is. The story makes sense, that is, offers an explanation of history in the telling, only if it occurs within a prior conceptual system aimed at and built on such explanations of human life. In short, historical knowledge presupposes a metaphysical theory of human life. Or to use Ortega's words, "History is the systematic science of the radical reality that is my life."[6] We can go a step further and state that because of this, historical reason cannot be understood or explained apart from this metaphysical basis. But it must remain clear that here we are not retreating into abstractions. Human life and historical reason converge precisely at the point of historical understanding. For as Ortega cautions, we are not to think of historical reason as an imported and imposed species of ratiocination about history. Historical reason is " . . . not an extrahistorical reason which appears to be fulfilled in history but, literally *a substantive reason constituted by what has happened to man,* the revelation of a reality transcending man's theories and which is himself, the self underlying his theories."[7]

If prior historiography had told us what Spain ideally or culturally ought to be but regrettably is not, this new way of reasoning proceeds without these editorial edicts to allow "what has happened to come to light and speak for itself." This means starting without preconditions where Spain is in order to begin without the usual preconceptions to understand what it is.

But this step is only the first of several. For where Spain is today is a function of where and what it has been, and this situation flows from the choice of certain options. But there is more: what Spain has chosen to be is also radically affected vectorially by what it could have been. Just as the understanding of individual human life involves both our real and possible trajectories, so a society can be understood only by referring its actual historical drama to the possible pathways that could have been taken in any given situation of its history.

Here we see a certain analogy with the structures of individual life. Within limits, societies, like individuals, have the unavoidable freedom to chart their collective course. I say within limits for one reason, because societies are limited to the choices implicit within their real possibilities. To illustrate with a simplistic example, seventeenth-century Spain could not have chosen to be an air power because airplanes had not been invented.

But this limitation is far from any sort of historical determinism, as another example may show. It was within Spain's possibilities to be an Islamic nation, perhaps by remoter circumstances in the early Modern Age even a Protestant power. It *chose* instead to be Catholic not as the path of least or no resistance, which is the way of determinism, but of maximum resistance to powers that otherwise would have pushed it toward either of those possible destinies.[8]

Just as in the case of individual life, we cannot ignore the workings of chance in the destiny of nations. Imagine, for example, what Spain and Europe would have been without the chance discovery of the Americas. Naturally we cannot, any more than we can image what a person would be if he had had different parents. America functioned as the maximum element of chance in the history of the Iberian nations. Perhaps it would be more accurate to say that what began as chance ended as destiny due to the choices that Spain and Portugal made in response to it.

By virtue of its decisions a society dramatizes in a characteristic way not only chance but also to some degree the otherwise inert elements of its circumstance (material, social, psychic, economic, juridical, etc.) and converts them into resources for its collective project.

Naturally, as we cautioned earlier, the limits of reasonable comparison of societies with individual life quickly become apparent. To begin with, individual life is empirically finite, as we have seen. We live from one stage to another, from one situation to the following, until we reach a final stage, an ultimate situation, beyond which there is no other in this life and world. But even though societies dwindle and die, there is no *a priori* reason that they must do so. Collectively speaking, no age or stage is necessarily the last one. Furthermore, we commit linguistic violence if we ask "who?" a society is. Upon reflection we realize that even though we are dealing with human life in speaking of societies, they are not fully personal. There is no social "I," and even the common social pronoun "we" is an inference drawn from the "who" that each person is. In individual life we find two elements, circumstance and vocation, that are not chosen but imposed, or in the case of the second, proposed. On the other hand, society *is* circumstance, that is, "my" primary human circumstance in which "I" find myself and from which I respond to my personal vocation. This illuminates Marías's prior caveat about societies: "It is human life we are dealing with, but life determined in an extremely high degree by forms of 'natural' circumstantiality, transformed by a series of projects that manifest themselves in realities more than in ideas or words. Do not forget that the vast majority of peoples who have existed in the world have been, or are, very silent, with a minimun of expression."[9]

The Spain That Could Have Been

This statement, which the earlier generations of his era almost always took to be a nostalgic reminder of squandered opportunities, takes on a new and positive nuance in Marías. He takes issue with Ortega, who had described modern Spanish history as "three and a half centuries of misguided wandering," by asking whether such a prolonged historical error, even if true, would be recognizable as such. For against what standard of "correct" Spanish history could it be judged? Naturally, Ortega and others assumed that a European standard existed, but because it was essentially foreign and alien to the specific circumstances of Spain, Marías found it unacceptable. Paradoxically, as we have already seen, it was alien to Ortega's own paradigm of historical reason. For Ortega, it would be necessary to burn the Spain that had been in order to find among its ashes the "iridiscent gem" of the Spain that could have been. But for Marías, the Spain that could have been was not a chance offered and missed once and for all time. At each juncture of history the understanding of what Spain was would include as an indispensable component its possible options, or as Marías calls them, its "trajectories."

But exactly which junctures do we mean? To begin with, they presuppose the prior existence and historical movement of the society we have called Spanish. Consequently, even though each of the following were to have varying degrees of impact on what *subsequently* would be Spain, Spanish society could not be defined by such things as the establishment of cities by Greeks and Phoenicians or the migrations of Iberians, Celts, Swabians, Vandals, or Visigoths. Not even the Islamic invasion, Marías tells us, belongs to the fund of authentic Spanish trajectories, although it profoundly affected and frustrated them.

At this point, Marías states his overarching thesis: "the Reconquest . . . is the original response to this tremendous trauma, the point of departure for the trajectories that effectively engender Spanish society in its maturity [and act] as a decisive factor in the projection of all its subsequent history."[10]

Here, in the form of a unique response to chance and circumstance, Spanish history begins as an unbroken social continuum, superseding Spanish prehistory with all its undeniably important but disparate elements. The story has begun, and from now on we find ourselves inside it. And because of this inner perspective, Marías tells us, we must look askance at extraneous factors that do not cohere with the main plot of the historical narrative. Naturally, this attention to the informing plot means that we must examine at each juncture how Spanish society sees itself and determine the degree to which its values and its aspirations coincide or diverge.

It is important to remember that even though a Spanish history and continuity exists from the time of the Reconquest, this is far from saying that

Spanish society sprang full-blown from that historical juncture. Marías identifies three phases of successive integration and levels of ascent toward a Spanish society in the full meaning of the term. The first is *Hispania,* the Romanized province, or provinces. Marías describes it as "the first version or prototype of 'Spain,'" which though certainly Hispanic is still not Spanish. In this early configuration *Hispania* was still a variation of Roman culture and language with certain features that, beginning as provincial peculiarities, eventually become "Spanish" in character.

When did these Hispanic Romans cross the line and become Spanish? To pick any absolute date would be a useless conjecture. Only in retrospect does it become apparent that in no way can the Spanish reality of today, or for that matter of the Middle Ages, be reduced to the Hispanic Roman cities of the third century A.D. On the other hand, there is no question about the continuity of those cities—Seville, Cadiz—from Roman times until the modern age.

The second phase of Spain, the beginning of which remains conjectural, as we have seen, could be defined as a Spanish society located in the geographic area associated with Spain but still far from the unity called "Spain." Because we are dealing with what Marías calls the "gestation" of a society, we seek in vain for the hasty transitions common to politics or war. It is a matter of developing *vigencias,* what we have occasionally referred to earlier as "binding observances," that is, predominant patterns of belief, conduct, and customs. The process is slow and uneven. As Marías describes it, ". . . the constitution of that 'Spanish society' in the unit called Spain is not simultaneous, but that its parts gradually joined as a sufficient level of custom was achieved, or as those customs spread from one nucleus—or several nuclei—to other areas that were backward or isolated for a longer or shorter period of time."[11]

Finally, the third phase dates from the founding of the *Spanish nation* in the full meaning of the term, in the second half of the fifteenth century. Because Spain was the first nation so constituted in Europe and the forerunner of the typical political structure of the Modern Age, its importance as a prototype can hardly be overstated. Yet Marías points out that the Spanish nation was not the final stage in Spain's development. Yet to come was the superstate articulated under the Hispanic Monarchy and composed of *las Españas* from the sixteenth century to the end of the nineteenth. With the separation of Cuba, Puerto Rico, and the Philippines in 1898, Spain *appeared* to return to the status of a nation. But on this point Marías has more to say, as we shall presently hear.

In order to understand the "Spain that could have been"—and let us add, at its various historical junctures—it is important to keep in mind that the Spain that is or has been is not reducible to its "aspects" nor even to the imprecise and much abused notion of "culture." Most of all, it is necessary to avoid the temptation to consider Spain in isolation. Marías notes that from the beginning of its history, Spain confronted others and what he calls "the other," a concept that we shall examine later.

This interaction with other societies, within and beyond the European system, creates a series of levels. Over against the current historicism which presupposes the essential equality of cultures despite their real or apparent differences, Marías points out that reality itself displays hierarchies insofar as effort, fortune, destiny, and creative power are concerned. "There are peoples who are more or less creative, original, fruitful, 'communicable,' and the same could be said of the historical periods, in connection with each of the great areas of the world, those that have a coherent historical meaning."[12]

Exploring the significance of interfacing cultural hierarchies, Marías points out that whereas many peoples may *contribute* to shaping a portion of the world, as many contributed to the formation of Spain, only a few can be said to *configure* it. Spain, he tells us, has been one of these "configuring" nations, and for this reason Spanish belongs to a select group of "universal" languages. This universality does not have to do primarily with how many millions speak a language but with how many diverse peoples communicate with one another through it. And this internal communication becomes at the same time a world dialogue with other languages of similar function.

The old nostalgic lament for the Spain that could have been always presupposed the European character of Spain, even though that character was thought to be defective and imperfectly expressed. This line of thinking is as easy to understand as it is hard to justify. Marías admits that Spain is unlike other European countries, but whereas his predecessors usually took this to mean that Spain was less European than its neighbors, he argues that in certain essential ways it was more so.

The Theme of "Lost Spain"

With the demise of Imperial Rome, *Hispania* experienced the first "decline of the West." Marías describes the situation of "Spain" in the fourth and fifth centuries: "Now Spain was on a remote frontier, torn away from a Rome that was no longer truly Rome, overshadowed by Byzantium, threatened on all sides. The decline of the Roman West affected its farthest point, its *finis terrae;* a danger that would reappear again and again, in response to changes in the balance of the world."[13]

Naturally, the focus of *Hispania* had always been Mediterranean. But this was soon to change. With the invasion of the Northern peoples—Vandals, Swabians, and Visigoths, principally—Europe made its first appearance in the history of the Iberian peninsula by way of France. Europe became a vast hinterland to the declining world of Imperial Rome. In Spain, a Romanized and

Catholic populace came under the rule of a much smaller Germanic aristocracy already essentially Latin-speaking but professing Arian Christianity. King Recaredo's conversion to Catholicism in 589 at the III Council of Toledo signaled an acceleration in the merging process of Visigoths and Hispanoromans. From this point on, the expression "Visigothic Spain" begins to have historical meaning as a European manifestation. For Europe was to be the combination of native, Roman, and Germanic elements. Ortega believed the Germanic element to be decisive because it had the power to decide and to organize, whereas the native and Romanized populations formed the masses who responded to the Germanic will and purposes. The problem that was to affect the future of Spain at the most basic level was the supposed diminished vitality of the Visigoths.

We have already seen how Marías took issue with the Ortegan hypothesis. It may have been true, Marías writes, that the Germanic impact was relatively less in Spain than in Gaul, but this was due to the correspondingly greater degree of Latinization in Iberia. Furthermore, the superior Latinization of Iberia and the prior assimilation of Latin civilization, including the language, by the Visigoths led to a smoother merger of natives and invaders and the *relatively* early rise of a functional society. Not that this coexistence was placid. *Hispania* saw much strife in the centuries when Visigothic Spain was being formed, but it was among the ruling Goths themselves, not between Goths and the Romanized Iberians.

Marías goes on to dismiss as specious Américo Castro's thesis that the Visigoths simply were not Spaniards. Here, history itself tells a different story. If it is true that the Visigoths were different from the native Iberians, it is also true that they soon became a part of *Visigothic Spain.* The superior Latinization of *Hispania,* including Lusitania, hastened the assimilation, or better, the Hispanization, of the Visigoths. France, Burgundy, England, and Lombardy, all less Latinized than *Hispania,* all took the names of their Germanic invaders. It is significant and symptomatic that Spain proved an exception to the general rule and retained its Latinized name, later becoming *Spania (España)* in Romance.

By the end of the seventh century, Visigothic Spain, its language, religion, and culture reasonably consolidated, was already on the verge of becoming a European country. Chance intervened to frustrate its further development. The Islamic invasion in 711 smashed the Visigothic kingdom but not its image and its appeal. At that point, despite all its real defects and imperfect realization, Visigothic Spain became an idealized and hence desirable "lost Spain." Thus was born the great collective quest of recovery, of reconquest, of restoration. The Spain "that could have been" now became the image of the Spain that had to be again.

Islam and "the Other"

Ortega writes in his *España invertebrada* that although the separation of the Mediterranean world into Christian and Islamic halves meant the end of the ancient Latin and Hellenic cultural hegemony predominant since the Punic Wars, it was compensated by the enormous gain of the European hinterland. Christian civilization moved northward, or at least began to look toward the Northern lands and to convert their barbaric peoples.

However, the cleavage of the Mediterranean *mare nostrum* did not mean that the southern boundary was simply lost. As Marías explains, "There it stayed, as something forbidden, hidden, inaccessible but present; and, in addition menacing, always lying in wait. Let us not forget that, quite apart from the great invasions, Moslem incursions and acts of aggression were constant and did not end until well into the the nineteenth century."[14] For a thousand years, the theme of Christian captives in Moorish or Turkish lands permeated European literature. Marías goes on to say that for this reason Europe cannot be understood apart from this long confrontation with Islam.

Yet this experience was all but forgotten in recent centuries as Islamic power waned and Europe became predominant in world affairs. Europeans of the eighteenth and nineteenth centuries saw the Spanish confrontation with Islam not as a feature more or less common to all European history but as a unique experience, more, an abnormality, of Spain. Whether other Europeans thought of the Islamic influence as, alternately, a contaminating or civilizing factor in Spain, their error lay in forgetting that it was an essential element in the formation of their own medieval history.

Spaniards never had such lapses of historical memory. For one thing, the Islamic presence in language, literature, toponymy, and architecture was too immediately evident to overlook. Other Europeans took this Islamic impact to be a contaminating or exotic feature peculiar to Spain, but since their presupposition of a "pure Europe" was a myth to start with, the supposed "abnormality" of Spain turns out to be, according to Marías, greater fidelity to historical reality. From this perspective, "Pure Europe" is simply a deluded and forgetful Europe.

Many modern historians speak of a blending of cultures in Spain, but even though Christianity and Islam were in tense proximity to each other for nearly a millennium, the relationship was one of polarity punctuated naturally by times of war, but also by instances of friendship and cooperation, yet always characterized by a fundamental rivalry.

There has been much insistence on the supposed "tolerance" shown by the Islamic conquerors toward their Christian and Jewish subjects. Even while indulging what likely amounts to an exaggeration, if chronicles of the time are a reliable guide, Marías finds that this view needs correcting. Islam was, and is, fiercely and polemically monotheistic. But a polemic assumes an opposition, which for Islam meant both Judaism and Christianity. On the other hand, for all its differences with and frequent hostility toward Judaism, or at least toward Jewish people, Christianity has always acknowledged its historical and theological priority. Even though Islam incorporates personalities and features of Judeo-Christian scriptures (the Prophets, Jesus, etc.), it recognizes no such theological priority but simply dismisses both Jews and Christians as "infidels."

Furthermore, even though Islam is a religion of the "Book" like Judaism and Christianity, it insists on the linguistic exclusivity of Arabic. Whereas the Bible exists in many translations and versions, Islam has always opposed translating the *Koran* into other languages, and its attachment to Arabic was not only a matter of tradition but of Islamic theology itself.

The exclusive, combative, and closed posture of Islam polarized the "other," the alien non-Moslem, and caused European Christianity, and especially the Spanish Church, to become in turn more rigid and vigilant. In Marías's words, "Europeans considered themselves primarily *Christians,* not only in religion but in all other orders of life, for the presence of the other faith and style of life solidified their belief and extended it to their whole horizon."[15]

The point Marías wishes to make following this line of reasoning is that Spanish nationality did not result from a cultural amalgamation of Christian and non-Christian elements, as Américo Castro and others claimed. The view that "Christians, Moors, and Jews," were essentially comparable and homogeneous elements in the formation of the Spanish ethos is untenable. What really happened, Marías insists, was that Spain came into being in reaction to those non-Christian and especially Islamic elements, to the "other" which was always experienced precisely as such, that is, as an aggressively alien and rival way of life.

In turn, the Christian reaction took the form of an aggressive rejection of Islam and a vigorous affirmation of its own doctrines. From an eighth-century perspective this opposition appeared utopian and doomed to failure before the invincible Islamic tide. From the first, therefore, a certain "Quixotic" note infiltrates the Spanish ideal, which could be defined as a refusal to be dismayed by the impossible. As Marías puts it, "Spain was born out of an extremely improbable project, out of an imaginative anticipation, an illusion."[16] We could say, then, that the search for a "lost Spain" became the specific and defining but seemingly unfeasible task of repelling Islam and affirming Christianity face to face with the "other."

Here, in stark juxtaposition, we must compare what Spain could have been with what it chose to be. No doubt to the deterministic mind an Islamic Spain would have seemed inevitable. Instead, within the surviving Christian pockets there surged what Marías describes as "an iron resolve to be Christ-ian," and being Christian meant also being European and Western.

From these conditions, and amid conventional suppositions about Span-ish history, Marías draws a startling conclusion: instead of being less Euro-pean than other countries, Spain is really more so. Spain is Christian and European not because it had no other choice but because it *chose to be so* de-spite the enormous weight of circumstances and the improbability that it could be so. Far from being a chaotic and supine result of kaleidoscopic influences, Spain has defined itself from its beginnings as a *project* chosen from among several possibilities as the most authentic option. For it collectively sensed in the most fundamental way that this project was its true calling, its vocation, that could not be betrayed. Therefore, "Spain, when adequately viewed, is the dramatic unfolding of a historical vocation, of a will that struggles to move foreward in the midst of uncertainty."[17]

We recall Marías' seminal work in defining the concepts of vector, tra-jectory, installation, and most of all, freedom as it applies to the individual drama of human life and to their analogous role in collective life. Once again, and this time in the history of Spain, Marías reminds us how far history cir-cumvents the static and predetermined. "The essential element of *freedom* shines forth here as it does in very rare cases. The 'Spain that might have been'—Oriental and Muslim—was there, before Spaniards' eyes, because it began to exist, and for at least a couple of centuries had much more factual re-ality than the other Spain; and let us add that later on, and twice in extremely vigorous form, it received reinforcements from Africa, while Christian Europe did not act even as a rear guard for the Spain that was laboriously carrying out the Reconquest. Which demonstrates once more that that history is not merely factual, is not reduced to facts and resources, but that its most important ingre-dient is *projects,* for whose sake those resources exist and for which they serve."[18]

The prolonged lapses in this Spanish will to be different from Islam, to be "other" than the "other, as it were, the puzzling eras of coexistence, satrapies, cross alliances, and mutual admiration all hint of moments of histor-ical, or better, human inauthenticity, of occasionally yielding to the continual temptations and virtues of "otherness." These are perhaps novel concepts to introduce into conventional historiography, but the novelty arises from the fact that, until now, history has not been treated as a manifestation of human life understood in all the philosophical and metaphysical rigor it holds for Marías.

Even though they make for misleading interpretations, in time these lapses pass and what García Morente calls *hispanidad* ["Spanishness"], or the Spanish spirit, reemerges with exceeding clarity. Marías describes it formally: "What we understand by Spain . . . is the Christian Spain that did not accept its islamization and struggled against it, with more or less success, with enthusiasm or with apathy, from early in the eighth century to the end of the fifteenth . . ."[19]

Such was the power of "lost Spain" to forge through successive "incorporations" the Spanish nation. But once achieved through victory over "the other," the informing project seemed complete. What was Spain, Christian and united, to do now? According to Marías, we must search within the programmatic structure of medieval Spain for the root causes of its hesitations, genius, and archaic tendencies in the modern age.

Castile

In the general debate by the Generations of 1898 on the "problem of Spain," probably no topic was discussed more than Castile. In an earlier chapter, we saw how in its "landscape lyricism" this first generation of the new epoch came to grips with the splendors and miseries of Spanish history and reality. In *España invertebrada,* Ortega states: "Castile has made Spain, and Castile has undone it." To which Sánchez-Albornoz responded many years later, "Castile made Spain and Spain undid Castile." For his part, Marías prefers to think that "Castile made itself into Spain," adding the clarification, "Castile dedicated itself not to making Spain, but to making itself into Spain."[20] Within this context, it is interesting to read what medieval Castilians themselves thought of Castile:

> But Castile is the best of all Spain,
> Because it was the beginning of all the others. . .[21]

Marías argues that it would have been impossible to bring about the unification of Spain merely through a process of "castilianization" [*castellanización*] of non-Castilian lands, for this would have contradicted the general incorporative spirit evident throughout the Middle Ages. This series of incorporations of non-Castilian areas was essential to the great common undertaking of Spain. For the Reconquest was always conceived not as a Castilian venture but a collective Spanish effort long before the dynastic unification of Spain became a fact.

As Marías sees it, in putting aside its local interests in favor of Spanish concerns, Castile took the first step toward defining the modern social enterprise we call nations. Antiquity had known minimal city-states and and colossal empires—Greece and Rome, respectively—but nothing that approximated the nation, even though modern historians may be tempted out of intellectual habit to apply the term to other kinds of polities such as the Islamic *taifas* or the tribal organizations of native Americans and Africans.

Therefore, it is important to remember that the process of nationalizing Spain was not Castilian but Spanish, even though Castile conceived it and put it into motion. Castile was never a nation and did not give its name to a nation, even though it was a kingdom among other kingdoms during the Middle Ages. In his *Cervantes clave española,* Marías says that Castile was never just a territory but an attitude. This brings up another point. Although under Castilian direction Spain emerged as the first European nation, its nationality presupposed others, for nations, like firstborn brothers, assume that others will follow to share a common home. And because they are all born of the European substratum, as Ortega so often insisted, and strive to manifest the abiding virtues of that heritage, an element of sibling-like rivalry characterizes their relationships.

In a factual or statistical sense, on which modern historiography depends almost exclusively, neither Castile nor Aragon, the major components whose merger gave rise to Spain, was economically or demographically impressive, much less so than, say, France. Neither abounded in resources. Marías describes their effective situation on the eve of unification as "lamentable." Neither had so far been able to resolve the economic decline, political dissension, and general demoralization so well documented in the second half of the fifteenth century. This being the case and the facts, how does one explain that in a few short decades Spain became the leading power in Europe and the world?

It was true, Marías writes, that there was no Castilian or Aragonese solution to these problems. But there was a *Spanish* solution. Time and again we find in Marías's writings the conviction, substantiated by argument and example, that real nations exceed—and occasionally fall short of—the sum of their parts and therefore cannot be reduced to, or explained by, a mere recounting of statistical or demographic facts, nor can their national aspirations be recounted as partisan or political agendas. Not quantitative accounts of resources nor appeals to ethnic heritage, but organizing programs of nationalization, which stir enthusiasm and capture human imagination and loyalty, hold the real secret of nation building and power. Where demoralization and disorganization had characterized Castile and Aragon a few decades before, "A new way of thinking about themselves was born, a new society, and a new sense of 'we.' It is no longer 'we Castilians' or 'we Aragonese' (still less 'we Old Castilians' or 'we Andalusians' or 'we Catalans'); it will be 'we Spaniards' with a 'we' that takes in everyone."[22]

Under Castilian leadership, Spain rose to universal greatness not only as the first modern nation but also as the originator of the first real *Weltpolitik* since Rome. For Spain did not simply become the first in what would be the European species of nations but went further and developed what Marías calls a "transEuropean Supernation." The Spanish themselves used to refer to it as *las Españas,* which, as we noted earlier, remains curiously resistant to translation.

For the most part, these advances have been denied, overlooked, or forgotten. Marías cannot suppress a certain indignation at the obstinate misreadings of Spanish history, and primarily by Spaniards themselves, whose readiness to believe the foreign slander of Spain seems but to grow with each twisting of the truth. He cites the preference for negative factors—poverty, depopulation, sloth, haughty claims of nobility, and religious fanaticism, for example—noting that were such claims true they would have rendered the actual history of Spain impossible *forever.*

Consequently, many dismiss Spain as "the country without a Renaissance." Havelock Ellis once tried to turn this supposed flaw to virtue by pointing out that the same features that prevented Spain from being a modern country would also allow her to flourish in a postmodern world. Such a prediction may prove true, but it arises from dubious assumptions. As Marías sees it, Spain did not simply have a Renaissance, it was itself a renaissance born out of fidelity to an ancient ideal.

Marías calls for a rereading of the facts and suggest a bold revision of Spanish history. He wonders whether it was Spain or the rest of Europe that veered away from the enterprise which it had so vigorously defined and championed. "Is there not an element of disappointment in the Spain of the seventeenth century, as she saw the enterprise which she had instigated in some sense 'betrayed'? Was it that Spain was 'left behind,' as has always been thought, or that she did not feel inclined to enter into certain trajectories that struck her as inauthentic?"[23] Elsewhere, he wonders why no one asks about "the Europe that could have been?" Does the rancorous, faithless, and nationalistic spirit of modern Europe, to which Spain naturally is not immune, lead toward its real destiny? In view of twentieth-century European history and its consequences, perhaps Marías is right to raise these questions.

Just what was the "Spanish project" proposed to the rest of Europe? It begins with the concept of *universitas christiana,* a Christian empire, considered divinely ordained and consisting in a harmonious coalition of Christian princes dedicated to warring against the infidel, converting the pagan, and imposing high and hard individual duties in alleviating "the ills of our religion." But what electrified the Spanish charge to greatness was undoubtedly the fervor and power that infused its Catholicism. Fresh from centuries of struggle to eliminate Islamic dominance and reestablish the full integrity of its Christian condition, Spanish Catholicism exhibited depths of commitment and reserves of vitality and fortitude that pervaded every aspect of Spanish life and astonished other Europeans. Other European nations were certainly "Christian," yet

Christianity was not the axis of their life, as it was for Spain. The old driving ideal of Spain as "one and Christian," now at last a reality, was offered as an enticement to Europe and subsequently to the world.

Under Spanish hegemony and largely Spanish in inspiration, new styles of diplomacy, trade, war, and alliances came into being which differed profoundly from anything the Middle Ages had known. For whereas medieval life was characterized by stability in the institutional ways of life, individual life was marked by extreme insecurity. According to Marías, the uncertainty of individual life was such that it could be counted on. Of medieval people, he notes that they had the security of insecurity. In other words, they lived in the paradoxical certainty of uncertainty.[24]

It is against this historical backdrop that the Spanish Renaissance and Spain's role in the formation of the modern ethos must be understood, if it is to be understood at all. For Marías, the Renaissance was precisely what the term implies: *rebirth*. This rebirth has usually been defined vaguely and probably erroneously as a return to the old (resurgence of Classical values, ancient texts, study of Greek, etc.) and, as a corollary, as a decline in the power of Medieval Christianity. But what we find is a paradoxical process that transformed the old Classical world into the new world order of the fifteenth century.

The limited, finite space of Medieval life and art, the *Finis Terrae* and *Non Plus Ultra* of Classical and Medieval man, now opened to infinity. Artists developed infinite perspective and explorers discovered the true vastness of the world. In many senses, and not just in geography, it was an age of discovery. In fact, Marías writes that unlike the belief-circumscribed and secure world of the Middle Ages, to Spaniards and Portuguese particularly ". . . life presented itself to them as discovery."[25]

Far from remaining indifferent to the Renaissance, Spain and Portugal embodied it. Their encounter with new cultures and races of people raised profound questions about the limits of the human kind. Were the inhabitants of those distant lands fully human and susceptible to salvation? The Hispanic response, especially by the Spanish, was resoundingly affirmative, and so the human condition was expanded far beyond the belief system and experience of Medieval peoples. It was an experience that gave new meaning to the old Spanish encounter with the "Other."

First nation, then discovery, expansion, exploration, and supernation, such were the eventual consequences of the old Castilian will to recover "lost Spain" and reaffirm through faith and arms its Christian condition. Perhaps the apogee of Spanish will, power, and faith is expressed in Hernando de Acuña's exuberant verse:

> One faith and a single shepherd in the land,
> One monarch, one empire and one sword.[26]

But if, on the one hand, this "Spanish project" was a decisive factor in shaping the Modern world, eventually modernity lost the ideal of Christian hegemony. The Spanish disillusionment with this modern turning away contrasts starkly with the triumphs of the Spanish ideal on several continents. Victorious over one phase of Islam, Spain now found itself in a protracted struggle against both a new form of Islam and a new and vigorous variety of Christianity itself. As we shall see, its reaction was as characteristically energetic as the outcome, like all fratricidal struggles, was predictably tragic. But even though chance and circumstances, which had so favored Spain at the beginning of modernity, would in time turn against her and much would be lost, at least a residue of will and spirit remained. Riding forth on his heroic but ironic quest near the end of the Spanish hegemony, Don Quixote seems to speak for his age when he says: "The enchanters may take fortune from me, but it is impossible for them to remove my striving and spirit." Can we not sense for the first time in these words a certain foreboding that Spain was nearing the human limits of its enormous enterprise?

The Christian Schism and Spanish Decadence

The Medieval will of Christian Spain to survive and prevail as a Christian people, embodied and directed by Castile as a nationalizing project, eventually reached fruition in a unified Spain and an international superstate we have called in clumsy English "the Spains." From the time of the Catholic Kings Ferdinand and Isabella, Spain seems to enter an age of limitless horizons. Beyond the seas, Hispanic countries are being formed with startling historical quickness. Throughout the Hispanic superstate philosophy and literature flourish within the powerfully expressive and fully developed Spanish language. Everything seemed possible and most things were.

These statements should not be taken for an idealistic vision of Spain. Statistically speaking, even in the halcyon days of world dominance, Spain was a relatively poor country without abundant natural resources and with a population well below that of France, for example. The oft-made accusation that Spain, and especially Castile, grew rich from plundering the New World has no basis in fact even though the lurid image remains in the popular imagination.

But as spectacular as it was, this projective yearning was not limited to a single prolonged expression of the native Christian will to withstand Islam but remained implanted in the Spanish spirit, ready to manifest itself anew with each great crisis in the Spanish experience.

These crises were not long in coming. Spain had created the conditions whereby Europe could have joined in the new *Weltpolitik,* which consisted in recently developed forms of military organization, diplomacy, and statesmanship aimed at forming a coalition of Christian princes in which the concerns of the faith would take precedence over regional and national interests. Marías notes that Phillip II thought of himself as a priest-king and despite his enormous power, authority, and personal culture lived in almost monkish austerity. The Escorial, Phillip's most characteristic architectural achievement, is a symbol of the Spanish will to defend Christendom. But the rise of nationalism and Protestantism frustrated this grand design.

Lutheranism reinforced the Spanish tendency toward exclusivity and purity in matters of faith. As chance would have it—chance, not determinism, Marías insists—just as the real or supposed differences between "old and new Christians" were beginning to die out, and with them the very *raison d'être* of the Inquisition, the Protestant movement rekindled them. Also by chance, Charles I of Spain was selected as Charles V of the Holy Roman Empire. This meant that Spain was thrust into the midst of a European struggle from which otherwise it might have remained detached.

Given the intensity with which Spain had identified itself historically as Christian and Catholic, it is not surprising that it reacted with such force and alacrity to the Protestant revolt. Marías describes it: "When the split occurred, Spain necessarily felt linked to the single Church for which she had done battle with the Muslims, until she had become what she had to be. The Reformation was not simply a movement of criticism, not even a heresy within the Christian community, but a drawing away, a breaking aprart; its acceptance by Spain would have seemed not only a sin against the faith, but an act of infidelity to the Spanish condition, a desertion of the very long historical project during which she had come into being."[27] There was yet another peril. Islam, defeated in Spain in its Arabic configuration, rose again under the Turkish regime to threaten anew the Christian world. For these reasons, Spain was compelled to prolong for two more centuries the original project of Christian affirmation, but under conditions vastly different from those under which it had fought in the Middle Ages.

For one thing, it was not Spain alone at risk. This time, the Spanish felt called to protect both Europe and the Church from external threats and internal heresy. In this context Spain proclaimed the Spanish-led victory of the Christian coalition at Lepanto (1571) as the culmination of its history. Perhaps it was no accident but an example of profound historical and personal synchronicity that Cervantes, who lost the use of an arm in the battle, considered it to be the high point of his life as well.

The defection of Francis I of France from the Catholic cause and his desultory alliances with Turks and Protestants dismayed the Spanish, whose foreign policy was based on the principle of Christian unity and collaboration and not, as Count-Duke Olivares put it, ". . . the loss and conquest of kingdoms." The first Spanish reaction to the nationalistic policies and deceptive intrigues of Cardinal Richelieu *against* the transnational Christian cause was one of disbelief rather than rivalry. Marías offers this explanation of the Spanish attitude: ". . . it was not that the trajectories of France and Spain clashed and entered into conflict: rather, it was that on the Spanish side the meaning of France's trajectory was not understood, for it was not subordinated to any higher purpose but responded to mere greed for aggrandizement and preponderance." He goes on to point out that as France began to guide the destinies of Europe in the seventeenth century, ". . . Spain felt more and more alienated and with increasing disappointment."[28]

Protestantism never seriously threatened Spanish Catholicism, and Spain itself was spared the carnage and atrocities of Northern Europe. Yet the influence of the religious struggles was apparent in other ways. To begin with, in the reign of Charles V there was the almost continuous Spanish military action against the German and Northern Protestant armies. Later, in the reign of Phillip II when the Empire was no longer linked to Spain, the military theater shifted to the Low Countries.

We have mentioned the relatively mild actions of the Spanish Inquisition, especially when compared to the atrocities that were occurring elsewhere in Europe. But this does not mean that its presence and influence can simply be dismissed as being inconsequential. Perhaps it would be more accurate to say that the Inquisition mattered because of certain things that did *not* take place. Marías believes that seventeenth-century Spanish thinkers declined to examine certain questions, Cartesian philosophy or budding new sciences, for example, so as to avoid harmful repercussions. After all, as men of learning and science they usually lacked the religious zealot's fanatical will for self-sacrifice. Besides, these new ways of thinking seemed paltry things at the moment, but in time they would become the glories of an age otherwise forever besmirched by almost unbelievable atrocities, indeed not to be surpassed in this dubious sense until our own century.

Thus, the theoretical predisposition which came to define the modern European mind did not take root or prosper in Spain. A persistent *décalage* in scientific and philosophic attitudes eventually became evident, but by that time the intellectual deficit could not be quickly overcome. But the actual decline, especially in thought and letters, came much later than is usually thought. During most of the seventeenth century, Spain was characterized by enormous creativity. Among many other illustrious figures the names of Quevedo, Saavedra Fajardo, Tirso de Molina, Gracián, Zurbarán, Velázquez, Lope de Vega, Moreto, and Calderón, whose life spanned most of the century, represent not a decline but the culmination of Spain's Golden Age of letters.

Nevertheless, by the eighteenth century the clearest Spanish minds (Feijóo, Jovellanos, Cadalso, among others) had slipped into a reactive or imitative mode. In many cases, they absorbed and even mastered European thought but, creatively speaking, did not add significantly to it. It would take two centuries and the Generations of 1898 before the intellectual gap between Spain and the cultural centers of Europe was finally closed.

In dealing with the theme of Spanish decadence, Marías notes that the Spanish perception of decline predated by decades any significant material losses. He suggests that the enormous successes of Spain in the sixteenth century made any later setback appear more ominous than it really was.

There is no denying that Spain itself suffered reverses; after the fall of the Count-Duke of Olivares in 1643 and the defeat at Rocroy, its decline was evident to all. Yet Spain was but one of "the Spains," and whereas Spain declined, the other "Spains" did not. Because its vision of the world was "intraEuropean," according to Marías, unlike the "transEuropean" perspective of Spain (and Portugal), Europe was unable to understand this broader "Hispanic" setting, just as later it could not—and therefore would not—distinguish between the system of "possessions" and dependent "colonies" of the British and French and the essentially self-administered Spanish system. Interestingly and sadly enough, in the nineteenth century the Spanish rejected their own creation and in imitation of the European models began to treat the remaining "Spains"—Cuba, Puerto Rico, Philippines—like colonies.

The ills of Spain during the Decadence, capitalized and generally acknowledged since the middle of the seventeenth century, have been treated mainly as Spanish problems. Certainly they were, for they were problems for the Spanish nation. But even though Spanish in fact, they were in many ways European in origin. Quevedo and Saavedra Fajardo, for instance, alluded to the European "madness," consisting of atrocities and irresponsible acts, and most of all, rejection of the pan-Christian Spanish ideal of diplomacy and international relations.

This rebuff and the multiple attacks from French-led Europe caused a retrenchment in Spain, the symptoms of which were noticeable as early as 1559, according to Marías, when in response minor Lutheran manifestations in Seville and Valladolid, Phillip II forbade Spanish students from attending most foreign universities. But the retrenchment began in earnest with the Thirty Years War and the Peace of Westphalia (1618–1648).

For Marías, the urge to turn its back on European affairs was a grievous mistake by Spain. As he sees it, Spain could not really withdraw from Europe because of its status as a "superpower." Like it or not, it was "everywhere" in a sense because of its presence and power. What it could and did do, however, was to indulge its tendency toward withdrawal and isolationism. This meant that instead of acting creatively in foreign affairs, it turned somewhat reluctant and passive and thus set in motion its long political and cultural pattern of reacting to initiatives instead of starting them.

There is another dimension to the Decadence that is rarely noticed.

When Spain emerged on the world scene already a nation and in the process of creating a superstate, the rest of Europe was still halfway living in the Middle Ages. The advantage clearly went to Spain. But as the other nations organized along national lines and grew in power, this advantage waned. Thus, in addition to being real the Decadence was also relative. The rest of Europe began to reach the level of Spain itself, although the American "Spains" are another matter that does not fit easily into this comparative paradigm.

For Marías, it makes sense to restrict the real decline to Spain to no more than sixty years, and particularly from 1640 to 1680. But it is important to keep in mind also that the so-called Decadence did not affect all segments of life in the same way or at the same time. Remember, for example, that Calderón was active throughout this period. Marías takes into account the material difficulties of those years—loss of population, navies, separatist movements, etc.—but the major institutions survived intact into the eighteenth century.

Then how are we to understand the Decadence? Marías explains: "Decadence was, above all, a crisis of expectation. The enormous reality of the Hispanic monarchy, scarcely broken in its largest part (America), preserved in its chief and nuclear portion with Europe, with a capacity for recovery that in the eighteen century turned out to be admirable, is passed over again and again, invalidated by a negative interpretation of overwhelming strength. What characterized this period was disillusionment."[29]

In summary, the physical and material changes in seventeenth-century Spain were important, certainly, but relatively secondary if we accept Marías's premise that the fundamental transformation in the Spanish trajectory, its project, as it were, was of a spiritual order.

Spain and the Enlightenment

From 1700, or 1714 at the latest, until 1808, Spain lived in relative peace within itself. No other prominent European nation has ever gone so long without experiencing a major war. According to conventional history, spent and exhausted after its Golden Age of exploration, conquest, and world hegemony, Spain settled down quietly under the cultural prepotency of France.

Marías suggests that historians have insisted too much on the Gallic influence, so much so in fact that often it seems that Spain became a cultural appendage of France. Certainly there were important links with France, including the Family Pact. But perhaps not enough has been said of the "Hispanization" and "Italianization" of the Bourbons. Not only did Phillip V come to Spain when he was seventeen and become thoroughly Spanish during his long reign, he was also descended from a long line of Spanish monarchs and furthermore, after 1714, married to the Italian Isabel of Farnesio. For his part,

Charles III was King of Naples for twenty-five years before coming to the throne in Spain.

Even conceding these foreign influences, it is obvious that "old Spain," a Spain little changed since the seventeenth century, remained very much alive for at least the first half of the eighteenth century.

But the change of dynasties did lessen the isolation of Spain. In addition to the intervention of foreign armies in the War of Sucession, Frenchmen and Italians were prominent early in the reign of Phillip V. French and Italian were important languages among the elite and educated classes, and newspapers began to introduce European topics. An overblown image of "advanced" and "enlightened" countries led many Spaniards to make unfavorable judgments of their own country.

In the eighteenth century, the Spanish story takes a different turn and before long a different tone. These foreign influences were to have an effect on what was emerging as the Spanish project of the eighteenth century: Spain itself. In earlier ages, the historical project of Spain had been the restoration of "lost Spain," that is, a Christian country whose foundation of religious unity had been broken by the Islamic invasion and occupation. After the Reconquest, this same driving zeal led to the founding of an overseas supernation and to the leadership of Catholic Christianity against both Protestant reformers and Turkish threats.

Eighteenth-century Spain was as religious as ever, but with a different trajectory. Marías points out that the proximity of other European nations with different political viewpoints caused Spain to begin an "examination of conscience," which in turn provoked a crisis of confidence. By now, nearly two centuries had gone by since the era of Spanish predominance. Europe had rejected the pan-Christian policies advocated in the days of the Count-Duke of Olivares and had inclined instead to nationalistic perspectives.

The result was that Spain began to think of its past as misguided and that most likely it, not Europe, had gone astray and now lagged behind its European neighbors. Insofar as this attention to Spain was reasonable and factually based, it had positive results. But often it went beyond criticism and despite the real advances by Spain, especially after 1750, became an unreasonable conviction of endemic inferiority that has lasted to our time.

Under the Bourbon dynasty, attention to the Spanish infrastructure led to greater national unity and a better standard of living. Among other administrative improvements, internal customs and barriers to trade with the Americas were eliminated, ancient legal codes inherited from the medieval kingdoms were integrated and modernized, industrialization increased, and population rose rapidly.

More subtle but equally meaningful from our perspective, by mid-century, the outlook and tone of life had changed. It is obvious that the eighteenth-century writers were generally less gifted and impressive than their Golden Age predecessors, but they wrote and thought in what we can only call a modern style. Marías finds much to admire in the balanced views of such writers as Melchor Macanaz and Father Jerónimo Feijóo. Taking Father Feijóo (1676–1764) as a model, he says: "He is the first of those eighteenth-century Spaniards whom we see today as 'post-conciliar,' with their faith intact but open and free, exempt from all fanaticism. They are less brilliant than the enlightened men of other countries, especially those of France, but seem to us today much less far from the truth, and at bottom more independent."[30]

In a movement that paralleled the renovation and modernization of the Spanish nation, the Monarchy consolidated its claim of "social legitimacy." Rather than acting as "Chief of State," the Bourbon monarchs were seen as the "Head of the Nation," and as such belonged more to the society and the people than to the political structure of government. In large part, it was due to these conditions of social legitimacy and national unity to which the moderate Spanish Enlightenment was dedicated that it glowed peacefully and productively, if unspectacularly, in the eighteenth century. Meanwhile, The French enlightenment flared brilliantly but destructively. Its malevolent repercussions were to have a profound effect on nineteenth-century Spain.

As in so many other cases, historical reason leads Marías to conclusions about eighteenth-century Spain that stand in startling contrast to the disparaging views popularized in the writings of Montesquieu and Voltaire, neither of whom had ever been in Spain. Yet the latter wrote that Spanish Catholicism had done more harm to the human race than Attila and Tamerlane. Even those with more knowledge and more moderate views thought of eighteenth-century Spain as little more than a French cultural and political puppet lacking original art, thought, and national stature. But upon examining the internal history of Spain, Marías responds: "The Hispanic world had never been more coherent and united, more peaceful, more prosperous, or better governed than in the eighteenth century."[31]

Marías asserts that Spain in the eighteenth century was "an enormous inertia crossed by critical currents." But it was precisely this inertia that stood in the way of the revolutionary fervor that was beginning to consume Europe. Despite the scorn heaped on Spain by the French *Philosophes* and their followers, attacks so virulent that Marías describes them as a resurgence of the "Black Legend," the Hispanic empire was still enormous, indeed, at the time the largest in the world. Not that Spain did anything to deserve this opprobrium. For this is precisely the point: it stood as an obstacle in the plan to eliminate medieval tradition, including organized Christianity. In the midst of the revolutionary movement, Spanish society and most of its enlightened intellectuals showed not the slightest inclination to renounce the faith that Spain had defended for more than a thousand years. And as long as Spain stood firm, revolution could not triumph completely in Europe. If Spain had rested uneasily with modernity itself, as we have seen, it was even more uncomfortable with the revolutionary ideal.

On the other hand, the Enlightenment advances in science and knowledge had considerable appeal. This is why the Spanish Enlightenment thinkers like Feijóo generally tried to avoid extremes and steer the country on a sensible middle course that shunned revolution, embraced science, and deferred to Christian authority in matters of faith. But this enthusiasm for Enlightenment advances remained tentative and fraught with certain reservations. This checked its creativity, leaving it imitative and reactive. Ultimately, the elite was unable to channel the energies of an exuberant populace and elevate them to true cultural excellence. While crediting many virtues and advances, we must also enter this failure as a debit on the ledgers of eighteenth-century Spain.

Spain in the Nineteenth Century

The long era of domestic peace and balanced enlightenment ended finally in 1808 with the fall of the Godoy government and the Napoleonic intervention. Given the turmoil that characterized nineteenth-century Spain, the question arises, how can so many calamities be explained? As Marías sees it, it becomes a question of seeking reasons to explain the fragility of the huge Hispanic domain.

To begin with, even though the eighteenth century was peaceful, it ended badly. After 1789, the extremes of the French Revolution rendered suspect and eventually untenable even the moderate enlightenment of Spain. Furthermore, to a certain degree the Monarchy itself was compromised by Godoy's personal immorality and what the Spanish people took to be the "arbitrary" policies of his government under Charles IV.

These misgivings coincided with the general perception by most intellectuals that even though peaceful, recent Spanish history was beset by failures. As Marías notes, "In short, they began to think that the Europe that regarded Spain with disdain and hostility might in some measure be right."[32]

But the same intellectuals who found flaws were unable to find much more. If calm times generally produce mediocre minds, the rule held true in the case of eighteenth-century Spain. Of limited abilities, the Spanish intellectuals were unable to react effectively to the European disqualification of the old Spanish project. Not that they themselves rejected the project as well. Rather, they relegated it, along with their Christian convictions, to private zones of life remote from the social and historical life of Spain. Nothing of old Spain was lost; it was simply withdrawn and rendered ineffective.

Thus, sorely aware of their real or reported inferiorities, these turn-of-the-century Spaniards lost sight of their superiorities. Or if they affirmed the latter, as was often the case, they did so insensitively, by obversely discrediting the real virtues and discoveries they saw in other peoples but lacked themselves. And before long this loss of confidence spread to the Americas. Marías often insists that until 1808, Hispanic America was in no way inferior to English-speaking North America. Indeed, if anything it was the other way around. Yet the disdain for Spain and things Spanish settled deeply into the collective psyches of Spanish-speaking America and produced lamentable results. "It led to a strange scorn for their own reality, which at its proper moment would be combined with an idealization of the possibilities of a future detached from Spain and the worth of those who proposed that future."[33] This condition, says Marías, caused the fragility within the Hispanic community of nations.

Over against the supposed failures of Spanish history which troubled the Enlightenment, the real failure, at bottom also an intellectual failure, was the inability to recognize that the original Spanish project, though accompanied by error, was not itself an error. This was aggravated by the inability to rescue this permanent project and translate it to new circumstances.

What had been a relatively calm Spain in the eighteenth century was agitated in the nineteenth by what Marías refers to as "induced radicalism." Without any obvious social changes, life became charged as though by an electrical current from the outside so that everything seemed changed. Thus, the moderate intellectuals of Spain, themselves pious and responsible in their writings and in their personal life, were associated because of popular hysteria with the dangerous radicals determined to bring down Church and State. The tranquil balance of the eighteenth century was lost. Around the spectacle of France, Spain and the Americas were polarized in horrified revulsion or enthusiastic approval. Thus was discord born. In Spain, there was fierce resistance to the French invaders; the Americas, left alone after the collapse of the Monarchy, moved under creole leadership toward independence, in some cases—Mexico for example—to resist the revolutionary ideology of France and the liberalism (the word itself was first used in Spanish) codified in the Constitution of Cadiz (1812); in others, to espouse those same causes.

The nineteenth century saw the rise of what we refer to today as "political life" and with it a new human type called "politician." Henceforth life itself, and especially public life, began to be understood and explained in political concepts, political figures received most of the attention, and everything else was relegated to subset status. History became political history. Public affairs became political affairs. The part, important as it is, had usurped the whole, which is of course more important.

Because nineteenth-century Spanish politics was characterized by instability and frequent incoherence, most people and perhaps more importantly for our purposes, most historians, came to believe that Spain itself was unstable and incoherent.

In Hispanic America there was even more political instability, often accompanied by violence. And as Marías notes, "Attention has been concentrated almost obsessively on that violence, and this has given rise to the present-day view of Hispanic America as something absolutely lamentable."[34]

The problem with the separation of Hispanic America was not independence, which in the long run was probably inevitable, but alienation from, and even repudiation of, Spain, which meant a loss of historical contact with its Hispanic roots. In extreme cases, the tendency has been to praise and prefer anything provided it is not Spanish. (The case of Mexico is particularly revealing.) For Marías, this alienation was the result of a morbid "politicization," which meant emphasizing the weakest and perhaps most misleading feature of Hispanic American life. For if Hispanic politics often leaves much to be desired, the reality of Hispanic life is of an altogether higher order, as anyone who has real contact with those societies senses immediately.

As a result of the violence, threats of violence, uprisings, and repressions, nineteenth-century Spaniards began to believe that such instability was innate. "Deep in the souls of Spaniards a suspicion began to develop that their country was made of some explosive substance, always ready to break out into violence. Those who did not feel inclined to violence felt fear, and, worse, a certain repugnance. By a mechanism very similar to that which inspires a black legend, this impression became general: beyond the concrete events that could justify it, it extended to the whole of Spanish society."[35] This, Marías goes on to say, was why Spaniards began to be afraid of themselves and to prefer public order at any price, even if that price was stagnation, or *marasmo*, a word that had considerable currency at the end of the nineteenth century.

The infatuation with politics, understood here as the political usurpation that relegated other realities to secondary planes, meant that historical reality itself tended to be ignored. Unamuno's insistence on "intrahistory" early in the twentieth century appears to be both a response to that reality and a protest against its political falsification.

In a previous chapter, we examined Marías's argument that conditions arising from the French invasion and the repressive actions in the reign of Fernando VII created a generational imbalance in certain dimensions of Spanish life that lasted throughout the nineteenth century.[36] This was especially true of the Romantic movement, which flourished literarily only in the last Romantic generation. But this imbalance did not exist at the popular level. Spaniards lived in Romantic modes at the same time as other Europeans. This discrepancy indicates, in turn, that an internal imbalance in Spanish life was at work. And if this was true in Spain, it was even truer of the American "Spains."

After separation from Spain, they sank into isolation, especially in relation to one another, and soon fell behind English-speaking North America. As Marías says elsewhere, the Americas not only separated from Spain, they separated from one another. And no wonder, for Spain and Hispanic institutions had been the common link among their disparate indigenous cultures.

For Marías, this political turmoil and instability can be traced in part to a declining system of binding observances, or *vigencias*. The values, beliefs, and assumptions that had been predominate in Spain since the Middle Ages began to weaken rapidly at the end of the eighteenth century, and this occurred simultaneously with rising uncertainties about the historical project that had always been the catalyst of Spanish life and policy. For example, new attitudes toward religion developed. No longer a belief in which one dwelt unquestioningly, religion became either a self-conscious posture one took or an ideology one defended or opposed.

If we translate these phenomena into the concepts of situation/condition, we could say that whereas eighteenth-century Spaniards were generally dissatisfied with their situation but delighted with and solidly planted in their condition as Spaniards, their nineteenth-century descendants tended to have grave doubts about their condition, to say nothing about their frequently turbulent situation. These doubts went even deeper in the Americas where, unlike Don Quixote, the newly independent inhabitants of mixed ethnicities and now-rejected heritage did not really know who they were. Instead of truly being themselves, they were reduced to being merely anti-Spanish. And instead of reasoning about their condition in an adequate philosophical way—in part because they had not developed a philosophical language—and lacking a solid belief system, they fell into the trap of living on borrowed foreign ideas, repeating in other circumstances the imitative inclinations of Spaniards in recent centuries. In effect, says Marías, the Hispanic countries of America broke away too soon from Spain and their immaturity became endemic.

Marías is much kinder to the Spanish Restoration than, say, the first "Generation of 1898," whose vituperative views we have commented on earlier. While lacking the passion and creative tensions of the Romantics, the Restoration nevertheless brought a level of civic harmony and stability unknown since 1808. Marías offers this view: "An accumulation of criticisms . . . has distorted the image of the Restoration, which to the eyes of our century appears as a lamentable, primitive, even ridiculous phase. A more careful examination of what was accomplished during it . . . leads to admiration for the period and a certain nostalgia for it, when we think of what was awaiting Spain within our own time."[37]

At the end, however, the inability of Restoration Spain to deal adroitly and intelligently with three major problems undid much of its work. Marías defines these as (1) domestic problems, including anarchy, summed up as the "social question," which had to do principally with the plight of workers and farm laborers, (2) the desire for autonomy among the remnants of the old empire, and (3) the regionalist or separatist movements, what Ortega called *particularism*.

Thus, in a somewhat circular fashion but from the new perspective and level reached through the dialectic of historical reason, we come again to the conditions that set in motion the "Generations of 1898." We shall recall our earlier comments on this period so as not to repeat them. But it is worth adding that having already rendered an intense significance from that localized historical viewpoint, they now acquire new meanings as we see them converge within the longer historical trajectory traced by the enduring Spanish "plot."

Conclusion: The Once and Future Plot

From time to time, Marías reminds us that his purpose is not to write a history of Spain but to retrieve and retrace the plot of its history. And he seems to feel the need to remind us of this specific intention because of the ease with which we may confuse historical plot with historical facts. Indeed, he deals with many of the same historical facts we find in conventional history. Furthermore, he emphasizes the same historical crossroads. What then is the difference between the two tasks? Marías explains: "History itself *gives an accounting* of reality, allows us to understand it; historical intelligibility is possible only through *narrative reason:* that is, the narration that is not reduced to mere events, that does not reduce human factors to 'things,' whether physical or psychic or social, but preserves their intrinsically projective and dramatic character."[38]

When historical reason comes to the aid of mute historical facts, by situating them in a historical plot, the result is understanding and intelligibility. This combination satisfies the requisites of reason, for reason (and living), Marías tells us, consists of apprehending things in their real connectedness.

Spain makes no sense at all if we mistake it for, say, France. As anything other than itself, it will appear abnormal, eccentric, perhaps merely exotic. But when its facts appear in a storied pattern, the result is a surprising degree of historical coherence. In fact, says Marías, "It would be difficult to find a people in whom the historical *project* that has constituted it has been more transparent and explicit, or held with greater constancy for centuries upon centuries."[39]

We have referred repeatedly to the historical Spanish *project* as both a defining movement of national purpose and an expression of the collective Spanish way of being. But a project by definition points beyond the present. And this brings us to certain question marks that hang suspended over everything yet to be. In view of their history, where are "the Spains" to go now? What ought to be their project for the future, or better, the project that is their future?

In one sense, it should be what it has always been in one form or another: the restoration of "lost Spain." But with an important difference that brings it to the actuality of the times: it should be restoration of "the Spains." Hear how Marías describes it: "The undertaking for our time can be none other than recomposition of 'the Spains'; from that decision depends whether the possibilities of each will multiply or be reduced to a minimum, further affected by their vulnerability."[40] This might well be utopian were not Spain (like Portugal) and Hispanic America (including Brazil) predisposed to a transnational (and not merely "international") existence by centuries of shared history and collective memory. Nor can this transnational ideal be considered apart from Christianity, in which the core of Spanish life has always resided.

But in the face of these compelling historical facts, Marías wrestles with the equally obvious objections against any imposed or coercive Christianity. That Spain was, or aimed to be, a Christian country and identified itself through that effort does not mean that each person must be Christian. This was a grievous error of Spain under the Hapsburgs.

However, even though the ideal of a universal Christianity cannot be applied to individual cases and probably cannot prosper if attempted in a secular setting, the problem may be resolved from another angle. Marías believes that regardless of whether Spain and Spaniards are Christian, the "historically fruitful core," which in earlier times consisted of an identification with Christianity, still survives outside a strictly religious context. "Spanish originality in the sphere of thought is consistent with the way in which Spaniards have understood themselves ever since they began to be Spaniards."[41]

And what expression does this "fruitful core" take today? The answer must be given in two parts. First, Spain has obstinately refused to lose sight of the inimitable *personhood* of each human life. The Other, whether Jew or Moor, American Indian or heretic, friend or foe, was always treated as a person, even when the treatment was harsh and implacable. Furthermore, the Spanish have risen to greatness only in those moments when they lived life as a personal mission. This is why the ill-advised but heroic sallies of Don Quixote must be seen as a quintessential Spanish trait. Most of all, the Spanish of both hemispheres have resisted with greater or lesser conviction the utilitarian spirit that would subjugate man to colossal abstractions of modernity (state, politics, ideologies, panworldism, science, etc.). If life is mission it is therefore an adventure with an ineradicable element of insecurity, to be sure, but also with the more or less remote chance of triumph. When at their best, the Spanish have known that the better hope of one's life is not worldly wealth but richness of spirit and the chance to live nobly and die honorably.

The philosophy to which Marías has devoted his life is astonishingly compatible with this secularized Christian view of life. But perhaps our astonishment is misplaced. For if this way of thinking arises from that same "fruitful core," then it stands to reason that it would veer in harmony with its source. Perhaps more than any other modern philosophy, the way of thinking we find in Marías has most faithfully and without pedantry incorporated the dynamic heritage of Classical and Modern philosophy. Its twin roots are extraordinarily deep, reaching to the Christian and Classical heart of the West, the seemingly inexhaustible sources of its genius and ingenuity.

10

In Consideration of Women

In earlier chapters, we considered at two successive but complementary levels, the analytical and the empirical, certain implications of the two sexuate modes of human life, progressing with Marías from the structures that constitute and allow a necessary interpretation of human life as such to those that characterize our bodily being as men and women. To put it another way, we began with a metaphysics of human life and ended with a fleshed-out metaphysical anthropology.

Two primary facts arise from our earlier study to concern us now: first, because the life of man has nearly always been understood as the normative standard of history, opinions about women have tended to veer either to the extraordinary or to the insipid. At certain historical moments, woman has seemed too lofty for man to reach and at others, too lowly to count in the chief matters of the world.

The second fact is a function of the first. In light of these pendular swings of opinion about women, most would agree that a persistent misunderstanding is at work at the most fundamental levels of sexuate life. This means that in an unexpectedly novel way the old cliché is true: men misunderstand women. But it means much more than that. In our earlier study we saw how each sex understands and interprets itself face to face with the other, which means that any substantial misunderstanding between the sexes becomes a misunderstanding of both sexes. If men do not understand women, then neither do they know themselves. And the reverse is true also. Or to look at the matter from a more disturbing perspective, by misunderstanding each other, men and women come to understand themselves in a deficient way that degrades the quality of life and the quotient of happiness for both sexes. It is a besetting problem that does not easily yield; ignorance that passes for knowledge exhibits a tenacious longevity.

It has been the destiny of this century to acknowledge with insistent and often strident honesty these persistent misreadings of women. Many of the old and once predominant assumptions, what Marías would call *vigencias,* have lost normative force and no longer prevail.[1] They have ceased to be unquestioned, unconscious beliefs and have become debatable and thus conflictive ideas. (For it seems to be the rule that whatever becomes possible also strives to become real.) Uprooted from the deep unconscious structures of life, *vigencias* rise to its surface, becoming visible and voiced and therefore literally "superficial." As conscious ideas which we may accept or reject, *vigencias* become stripped of their regulatory authority, preserving only the appeal of an always-modest logical dialectic, which proves customarily timid before emotional bias and desiderative urges. Hence a principal reason for the frequent carelessness and disdain with which we treat ideas, and not just those of shoddy appearance but even those of sound construction.

Even as the old belief structure was dissolving, another factor was deepening this crisis: the divergence of feminine sexuality from its traditional reproductive context. Marías describes the change: "This is a fact of enormous weight the consequences of which we have not yet become aware. (I am afraid we have not even started.) Men and women live immersed in a system of assumptions which for thousands of years have associated sexuality and reproduction. But now in this century and not before both things have been separated."[2]

Although this change is biological in its manifestations, it is not biological in origin. No mutation has occurred to change human sexuality. Rather, we must look to medical science, psychology, sociology, aesthetics, morality, and religion in order to account for this change. In other words, the change is biographical and historical and therefore affects men and women in an intensely personal way. This is why it deserves to be called a crisis in the first place.

Naturally, as a reaction to a human crisis of this magnitude, an imperative quickly arises to understand its causes and consequences and to reestablish a solid plane of new certainties. But to respond to this imperative using antique analytical and statistical methodologies, never suited to dealing with personal reality to start with, is not only to fail to state the problem in workable terms but also to invite certain miscalculations that distort contemporary feminism. Without an adequate anthropology able to account for life's actual dynamics and complexity, we risk lurching from a human crisis to general historical tragedy.

Almost from the beginning of his philosophical work, Marías labored to anticipate these possible errors of overanxious but myopic zeal by developing adequate anthropological methods and concepts. In many ways the culmination of his theoretical advances, *Metaphysical Anthropology* (1970), explores the complementary and inseparable relationships between men and women. But the first of his many writings on women date from as early as 1947, and they have continued since as an unbroken labor of love and enthusiasm. His first complete book on women, *La mujer en el siglo XX* [Woman in the Twentieth Century], was published in 1979 after the authorial hiatus brought on by personal trauma and at the start of what we have called here his "second voyage" into philosophy. In his Prologue, Marías admits that this book ". . . does not owe a great deal to other books but an indiscribable amount to many women: one above all others, but also to women of all ages and several countries who are my friends."[3]

Even as we acknowledge his heartfelt gratitude and appreciation, we are obliged to admit that by today's feminist criteria, especially in the United States and the English-speaking countries, his would be, to many, a misunderstood and unwelcome effort. For this reason, it seems worthwhile to address the issue briefly before proceeding.

According to a widespread but obviously specious logic, only women—and preferably feminists—can write authoritatively, that is, truthfully, about women, just as many ethnic minorities claim the exclusive right to speak for their particular ethnicity or cause. In both cases, they justify this "Insider Doctrine" by pointing to the unique nature of their experience. Men, we are told summarily, cannot understand women because men are not women, just as a non-minority person cannot comprehend what it means to be a member of a minority group. But the reverse consideration does not hold: feminists blithely take it for granted that they understand men; minorities assume the same in the case of the larger society; and neither grouping seems concerned about the ironic contradiction implicit in their assumptions.

As I said, the logic is specious. For if it were true, then no male novelist could ever create a believable feminine character. (And naturally the reverse would be true for a female writer.) Nor could we hope to reach any understanding whatsoever of, say, Medieval society or Classical Greece, for we are not Medieval people or Classical Greeks. Taken to an extreme—and naturally extremist ideas always are—the world would be reduced to a series of hermetic compartments without hope of communicability. Fortunately for us, imagination and sympathy demolish all such notions and permit us to understand to a greater or lesser degree humanity in all its dimensions and groupings. To admit that this understanding is far from perfect is not to say that it is far from possible.

For his part, Marías has never deferred to these tempting prejudices. He writes of women from a lifelong fund of sympathy and enthusiasm built on many friendships. He is concerned for contemporary women in general, who in trying to escape the tribulations of the past risk falling victim to the ominous perils of today.

The Historical Setting

According to the basic premises of historical reason, the deepest and most complete human understanding of a phenomenon happens when we see it emerge from a prior situation and move in vectorial fashion toward potential future configurations.[4] Epistemologically speaking, we could say that understanding occurs insofar as we see the dramatic emergence and unfolding of human realities and are able to describe their trajectories and anticipate their eventualities.

Applying this procedure to the case of contemporary women, Marías discovers that he must examine the Victorian context against which contemporary feminism has arisen in polemic revolt. Because the once unquestioned *vigencias* have lost their predominance (or at least have weakened), women have had no choice but to raise questions about themselves, the most basic of which is this: what does it mean to be a woman in today's world? Naturally, for women to ask the question, that is, to ask it seriously and personally, is to admit a great deal of doubt about their roles, expectations, and possibilities. And because of the intricate reciprocal relationships between the sexes, to raise these doubts about women is to raise them necessarily though secondarily about men as well.

Consider the following factors also. First, increased longevity. In former times and until recent decades, women (and men) aged much more rapidly than they do today. What is more, they accepted consequently the stages and rhythm of life associated with this brevity. If a married woman of thirty or thirty-five with children was thought "matronly" in the Romantic or Victorian era, today she seems almost "girlish" in the double sense of still being young in years and youthful in temperament, outlook, and expectations. Perhaps it would be more accurate to say that even if women of previous generations did not physically age quickly, they did so socially and psychologically. In other words, they acted, and were expected to act as old as they could, that is, old before their time. Marías adds this telling detail: ". . . she soon settled into the ways of life which, without actually being old age, appeared to be in the most crucial way: the elimination of the future."[5] Without necessarily believing that life was over, women thought its excitement was and that nothing new would happen to them.

Obviously, things have changed for women. But does this mean that women themselves have changed? The tendency has been to attempt to answer such questions biologically or perhaps psychologically, for biology and behavioral psychology are the foundation of most modern theories about human life. Marías disagrees: "The existence in permanent form of the feminine condition is cultural and historical, not biological, I mean not just biological."[6]

These historical variations in the condition of women mean that a history of women is possible. And more than possible, real, if we take seriously the titles of works published in recent years. But here we must be cautious. For lacking adequate anthropological and philosophical underpinnings, these histories have tended for the most part to treat feminine history as either a sub-set or repudiation of the masculine and, consequently, as an emotional rejec-tion of what was perceived to be the sorry role of women in the past.

Above all, contemporary feminists despise the Victorian age with its im-ages of restricted and repressed women. On the one hand, this antipathy arises from the old progressive notion that all past eras were but a preparation for today and that with the advent of each new age the past is seen to be immedi-ately expendable and superannuated. Thus, the nineteenth century looked down on the eighteenth century as a necessary but *déclassé* stage preparatory to its own splendor, and, in turn, the eighteenth century exaggerated the vices and ignored the virtues of those centuries it derogatorily called the "dark ages." But following the same progressive ideology, today's feminists of both sexes heap scorn on the Victorian era, itself once so proud of its enlightened advances. And if the same pattern holds, then in the twenty-first century peo-ple will take similar views of us and our time. For the obverse side of progres-sivism is a series of retroapplicable disqualifications of human history.

At the same time, this disqualification of the recent feminine past also presupposes that because women were limited in what they could do and bound by what they could not do, they were therefore wretched and unhappy. No doubt they were to a certain degree, as all persons are more or less, but the question is to what degree. And to ask this question is to imply another of an opposite sign: to what degree were they happy?

The prevailing assumption today is that because women in the nine-teenth century and for most of the twentieth did not have the political and eco-nomic rights of today's women, they had to be miserable. By our standards perhaps, but not necessarily by theirs; and because, after all, it was their age, their standards must take precedence, unless we rudely impose our own crite-ria, as lately we seem to be in the habit of doing. Women of that era could not and did not do just anything they wanted or go anywhere they pleased. Today this description of life seems barbaric, but the same statement points toward a happier interpretation when seen from another perspective. Because they did not do just anything and thus did not have to do everything, women of the past were selective in what they chose to do. Women did not have to, were not ex-pected to, were perhaps not permitted to involve themselves in the coarse, vul-gar, and degrading things that men had to confront. Unlike men, who had to interact with everything, women necessarily made distinctions and adhered to limited "elective," or "elegant," priorities (both terms derive from *eligens,* or "selective"). We could say therefore that women tried to be "women of dis-tinction" in the several senses of the phrase.

Nevertheless, the negative expectations, what Marías calls with a useful neologism *solencias,* weighed heavily on the life of women. *Solencias,* or "so-lences" in English (from the verb *soler,* to be usual), are to be understood as the missing opposite to "insolence" (literally, that which is unusual, uncalled for, and, generally speaking, intolerable). Freed from the more onerous of these "solences," women have enjoyed an enhanced "humanization" of their lives. Particularly since about 1945, Western women have been in a position to take possession of their condition as feminine persons. Have they done so? Perhaps not, for reasons we shall examine.

Even as this humanization has been occurring, there is also a tendency to discount the adjective "feminine" and to assume that women are simply persons and nothing else. Marías disagrees by noting that there is really no such being as a person per se, but only men and women and therefore only masculine and feminine persons in their sexuate corporality.

We all know this sexuate omission has not gone unnoticed. But the common assumption (often expressed as an accusation against feminists) is that if women deny or overlook their feminine condition, they simply become masculinized and start acting like men. But if we follow Marías's logic, then we would have to conclude that instead of a masculinization there occurs a depersonalization of women. Naturally, feminists are not consciously interested in acting like men, but they may not want to act like women either, at least not like the women of earlier generations. For this reason, notes Marías, "It is astonishing the number of women who do not come across as women. But since they cannot really be anything else, because they are not anything else, they turn out to be insipid."[7]

Thus, an unresolved tension has arisen between the urge to humanize their life as women and the opposite tendency toward depersonalization and disregard, in extreme cases even disavowal, of the feminine condition. Yet if women do not choose to be fulfilled as women, then what options are left? The stock answer would be, fulfillment as persons or individuals without consideration of one's sex. But we have already seen that personhood and humanity occur only in masculine and feminine modes.

As Marías sees it, the great opportunity for contemporary women lies in seizing those feminine possibilities for human fulfillment the complements of which hitherto could be realized only in masculine life. Later, we shall look at some of these possibilities, but from the outset we can say that none exists in definitive form. Their realization depends—as do all truly human realities—on imaginative creativity. Without imagination, women may claim their civil or legal rights through pure zeal, but if they stop there they risk forfeiting their infinitely richer human potentiality.

The Matter of Equality

Since its appearance, the main thrust of feminism has been to break down masculine barriers and see to it that women do the same things as men under similar conditions and with the same rewards. Naturally, though it has not been loudly said, they also expose themselves to similar corrosive risks and rivalries. The economic and social legitimacy of this effort cannot be denied, as Marías points out. Yet he goes on to argue that real feminism cannot be reduced to a formula for making women act and live like men; it is not a matter of laying claim to what men have, but of seeking what women perhaps have never had but ought to enjoy: the plenitude of the feminine condition.

The recent weakening of the old binding beliefs and "solences" has shifted the center of feminine life from a solid belief system, what Marías would call a "credential" foundation ("credential" from Latin *credere,* to believe), to a correspondingly greater reliance on ideas. In this aspect, women seem more masculine. Perhaps this is the reason for such accusations against them, for men have traditionally been more caught up in ideas than women. And because historically women have been grounded much more deeply in beliefs and subjected to the negative "solences" that regulated feminine behavior, their lives were more stable and less prone to drastic upheavals than men. If men made the epochal history of change, women created the unchanging intrahistory of daily life on which Unamuno insisted so much.

Consequently, men and society in general depended on women to maintain the real context of social life: good manners, stable homes, and, in many cases, even the religious integrity of the family. In America, for example, and probably elsewhere, men who "never darkened church door" depended on the religious devotion of their wives, mothers, sisters, and daughters to cast over them a reflected ecclesiastical virtue they perhaps did not personally possess. In effect, countless men lived "on credit" earned by the distaff side, reassured that the "better half" of humanity could be counted on to maintain high standards even though men themselves did not necessarily measure up. This is why the so-called "weaker sex," often thought of as passive, actually exhibited impressive firmness and resoluteness. Men were usually physically stronger, but women demonstrated greater steadfastness in times of illness, bereavement, or financial calamities.

Thus, if men were busied with historical innovation and discontinuity, women gave life an abiding cohesiveness at its everyday level. Perhaps woman's greatest achievement was her ability to lay a solid foundation from which these grandiose masculine projects could be launched in the first place. Men often dreamed of great future deeds and fantastic tomorrows, but women knew that life must be lived—first and finally—one day at a time. Whereas men were prone to overlook everyday life in hopes of beginning it in earnest on some ideal future plane, women knew that the real point of contact with the world was only and always here and now. And women knew also that the innovative schemes of men were valid only insofar as they could be transmuted into the stuff of common life. In this process women have always been crucial: "Nothing comes to pass until it is assumed, adopted, and transformed by woman."[8]

Insofar as ideas and beliefs are concerned, Marías notes that ideas, the traditional province of men, may be transmitted through books and schools, reaching their extreme and perhaps pathological expression either as revolutionary upheaval or reactionary resistance to change. On the other hand, women have been the primary agency whereby ideas achieve the status of beliefs. And because this transformation has normally taken place at the level of everyday relationships, beliefs have nearly always tended to be more forgiving than dogma and ideology, which as idea systems veer more to harsh abstractions and unforgiving schematics.

This is why neither revolution nor immobility is possible where beliefs are concerned. Their oceanic rhythm has little to do with immediacy and conscious impatience. Rather, they underlie and condition life's dramatic flow within which ideas appear as mutable and problematic temporal options destined either to subside and disappear in time or to be themselves absorbed into the belief system.

What happens as women seek to abandon their traditional dwelling place in beliefs in favor of ideas? To begin with, the attempt is utopian. The truth is that neither men nor women can live primarily on ideas alone, for only beliefs can contain and sustain our life—and our ideas. This means that the effort to do so is a false attempt. Many things seem to happen (and may even be proclaimed as fact), Marías reminds us, that simply cannot and do not happen. Consequently, to assume facts not in evidence introduces a disturbing element of falsification into life.

Paradoxically, this falsification applies first to ideas themselves. In achieving what Marías calls "credential" status, ideas begin to function as if they were beliefs, that is, as unquestioned assumptions to which little or no corrective thought is given. But by their very nature ideas call for examination and competitive comparison with other ideas. Without these conditions, ideas become pseudo-ideas lacking rigor and intellectual precision. Hence the crude and rough appearance of so many contemporary ideas. They circulate unfinished, unpolished, but unchallenged, and naturally seem half-baked whenever anyone takes the trouble to subject them to intelligent scrutiny. Think, for example, of today's coarse notions of human sexuality or our dysfunctional ideas about sexuate relationships.

Because ideas are by nature debatable, even in their most refined forms they are bound to clash with others and therefore cannot really constitute a harmonious foundation for life. Therefore, to propose living solely from an idea system is to be subject to constant structural tensions and antagonisms. In this regard women have proven to be a fascinating exception. "One of the strongest reasons," Marías explains, "for man's interest in woman has been that in her he found another way, another configuration of human life in which belief as such predominated. That which is different always attracts, and the more different it is, the better, as long as there is enough of an analogy for dialogue and communication to be possible."[9]

Without such differences there can be no dialogue, for communication flows when what Marías calls a difference of human voltage comes into play. Because communication is always a transfer of differences (of opinions, perspectives, emotions, knowledge, conflicts, etc.), it cannot occur, or at least has no pressing reason to occur, when all are on the same level.

In recent decades, the trend has been to advocate absolute equality of the sexes, or in current jargon, "to level the playing field." But what kind of levelling do we mean? Obviously, it refers to abstract personhood and citizenship where one's sex is irrelevant: basic civil rights, education, legal protection under the law, and equal professional opportunities. (Naturally, there are limits to the latter: a man could not be a wet nurse, for instance, and it is unlikely that a woman could be a heavyweight boxing champion.)

But serious problems arise when the levelling goes beyond mere abstract rights and touches the human reality of men and women. Naturally, if men and women as such, leaving aside for the moment the matter of impersonal rights, really are equal from the start, then the levelling amounts to an acknowledgment and liberation of the true human condition. But if they are not equal, then the pressure to level the sexes constitutes an injustice—to both sexes.

For Marías, the question of equality depends too much on the flawed premise that because men and women are, or ought to be, treated equally before God and the law, they should be equal in everything. The ideal of equal personal value thus risks becoming a doctrine of forced equality of attributes and outcomes. The problem is that equality then tends toward a mandated sameness. Yet men and women are not the same. This is why we call them men and women in the first place and not simply human beings. Their relation is not based on sameness but on dynamic complementarity. Marías observes: "Equality in the area of sexual life automatically means a decrease of the sexual element in human life, because this difference of charge, this irreducible polarity, is precisely what energizes it."[10]

For this reason, the conventional notion of men and women as mirror images of each other separated only by the symbols of their respective sexes strays far from the reality of their condition. According to Marías, not only do men and women understand the same things in different ways but they understand different things, even if they call them by the same name.

In any case, this differentiation is not primarily a function of attributes but of interests. For example, one may have the physique of an athlete but have no interest in athletics. Our projects, insists Marías, are infinitely more interesting than our gifts. "Man is not the sum of his talents but what he does with them . . ."[11] For this reason, the ubiquitous statistical studies, graphs, measurements, and comparisons so dear to the social sciences fail to give us a true *personal* account of human life, any more than an analysis of the ashes of a cremated body could tell us anything really significant about the deceased *person*.

The Feminist Paradox

Victorian woman could not do certain things, hold certain jobs, or go to certain places because she was a woman. In effect, her personal restriction was also a suppression of her full womanhood. Paradoxically, womanhood is still being denied today, only now willingly and willfully. As Marías puts it, "Woman can do or be anything, which is fine, but with the condition that she act not as a woman but in a neutral manner." Now she can enter these once forbidden precincts, but in order to do so she must leave her femininity at the door, ". . . as one leaves an umbrella."[12] Therefore, for different reasons, both the Victorians of yesterday and the feminists of today deny the full expression of woman as a *feminine* person.

In order to accommodate the contradictory trends in the life of contemporary women, feminists have turned to an inverted form of an old and failed American racist formula: equal but separate. On the one hand, feminists contend that men and women are exactly the same, but on the other, they insist on hanging a "women only" sign on certain areas of life: journals, congressional caucuses, national and international organizations, feminist movements, etc.

But this separatist ideology violates the very nature of the human enterprise, which consists basically in a reciprocal, dynamic, and constant relationship between men and women. The so-called "war of the sexes" is at best an impious fraud. Our sexuate relationships constitute an identifying and unifying dichotomy. At the most fundamental level of human life we know ourselves as men or women *in view* of the other sex. If we lived in a world without the other sex, we would be unaware of our own and would not think of ourselves as men or women, just as we would not know to call one hand our right if we did not have another we call our left.

The Freudian Imperative

The Freudian imperative is the theoretical and clinical determination to explain human behavior, especially its aberrant forms, as a function of infantile sexuality and subconscious and often repressed desires and taboos.

We can sometimes reconstruct the spirit of an earlier period of history by reversing the priorities of the succeeding age, especially if the latter takes a rebellious or polemic posture. Thus, if we knew nothing of the Victorian era, we could probably deduce that it had little to say (publicly at least) of human sexuality. Why? Because under the aegis of Freudianism so much is said of it in our time. And if we were entirely ignorant of the more distant past, we could retrace a staged involution from these stiff-lipped Victorian codes to a more ribald and licentious age in former times, which is exactly the tone of life we find in Elizabethan and Renaissance times. History, we must conclude, exhibits not only linear constants of continuity but also wide pendular swings in reactive modification of what has gone before.

In late years, and particularly among feminists, there is much talk of the "sexual revolution." But in many ways the talk is but an echo of a much older fact. For the truth is that Freudianism has long since drastically altered our views on human sexuality. Freud reversed the moral priorities of the Victorian era by converting forbidden sexual themes into therapeutic strategies. And it was not long before these ideas spread beyond mere clinical applications and made their appearance in art and literature. Surrealism, for example, is one version of artistic Freudianism. All this happened decades ago.

Yet it is true that although Freud was revolutionary about sexuality, he was, to use his own terminology, repressed when it came to women. As Marías notes, "It is curious that a man who centers his interpretation of humanity on the sexual dimension has so little to say about women."[13] Marías also faults his theories for their mechanistic, deterministic bent, heavily drawn from notions of primal instincts and anatomical references. Like all determinisms, Marxism for example, Freudianism represents an extraordinary oversimplification of human reality.

But if Freud's theories rested on a deficient philosophy of human life, Marías notes approvingly that his clinical practice was based on the biographies of his patients, even though certain essential dimensions were omitted from his analysis. For example, he makes no mention of the future. Yet Marías would argue that one's biography, one's story, makes sense only from the standpoint of the future, that is, from the projective reality of human life.

Freud fails to separate the specifically erotic and sexual from the diffuse and problematic infantile sensations of the libido. On the other hand, he insists on the priority of the naturalistic and instinctual and remains conspicuously inept in accounting for feminine sexuality, turning to such problematic and unscientific concepts as "penis envy" and "narcissism" to cover his own intellectual clumsiness. In doing so, he remains far from the *personal* understanding of human sexuality we find in Marías.

In summary, Freud reduces human life to libidinous pleasure principles, oedipal and other complexes, instincts, notions of the *uber ich, ich,* and *es* (super-ego, ego, and id, respectively), which make even less sense in their Latinized English versions than in the original German. Like Marx, he defines both social structure and its final purposes in terms of economic necessity and in general follows a line of thought, beginning with Rousseau, that cleverly extols natural, instinct-driven man at the expense of the rational and the historically conditioned mind. The inherent dialectical paradox continues. With the possible exception of Rousseau himself, probably no one has reasoned more persuasively than Freud to convince us of our unappealable unreasonableness. In the present context, Freudianism assumes a preponderant importance since it is one of the immediate sources of contemporary feminism and lies at its ideological core.

A Summary of Views

If in *La mujer en el siglo XX* Marías dealt with historical and sociological factors that have radically altered the feminine condition in the twentieth century, in *La mujer y su sombra* he acknowledges these changes and examines their consequences in the life of today's women. Specifically it moves dialectically within the sphere of personal relations, which is where men and women experience one another. This means first of all that the primary knowledge of the sexes comes from their reciprocal experience of living together.

This experience, Marías tells us, cannot really be considered apart from bodily being. We neither encounter persons of the other sex as bodiless souls nor as soulless bodies. Rather, to use Marías's expression, men and women are always *alguien corporal,* or, a "corporeal somebody," that is, someone who is also some-body. For this reason, Marías points out, "The exploration of woman requires especially an energetic personalization."[14]

What does this mean? It might seem to imply that we are back to the "insider" notion that only women can say meaningful things about themselves. Most likely, so-called "radical feminists" would readily agree, but perhaps in the majority of cases their statements, books, and concepts either derive from or owe much to scientific and economic assumptions made by men. Freud, Darwin, Watson, and Skinner come to mind as immediate examples.

Western thought, notes Marías, has long been characterized by a substantialism that takes tangible things and objects to be the model of reality. It rests uneasily with other realities not readily susceptible to quantitative mensurability. Consequently, in one form or another it has sought to explain human reality by reducing it either to the level of things or, secondarily, to a subset of animal or biological categories. No wonder, then, that science has lagged well behind art in understanding and respecting human life. The best these scientific theories could offer were zoological, biological, economic, or psychological paradigms of an abstract "human being."

What does this mean for woman? In Marías' words, ". . . the present task in seeking to understand woman is to snatch her away from zoology, which seems ever more invasive, at times under the guise of sociology, and to consider her *biographically,* as one of the two forms in which human life exists and is fulfilled."[15] This life should not be understood simply as an objective "way of being," not as static existence, as we might understand a physical object. Rather, we must come to see woman as a personal and absolutely unique "somebody" who is, but at the same time is always becoming, as someone both real and unreal, with an imaginative dimension that can only be appreciated biographically because it can only be understood narratively.

Paradoxically, although Marías does not expressly say so, we can deduce from his essays on women that he believes that contemporary feminism has largely served to defeminize society and overly masculinize the world. Not only is it based essentially on the express *ideas* put forth by men instead of the inchoate *beliefs* of women themselves, but its effects have been to sweep women into the general pattern of male preoccupation with ideology and revolutionary change and to encourage an equally masculine tendency to enunciate life rather than live it. In short, women are tending toward the same instability and restlessness traditionally characteristic of masculine life. Whereas women have traditionally dwelt within themselves, in the intrahistory of life, exhibiting an attractive reservoir of inner serenity, peace, and hospitality, today they are often beside themselves in varying but unattractive states of urgency, agitation, and haste. Consequently, as Marías notes, "The fearful *personal* instability of our time, before which all other varieties pale in comparison, for example, those concerning love within or without marriage, has one of its causes, and probably the principal one, in this loss of the deep roots of intrahistory. Is this a matter for women or men? Of course it concerns both, but since this intrahistory is primarily the domain of woman, the loss especially affects her. That it has been induced in large measure by men seems apparent to me."[16]

As a consequence of abandoning her intrahistorical role, including certain of its moral dimensions, today's woman is less desirable—and less desired—than the women of other eras. And for a basic reason: she satisfies fewer of man's desires and responds to fewer of his needs. Furthermore, because she is desired less, she in turn desires less, for woman, Marías believes, desires and is rendered desirable when she is desired by man. Consequently, today and in decreasing circularity, she does not create those needs and desires in men so that she and she alone can satisfy them.

Perhaps the most heated protest of modern feminism has been against woman's dependency on men. Yet as Marías points out, it was within this so-called dependency that women exercised their traditional predominance. If men claimed a nominal authority, which they summoned only exceptionally and sporadically, women controlled the unbroken skein of life in its daily and hourly rhythms, assigning tasks, enforcing behavior, setting standards, and transmitting knowledge and values. This is why as these duties are shunned, despite all appearances and claims to the contrary, Marías believes ". . . the dominion exercised by women is at one of its lowest moments of history."[17]

Perhaps we need look no further than the current disparagement of motherhood to find the root cause of an equally dramatic decline in personal stability, basic knowledge, and ethical standards in our time. As Marías describes it, "The temptation of woman in our time . . . is to diminish, weaken, or compromise her maternal function and to exchange it for others that seem to her more attractive or important but which perhaps are not. Less important, because their consequences do not have a comparable scope; less attractive, because they usually leave a woman empty, especially when she senses that she gave up something better and more closely personal for them."[18] Of course, she may have made such an unhappy choice in the first place because of the disrespect men showed for her maternal role.

The Possibilities of Feminine Life

But having pointed to several negative aspects of contemporary feminism—its masculine antecedents and consequences, its destabilizing personal and social tendencies, and its role in marginalizing women and rendering them ineffectual—we come now to some of its more promising features. Let us begin with the most obvious fact. If in the Victorian era "good" women were supposed to go to few places but Heaven, today's women go everywhere. Whereas throughout most of known history, women were usually "off limits" to most men, today they are readily and daily accessible.

This raises the delightful possibility of a whole range of intersexuate relationships unknown or at least rare in other eras. It is important to emphasize the adjective "intersexuate" instead of giving a Freudian "intersexual" coloring to these relationships. In any case, given the multiplicity of intersexuate contacts, a generalized "sexual" relationship—real or inchoate—would be impossible and therefore would, and does, amount to a falsification of life at its most basic level.

Here we reprise in a new context the concept of the "amorous" or "lovely" condition of human life, which was implied in our first encounter with the analytical theory and introduced formally when we moved to the empirical theory of embodied human life. This "lovely" condition appears within and as a feature of an even more general human condition that we have described as "sexuate." From our sexuate condition we experience our primary needs, especially the primordial need to be a man or woman. For we can only know ourself to be so in view of the other sex. In short, our personal needs are necessarily heterosexuate, including our specifically sexual need.

Therefore, all personal relationships between men and women are constituted within the amorous condition, that is, within the element or ambit of love, or its inchoative and seldom-realized possibility. For this reason, merely "being with" *(estar con)* is sufficient cause for such relationships to exist, whereas with members of one's own sex this "being with" must involve some further task undertaken together. On the other hand, it must not be thought that such "togetherness" with a member of the other sex is necessarily sexual in nature, even though it must include a note of *ilusión,* or enthusiastic anticipation between them.[19]

What Marías calls the "concrete nucleus" of the amorous condition is, however, the heterosexuate love between man and woman. By this, he does not mean that other forms of love are mere transformations or sublimations of heterosexuate love, but that they are rooted in and radiate from this heterosexuate structure. To look at it in a way we have examined before, men and women are installed vectorially and therefore project themselves within this amorous or lovely condition with multiple and variable intensities and directions, which are subject to error, age, experience, rectification, ruptures, apathies, and lack or excess of imagination. In a word, they are biographical. This is why it is a great oversimplification to label all such movements sexual and attempt to assign them to a single outcome.

This brings us to the possibilities of intersexual friendships and to a telling admission by Marías: "I have always believed that intersexual friendship is the most important and though not very likely or frequent in most countries or eras, the truest *friendship* of all."[20]

Even though we have been warned repeatedly not to follow the simplistic Freudian dialectic and reduce intersexual friendship to a sexual nature, neither are we justified in inclining toward an asexual interpretation. Rather, such friendships occur in the sexuate dimension and have a sexuate cast, yet because they are friendships, they cannot be invasive but must exhibit an unbreachable respect not only for the other person but for that person's privacy and intimacy.

The frequency of personal communication and contact is a necessary condition for friendships in general, and no less so for those between men and women. Nor can friendship be considered a finished relationship. Rather, it consists of a process of mutual discovery, because the persons involved are always coming to be in vectorial, biographical, and dramatic fashion. And the discovery has to do not so much with *how* the other person is but *who* he or she is.

We interpret and understand our life through language, spoken primarily but also nonverbal, and this means that dialogue is necessary between friends and lovers. But unlike love, which may or may not be mutual, friendship presupposes a reciprocity of dialogue and interest, along with an indispensable quality of mutual generosity. Not that dialogue is all talk. Instead, it includes intervals of silences, as well as times of what Marías calls "active listening."

What do men and women talk about in such friendships? Perhaps nothing that others would call "important topics." The only absolute requirement, notes Marías, is that the talk be from the heart, or as he puts it, from one's own intimacy. In those cases where there is a significant difference of age, the talk is more likely to center on matters of importance to the older person, who is more likely to feel an urgency to transmit accumulated knowledge or things in jeopardy of being lost in the onrush of time.

These friendships can be especially enriching because they allow us to live vicariously through our friend either the world of younger generations or the past of the elderly. In either case, it is a means of expanding our experience beyond the rigid limits of our own life.

Yet while the possibilities of intersexual friendship promise a rich new dimension in human relations, other factors work to suppress it. For example, ours has become a hasty world—probably because it knows itself to be in reality so slow. There is no time for letters, long conversations, and hours of togetherness, and even less time perhaps for the words we do exchange to settle and deposit their final significance in our life.

We are engaged in so many things that we do almost nothing well or completely. The old American saying of giving things "a lick and promise" has taken on a sad but real meaning in today's circumstances. This incessant pace is especially detrimental to the feminine condition, says Marías, which has always consisted of "being there" [*estar*]. Hence the serenity, peace, and hospitable qualities earlier associated with her. Women have always done many things, probably more than men at any given time, but in order to "do" herself, to shape her life as a woman, she needed time to be, that is, enough time for her "slow crystalization" to reach fruition. Without this completion, and given the disruptive haste of our time, the maturing process stands in danger of being definitively compromised.

According to Marías, the value or damage of what is said—or not said —to women is incalculable—to both men and women. The decline of lyric language, indeed the scorn for words themselves, introduces a note of crudeness into the delicate process of friendship between men and women—to say nothing of love. In the name of crass realism, whole dimensions of imaginative reality are in danger of being lost, among them the true image of women and with it the possibilities of human relationships that otherwise could bring about a human plenitude in our time.

We said that the feminine condition implies a relatively serene and hospitable "being there." Now we can add that her home is, or has been, the normal surrounding or context for her life. "The home," says Marías, "is the great creation of woman."[21] The metaphorical affinity of home to womanly life is striking. Man comes calling at the doorway of her life, as he does at the doorway of her home, seeking a hospitable reception. But her response is not simply passive, as is often supposed. She does not open her door or her life to just anyone, for she is "elegant" in the selective sense we saw earlier. Rather, she provokes or incites man to come calling. We could say that he takes the initiative—which she offers him in the first place.

For some, however, this physical and figurative quality of "being at home" is taken to mean unilaterally that woman has been simply a prisoner in her home, unable to come and go as she pleased, and that now it is time for her to escape. To which Marías responds: "To a large degree this is the history of the twentieth century and the justification of many attitudes of our time, which consist of protesting and doing away with what is supposed to be the 'condition' of woman. The problem is that all too often there is little inkling of what this condition consists of, and has consisted of historically; instead it is replaced by a caricature and reacted to accordingly."[22]

As a result, in many instances women of today are no longer "at home"—anywhere—but in several senses outside the home. And this is precisely the crux of the feminine crisis in our time. It is no longer just a question of wanting to be out of the house; today there is an assumption, what Marías has called a *vigencia,* that, regardless of any personal desire to the contrary, she must work outside the home in order to be respected as a "productive" member of society. Naturally, when she does return she usually has to do the work she always did at home. Only now, far from being a labor of love, it tends to become resented drudgery that poisons the hospitable atmosphere and renders the home—and with sad frequency the woman also—repellent instead of enticing. The world seems to be filling with solitary houses, occupied by solitary women, that once were, or could have been, homes.

By abandoning the home, woman has lost her base without gaining any comparable compensation, and this has weakened her chances for exerting a specifically *feminine* influence on the world. Under these circumstances her actions, undertaken in a largely neutral or masculine setting, differ in no essential way from those of men. Yet these specifically feminine influences are sorely needed. Marías describes the need with these words: "I have an exalted idea of feminine possibilities, among them woman's intelligence. I have formulated with philosophic rigor the idea that there are two forms of vital reason, masculine and feminine, both profoundly different, but complementary and necessary for planning and perhaps resolving problems in an adequate way."[23]

Marías remains convinced that human actions conceived and executed only at the public level will probably have little lasting value. Without the private setting and enrichment, they will prove to be too fragile and rootless to endure. In the case of woman this is doubly true, for her grounding in a private world is, according to Marías, the *sine qua non* of her efficacy, as well as a buffer against any destructive aftershocks her public work might otherwise have on her life.

We have been speaking in general social terms. In a more concrete sense, Marías notes that livable features of cities depend in large measure on the presence and pervasive work of women. For cities are not simply an aggregate of abstracted statistics, populations, or publics; before and underneath all that they are places where people live together, or failing that, coexist in lonely and sterile proximity. Certain great cities—Vienna, Paris, for example—and probably many smaller ones, were once associated with the beauty, grace, and civilizing action of women. The fact that these qualities no longer seem important and do not constitute a standard of excellence seems highly significant. Some would take it to mean that a gilded but false lyricism has given way to a more verifiable and measurable realism. For others, perhaps including Marías, it may signify a real human loss.

When women are not at home with themselves, when they turn away from from their immemorial dominion of concrete human intrahistory, the inherent restlessness of men increases to tragic proportions. Because without women, men cannot "stay put" but are condemned to wander and roam—usually into viciousness, almost never toward virtue.

Conclusion

We still repeat the notion that men do not understand women. But we take it as a cliché and discount it as a truth. For today it seems that men have little curiosity about women. Perhaps woman's greatest loss in recent decades has been her aura of ultimate mystery, of final intimacy, which surely has been one of the great motivating factors of history. In short, men think they know women and reveal this conviction if not in words then in their indifference.

For their part, in recent decades women have presented men and society a number of theories inspired or suggested, as we have seen, by certain men, which have had the general effect of diminishing feminine attractiveness to perhaps its lowest state in recent centuries. The most telling proofs of this waning enthusiasm are no doubt the fragility of unions, matrimonial or not, the declining birthrate, and the growing number of people of both sexes who have either chosen or been condemned to solitary loneliness.

Yet, as Marías sees it, this condition arises from a grievous misunderstanding of woman—by both men and women. "Woman represents a maximum of *intelligibility,* because she is a person, and human life is the only truly rational reality known. At the same time, she represents a maximum of *difference* with respect to man, because she is the other form in which human life occurs in its irreducible peculiarity. To put it another way, she is a *mystery* but with the possibility of being *understood*."[24]

How does this understanding come about? Not by concentrating on her wants but first on her desires, for while she may be able to express what she wants, her desires may lie too deep for words. "This," says Marías, "is probably the most exciting task man can take on, and perhaps the hardest. It takes time, and he is usually stingy with his time, but even more it requires attention, curiosity, and interest, that paradoxical 'unselfish interest' that so attracted Ortega."[25]

In the end, his search for understanding of the abiding feminine mystery leads Marías to the superlative love between a man and women, what he calls *enamoramiento* and which English would best render perhaps not as simply "falling in love" but as "being in love." It consists not of directing attention to the beloved in order simply to make her the "object of affection" but of an ontological shift to a state of being in which the beloved becomes the "project" of one's life, as Soledad was the reason for the being of the man we know only as "A."

And here, finally, woman begins to reveal herself so that man can know himself. Not totally and not once and for all, for personhood always retains an ultimate opaqueness and human life is always in a state of coming to be, of becoming. Hear Marías's summary of the matter: "And only then, as he puts into play the final wellsprings of his personality, as he stakes his life on the turn of a card, does man have the impression that he has 'touched bottom' and has discovered also who he really is. But not alone, of course, for woman reveals to him, as in a mirror, his own reality."[26] For Marías, the importance of this discovery can hardly be overstated. He calls woman "the mysterious continent" and believes her worthy of a lifetime of effort in this world, and hopefully in the next as well.

In his *Crossing the Threshold of Hope*, Pope John Paul II speaks approvingly of a "*. . . symptomatic return to metaphysics . . . through an integral anthropology.*"[27] This could be a summary of Marías's way of thinking. *For not before Marías has there existed an adequate philosophical accounting of the fact that human life occurs disjunctively in two inseparable but radically different forms. We call them men and women. With Marías, therefore, we have reached a significant turning point where an anthropological metaphysics is not only possible and indicated but now real. Perhaps it is also the point where science, religion, and art can once again find the common ground they abandoned at the outset of modernity to go their disparate ways.*

For centuries, it seemed that with every great discovery human life was relegated to ever remoter insignificance. At the height of modernity, its unappealing fate appeared to have dwindled either to a solipsistic relativism be-

yond hope of understanding or to the simple indignity of inescapable confine-
ment to the natural, material, and zoological world. (It is a telling and troubling fact that most contemporary theories about human life, theories that
have enjoyed almost uncontested sway for scores of years, depend heavily on
research done either on lower species of life or primitive and prehistoric
human cultures.)

The line of thought that Marías represents has rescued human life from
the anecdotal and elevated it to the dignity of a metaphysical method. But
Marías has gone further: through his discovery of the empirical structure of
human life he has developed concepts of personal, embodied life that accommodate both historical variation and metaphysical permanence with full intellectual rigor. Best of all, his methods work most effectively at the level at
which we really live life as men and women. I take this to be the best and final
proof that we have before us the long-sought "integral anthropology."

11

THE PURSUIT OF HAPPINESS

In the introductory chapter, I wrote that a "residue of happiness" lay at the core of authentic philosophy. At that point the claim probably seemed little more than a rhetorical gesture, supported certainly by personal conviction but understandable perhaps only as a universal characteristic of any valid philosophic enterprise or, textually, as a hint of coming developments in Marías's own thought. In the interim, other matters concerned us, but now near the end of this book, it is time to take up that early theme and flesh it out with specifics and consequences in the thought of Marías, in effect to show that happiness must be an ultimate theme of the philosophy espoused by Marías because it touches the whole continuum of human life.

Whereas in Classical times happiness was generally thought to be the reward of the wise and virtuous, today we are more likely to concede it to the frivolous and foolish. And no wonder, Marías reminds us, for with indifference things decline, especially the most precious and delicate.[1] Along with such neglected themes as personhood, human life, love, freedom, and personal death (unlike biological death), happiness is one of the *grandes ausencias,* or "great lacunae" of modern thought.[2] While modernity has dwelt insistently on things in the questionable—but rarely questioned—assumption that they constitute the primary and proper reality, the themes that affect us most deeply, personally, and directly are shunted off to unsupervised conjecture. But Marías does not tire of reminding us that unless we have a clear idea of these intimate matters, we shall not understand our world or our life.

Marías himself needed no clearer incentive to launch into the topic and "to think seriously" about the theme of happiness in his *La felicidad humana.* For the elusive but urgent human matters have always interested him the most. It was a daring venture, or better, adventure, yet one he undertook with an enormous sense of responsibility. To this he adds a passion and verve which the sensitive reader must surely take as suggestive hints of Marías's own life experience.

While almost no other contemporary philosopher joins Marías in writing of happiness itself, personally or vicariously we readily acknowledge every day its parasitical and derivative alter ego known as unhappiness. And like unhappiness, there are similar terms derived from positive concepts that apply only to humans: mis-fortune, un-lucky, dis-grace, dis-content, etc. This means that the bad descends from the good, as the absurd presupposes the sensible, and alerts us at once that the positive is in each case the fundamental quality.

Thus, we are inclined to believe that in some still undetermined way happiness is or ought to be intrinsic to our life, and even if we appear condemned to unhappiness by the very conditions of this world, we protest the indignity and cannot bring ourselves to think that our state is normal, just, or desirable. These qualities we reserve for happiness, even if we seldom experience them. In other words, happiness remains normative even if it is not very normal.

This is why we do not gainsay Alexander Pope when he states that happiness is that "For which we bear to live, or dare to die." And the intensity with which we seek happiness often translates paradoxically into a willingness to endure unhappiness and to forfeit our very lives in the quest. Only what we truly live for do we willingly die for. Happiness is such a matter of life and death. It overshadows our life even though it may never illuminate it. Marías says that all the things we pursue, all that interests us, reveal a background of happiness. "They interest us insofar as they contribute to our happiness, or make it more likely, or restore it if it has been lost. And this shows how disproportionate the intellectual attention it has received is to the absorbing and immense real weight it has in our life."[3]

On the other hand, under heavy philosophical scrutiny happiness tends to glide off into provocative semantics, and this has created in modern peoples a readiness to settle for its more docile substitutes, especially if they can administered in the abstract and on a colossal scale. As Gabriel Marcel has said, we have become the willing dupes of words. Yet Marías insists that happiness in the abstract remains a contradiction, more to the point, a personal contradiction. It is not transferable but, if anything at all, a function of "my" untransferable life. It is not something we do, for in most languages there is no verb of happiness: perhaps I can "be" more or less happy but I cannot "happy." As Marías summarizes the parameters of happiness and sets the stage for what is to come, "One cannot be satisfied with its social, psychological, or circumstantial features. All this may constitute the setting and the borders of happiness, or the forms in which it may or may not be realized. Under certain circumstances happiness is more or less probable, but in the final sense it is always strictly personal."[4]

Happiness, then, is not an isolated or separable feature of my life. It is not something I do or is done to me. Instead, we could say that happiness affects life in its core unity and not just its partial or particular contents or dimensions. It is that to which in our personal integrity we can say "yes" whole-heartedly and intensely.

The Impossible Dimensions of Happiness

Fully aware of the paradox, Marías calls happiness *el imposible nece-sario*, "the necessary impossibility." Unlike animals, man is the creature who aspires to be happy in order to be himself. But that aspiration, which is consti-tutive of human life, involves multiplicities of projects, options, desires, and trajectories. Even in the best of circumstances, only some of these can be real-ized, while others languish denied, frustrated, forgotten, or postponed. There-fore, happiness itself, insofar as it is the fulfillment of this general aspiration, remains fractionalized and partial. And this is what we call unhappiness, which we perceive as dissatisfaction.

But having said this, we must not forgot that life "moves in the element of satisfaction," just as we must not overlook the companion truth that to be unhappy is to acknowledge that happiness is inherent in our life. We could not be unhappy if we did not already have an image and ideal of happiness.

Because we can neither renounce happiness nor know it fully in this world, it follows formally that "Man consists in trying to be what he cannot be, and this, using an excellent verb, is what we call *living*."[5] We live, then, with an internal contradiction: all our efforts are directed toward happiness and contentment, yet we are unavoidably discontent.

"Had we but world enough and time," says Marvell in his celebrated verse, our errors and dilatory tactics would have no final consequences. In the fullness of time we could make up for all our mistakes and missed opportuni-ties. But our days are numbered, or at least finite. And what is equally impor-tant, Marías insists, they come in staged, or "aged" sequences. Certain acts and decisions belong to certain ages and would be grotesque if attempted at other stages of life. Our life exhibits a systematic temporal order which, within ample limits, qualifies cosmic time and converts it to livable and lived human temporality with tones and levels.

Life is a dynamic structure. Things happen to us and we "happen" to them in such a way that each portion of our life weighs on all the others. "When we wager a fragment of life on something to a certain degree we are gambling with our entire life. It is characteristic of human life in its fullest and most intense moments for us to stake everything on a single draw of the cards. We may win or lose (and we may also choose not to play, but not to play is to lose even the hope of winning)."[6]

From all this, we draw the conclusion that having placed our bets we cannot take them back. Life is irreversible and irrevocable, an unarguable fact against which, nevertheless, modern people argue incessantly, often to the point of disqualifying their life.

Even in the best of circumstances nothing is enough, because nothing, that is, no one thing, brings us our sought-after happiness. Before a variety of things and a series of possible pathways I have no choice but to choose one or some and reject others. Yet to prefer what seems best is also to spurn that which appears good. "The road not taken," to recall Robert Frost's melancholy verse, is a requiem for forfeited life; for it reminds us of other callings, other possible lives, we could have chosen but instead left to languish as nostalgic, bygone chances. Even though we may have no doubt that the road taken was the best choice of those available, it is proper to lament the happiness they could have meant. For they are, or were, also *our* choices, and in leaving them behind we must also leave and lose a part of ourself.

Because life is frontal and futuristic, coming events enhance or diminish our happiness. We cannot be happy today if we know that we shall be unhappy tomorrow. But if we know that happiness is on the way, then we are happy already. Therefore, because happiness involves the whole of life rather than its separate dimensions, we can say that it is prospective and primarily affects the future. We confront the prospect of happiness because we face the future.

On the other hand, pleasure—and perhaps pain—exhibit an instantaneous character. The prophet Isaiah's advice, "let us eat and drink, for tomorrow we die" (*Isaiah*, 22:13), is a frenzied grab for momentary pleasure, not a guarantee for happiness, as the prophetic words of God make plain in succeeding verses. What happens is that we try to eternalize pleasure, to "make the moment last." Naturally, it never does.

Because happiness is a function of personal life in its projective or prospective wholeness, it cannot be automatically assumed apart from that unity. In our day, we come close to legislating happiness. For example, it is often taken for granted that given certain generic social and economic conditions—education, health care, a certain standard of living, etc.—individual happiness inevitably follows as a result. Yet if we think about it, we know this is not true, at least not necessarily true. Happiness may occur in the most unlikely circumstances—poverty, illness, etc.—just as unhappiness may be found in the midst of opulence, in a life full of things dear to one's heart perhaps but antithetical to one's dreams.

Of course, in both plenty or poverty happiness may also be sacrificed to the pursuit of pleasure, in the first place because pleasure is readily available and thus represents the easy path of least resistance, and in the second, because one assumes beforehand that happiness cannot stoop this low and that moments of pleasure are the best one can hope for.

For these and other reasons, before any determination of happiness can be made, one must know something of what constitutes, or could constitute, happiness for each society and, strictly speaking, for each person. For as Marías insists time and again, our aims are more defining than our ambience.

Measures of Happiness

A formula for measuring happiness, Marías tells us, might be stated as a fraction, with a numerator to represent our reality and a denominator to signify our aim. In an ideal case they would be equal, but since life with all its idealism unfolds in a real world, the "denominator" would nearly always remain larger than the "numerator." From this, we see that happiness depends much less on abstract conditions or personal attributes than on the magnitude of our "happiness denominator." Nor does the ratio of difference mean that happiness is completely lacking. One may know considerable happiness, or least good fortune, by impersonal or external measurements, but if the aspiration to happiness is exceptionally high, then unhappiness for that person is the inevitable result. The question is, how do we determine the relative values of such an equation?

Our individual reality is primary and radical, as we have seen, but only within a given historical and social setting does it make sense to speak of it in concrete and personal terms. The degree and angle of personal insertion into a collectivity may vary widely, from Western societies which permit a maximum of personal expression to primitive or totalitarian systems in which individuality may be either unthinkable or highly suspect. In still others, spiritual or psychological awareness of individual autonomy may exist but is checked or even suffocated by countervailing forces, for example, in a dictatorship.

A peculiar form of what we could call "induced unhappiness" may occur when societies of limited resources become aware of the material abundance of others. Exposed to the example of materially affluent societies, say the United States, other peoples suddenly feel themselves deprived. Of what? The things they have never had and probably never desired but now want. The discontent arising from this awareness can be a stimulus to work for a more satisfactory life, but it may also condemn whole generations to have to live with the unhappiness brought on by their induced sense of poverty. This is especially true in those societies restricted by rigid ideologies that equate individual betterment with betrayal of a revolutionary cause.

The material success of so-called "advanced" countries has been taken as a model to follow toward that collective economic fulfillment assumed today to be synonymous with happiness. Economics thus tends to become a moral imperative to be applied to the rest of world. Inherent cultural and personal differences and aspirations are swept aside in the name of a one-world vision. Happiness becomes a generic, mandated program, not the realization of one's intimate feelings.

It is not true, argues Marías, that all societies manifest the same intensity or level of felicitary expectation. In some, happiness is looked on almost as an indecency, and for an individual to aspire to a greater quota of happiness than that sanctioned by the social *vigencias* is to be insolent. In his day, Stendhal preferred Italy and Spain over his native France because he found in those societies a greater passion for life. He knew that people who cannot stand much pain cannot tolerate much happiness.

On the other hand, in the interest of generic paradigms of happiness whole generations are called on to sacrifice their lives for the general future welfare. In other words, one is asked to forego present happiness and fulfillment so that a greater number of unborn persons will one day know a supposedly greater happiness. Marías is bluntly critical of this sacrifice: "By what right can living men and women be sacrificed in the name of their children who may never even be born because those who would have been their parents will have died?"[7]

What Marías calls "modes of insertion" involve the possibility of happiness that depends on how nearly one's aim coheres with the general aims of the society. There are wide modal variations in this social insertion, from the ancient view that life in exile from one's native land was a fate as grim as death itself, to the modern social fluidity whereby people willingly migrate from the land of their origin to the country of their choice.

But this fluidity also conceals other risks to our happiness. The abstract paradigms that give a preponderant value to economic or perhaps political factors also omit others, seemingly too humble to count seriously, that in reality matter a great deal and may be decisive: friends, family, climate, language, the human and physical setting of city, village, or the landscape itself. Such lifelong intimate realities, unnoticed through sheer habit, leave an incredible void when taken away, as though a portion of the earth had dropped away under our feet or a part of the sky had fallen. For without them daily life loses its savor, zest, and depth, and yet it is precisely the quality of our daily life, says Marías, that determines the probability of our happiness.

This diurnal quality of happiness may be formulated as a question: what is our daily expectation of life? This question, with its innumerable possible responses, allows us to understand the personal modulations of happiness and the infinite distance that separates it from all abstract paradigms. The same question persists throughout life, but its possible answers tend to vary with each age. With the passing of the years, it is not unusual for a certain disillusionment to settle in one's life. (In some eras, the Romantic, for instance, this disenchantment may come very early. The Romantics were not only precocious in youth but also precociously old. Goethe's *The Sorrows of Young Werther* offers a well-known example.) Yet to declare happiness to be an impossibility does not annul its necessity but only intensifies its tragic urgency. Perhaps this is one reason why the Romantics were so fascinated by suicide.

But what happens when all our expectations come true? If the expectations are modelled on the generic paradigms we mentioned earlier, for example, economic success, power, or fame, then with disturbing frequency the results are disappointing. In such cases, instead of happiness one experiences an excruciating and seemingly unreasonable dissatisfaction with life. But the reason for this dissatisfaction surfaces once we realize that the image of happiness was shaped by a generic template indifferent to our native desires.

The person who "has arrived" and "has it made" in the opinion of society often wonders inwardly, is this all there is? Marías would argue that this state of "arrival" may be the deepest threat to happiness. The very notion of ultimate accomplishment is a radical biographical contradiction. For human life consists not of deeds and arrivals but of always doing and ever arriving.

The unreal, "arriving" dimensions of life make it impossible to resort to any sort of mathematical or statistical analysis in order to sketch a profile of happiness. We have already seen how Marías protests the scandalous application of such methodologies to human life. It is not that these methods fail to yield information but that they offer information about *something else* that is not life and therefore not happiness. Indeed, there is no prescribed method at all for ascertaining happiness. As Marías sees it, "In order to understand what happiness is there is no choice but to *think*, which in the final analysis is the only method."[8] And if this thinking is to be intelligent and discerning, then we must turn to the subject affected by happiness, that is, to the person engaged in the consuming search for happiness, and ask what it is he seeks in the name of happiness and what he discovers when he finds it, or, alternately, fails to find it. This confines the "field of study" to the contents of our own or others' experience, including the imaginary persons of fiction.

Because happiness comes associated not with things but with life in the making and arriving, the element of risk and possibility of failure are inherent in its pursuit. Happiness, therefore, requires a certain amount of imagination and daring. In order to be eligible for happiness we must be brave enough to desire and courageous enough to risk fulfilling our desire. Yet this is far less common than we think in this age that values security above all else. "Many do not dare desire what they truly desire because it is not what *is* desired . . . and we find that the chances for happiness are rendered improbable by this dual lack of daring."[9]

The Social Parameters of Happiness

Without withdrawing the earlier argument for the personal nature of happiness, we must add that a general social level or ambience of happiness bears directly on its individual manifestations. In recent years a series of statistical and demographic studies have attempted to identify those areas with the optimal conditions and highest probabilities of the "good life." But such data are extracted with questions and categories that predetermine some responses while excluding others.

Given his abiding skepticism of objective categories when it comes to human reality, it is not surprising to hear Marías suggesting a more "visual" approach to collective happiness. In the case of cities, for instance, he notes that it is necessary first of all to *see* its streets and districts and to consider this visual contact as the primary datum. In comparing cities, there are, he insists, enormous differences "In spontaneity, in the interactive presence of persons, in communication, and in what we could call the ambient cheerfulness (which does not coincide with the personal cheerfulness of each person which is a personal and variable matter). And this cheerfulness of the streets and the city flows over the individual."[10] All this can be seen and sensed but hardly measured in any objective fashion. Likewise, fear is impalpable, even though in some societies it is so generalized as to become a way of life.

In our day, we set "gainful employment" or "meaningful work" as two conditions for happiness, which they certainly are. But leisure, of which there seems to be so little, is at least equally important, and in many cases probably much more so. This despite the fact, as Marías points out, that the very concept of the Spanish *holgura*—now tending significantly to fall into disuse—is hard to express in most European languages. Only the English "leisure" comes close, although it lacks the added meaning of being at ease in dealing with people and conditions.

Another factor that affects the social setting for happiness is the general level of expectation, and no less so its opposite, the assumption that everything that can be already is, that we know it all, and that nothing new or unexpected will emerge. Paradoxically, happiness presupposes counting on a measure of the unexpected, otherwise when it comes we may not even be aware of it.

From all this what we know experientially becomes evident dialectically: happiness is more probable in some social settings than in others. But probabilities are not happiness. In reality, happiness itself is an abstraction; what we find are relatively happy—or unhappy—persons. Happiness, Marías reminds us again, is a personal matter. But this does not mean that we can disqualify everything we have said about the social background of happiness. For whereas societies and governments cannot give me happiness, they can readily provoke unhappiness by invasions of privacy and the imposition of unreasonable restrictions on personal life. This is why, says Marías, those regimes that formally promise happiness for their people propagate an untenable lie. No wonder they usually bring only unhappiness and disillusionment.

The only possible personal happiness, which we must remember is also more or less impossible, cannot be quantified in conformity to objective measurements. Yet it is susceptible to qualification. For example, it is possible to speak of happiness in terms of vectorial intensity. Indeed, Marías gives it this formal qualification: "Happiness consists primarily in the *intensity of life*."[11]

The Classical Understanding of Happiness

If the nature of happiness is elusive, to attempt its history would seem utopian. Yet within the Classical Greek and Roman cultures in which the Western ethos is grounded, Marías finds assumptions and theories that form the background of our modern notions of happiness.

Restating an intuition deeply rooted in Greek thought, Aristotle says that all knowledge and every pursuit tends toward or culminates in the highest good and ". . . the general run of men and people of superior refinement say that it is happiness . . . ," adding that they ". . . identify living well and doing well with being happy; but with regard to what happiness is they differ, and the many do not give the same account as the wise."[12] This uncertainty over the nature of happiness leads Aristotle to examine its possible forms—various pleasures, virtue, friendship, etc.—and to conclude that the supreme happiness consists in an enduring self-sufficiency, or autarky.

Yet Marías points out that this autarky does not consist of a mere contemplative disposition but of an activity that culminates in *theoria*. But unlike the moderns, who distinguish between *theoria* and *praxis,* Aristotle held that *theoria* was the highest form of *praxis* because it was self-contained, self-sufficient, and therefore divine.

Nevertheless, Aristotle and Plato agreed that this self-sufficiency must not be interpreted to mean a solitary life. Aristotle states that friendship was the most necessary thing in life. The Greek insistence on lifetime duration and the social setting of happiness in its two Greek expressions, *eudaimonia* and *makarios,* implicitly points beyond any abstract or solipsistic theoria to the social needs of one's life. To put it another way, *theoria* was self-sufficient and needful of nothing beyond itself, but man himself was not. As Marías summarizes: ". . . the Greeks speak of autarky, self-sufficiency, etc., but the need to have friendship causes man not to be self-sufficient but needy and indigent."[13] When the Greeks began to think directly in non-categorical terms of life itself, this sufficiency was taken to mean an independence bordering on indifference in the face of circumstances, a concept that was to have wide circulation among the Stoics and others.

Given Marías's orientation, his insistence on the fact that man's very life and being are circumstantially conditioned, it is no wonder that he finds the supposed Stoic indifference to the world to be excessive. For the Stoics, among them Seneca, to admit neediness was to confess a lack of self-mastery and self-sufficiency and hence to be less than serene and happy. For Marías, our ontological indigence, while unavoidable, does not necessarily prejudice our peace of mind or place in jeopardy the self-mastery of life. After all, it is not that things impose themselves on me, but rather that I personally and executively initiate, guide, and come to terms with my neediness. Understood from this viewpoint, my need does not act reductionistically, nor is my circumstantial condition any less promising of happiness than the hermetic, distrustful, perhaps even fearful Stoic indifference or the Epicurean search for unsullied and imperishable pleasure.

Marías writes of the "profound sadness" that permeated ancient society in the time of Seneca. As the Classical world waned, men no longer believed in the gods and did not yet believe in God. Alternately, they sought pleasure or professed indifference to fate as a means of avoiding their always-looming existential grief. Faced with the perplexity of personal annihilation, the men of the late Classical Age were "avid for fame" and fearful of death, and given the very real likelihood that happiness was not possible in their shrinking life and disillusioned world, they tended to reduce it to fit their diminishing expectations. The question was whether this "reductionist" happiness was really happiness at all. As Marías sees it, Christianity was soon to introduce the elements of futuristic project and love which pointed to an altogether different plane and magnitude of happiness.

The Christian Views of Happiness

Whereas the Greek *eudaimonia* suggested an essentially human agency in happiness, *makaria* indicated a more elevated and even divine realm. The eight beatitudes of the New Testament are linguistically based on its derivatives *(makar, makarioi)*. The Spanish translation of the term as *bienaventuranza* turns out to be particularly fortunate, says Marías, since it includes an etymological reference to the future (Latin *venturus,* "that which is to come"). Unlike *fatum,* "fate" or Spanish *dicha,* which has to do with the personal destiny that is "spoken" into being at one's birth by the Parcae or Fates, the *bienaventuranzas* were those eight forms or aspects of "blessed" happiness that Christ taught to his disciples and that, therefore, may be learned and achieved in this life. As Marías writes, ". . . the essential thing is their dual character: the reference to the future and the connection with something proper to man, an attitude, installation, or form of behavior."[14]

According to Marías, theologians may have been too hasty in translating this blessed state to a paradisical setting beyond this earthly life. In keeping with his insistence that our understanding of human reality must begin from its circumstantiality, Marías says the Beatitudes must first be considered from the standpoint of those who heard them from the lips of Christ, just as they must be circumstantially related to all subsequent generations. In each of what we may call the "felicitary categories," the "blessedness" has a direct causal connection with one's attitude and behavior in this life. ("Blessed are they which do hunger and thirst after righteousness: *for* they shall be filled.") Marías notes that Christ did not offer theories but made direct reference to the lives of unsophisticated men and women in their daily circumstances.

Instead of theorizing about the happy life, Christ illustrated it through his celebrated parables. These supreme examples not only corroborate to Marías's satisfaction his belief that the narrative emerges as the superior form of reason we have described elsewhere in its various aspects as "narrative" and "historical" reason, but also strengthens his argument that it functions as an immediate form of knowledge.

Furthermore, this direct, concrete formulation lends a futuristic slant to the promise of happiness. "He who listened to the Sermon on the Mount, or he who reads the Gospel of Saint Matthew today begins to hope, to take on an expectant, desiderative attitude, and to await the fulfillment of a promise."[15] Thus, the concrete, circumstantial reality of this life reveals a hopeful link to the life to come. As we have seen before and will see again, Marías believes this personal connection to be essential if the life to come is also *our* life. Just as these blessings are promised to each person, in all matters of supreme importance the personal and concrete life of each person must take precedence over abstract constructs. No intuition is stronger in Marías or closer to the heart of his doctrine.

Unamuno protested that immortality of the soul alone was not enough. His hopes—and his doubts—centered on the resurrection of his own body and the continuation of life as himself with his own name. And this hope, Marías reminds us, is precisely the promise of Christ, the assurance, linked to his own resurrection, that not only shall we live forever in spirit but also in a resurrected body. For Christ returned to his disciples not as a disembodied spirit but as the man they had known and called by name. This personal assurance makes temporal inconvenience bearable and colors every earthly sadness with a faint prophecy of joy. But every temporal happiness is dragged down toward despair if we know, or think we know, that tomorrow, some final tomorrow, we must die utterly.

Another Christian variant of this earthly experience of joy is found as early as the writings of Saint Paul (*II Corinthians*, 12,4), but it abounds in the Mystics, including Ruysbroeck, Angelus Silesius, Saint Teresa, and Saint John of the Cross. As Marías explains, "The idea of the ineffable accompanies mysticism. The Mystic has seen or experienced something that cannot be uttered, and yet he speaks and tells something of it, and for this reason we have some knowledge of his experience."[16]

Because the Mystics speak of the sublime divine love and the unspeakable happiness it produces, using a language that often approximates the amorous terminology of lovers, there is a tendency to interpret the mystical experience as a sublimation of the sexual. For Marías, this interpretation of covert sexuality is no less erroneous than a disregard of the literal language and the resulting reduction of the terminology of love to religious or theological symbolism. In the mystical texts, "There can be as much symbolism as one wishes and all the theology that underlies them, but without losing sight of the immediate, direct, and amorous sense and the association of this love with happiness . . ."[17]

Referring to Saint John of the Cross, Marías explains that the proper way to begin to understand the Mystics is to take seriously what they say. For example, Saint John of the Cross writes of the lover and his beloved, using the terminology of human gender. For Marías, this means that we must begin with the sexuate condition of human life, which is where we encounter the primary and concrete form of love between man and woman. As we saw earlier in Marías's thought, this is the context in which all other loves, including the divine and irreducible love, may be understood.

Religion is often reproached for this anthropomorphism, but Marías reminds us that the very divinity of Christ makes it possible to preserve the human component in at least one dimension of the love of God. Yet he hastens to add that this love of God is by no means a mere sublimation of love between a man or woman. "The fact is that without this anthropological dimension human reality and the nature of human love would be different."[18] This human love, he reminds us again, originates in the radical indigence of man and woman who, need each other in order to be who they are.

Although the ends of this divine love lie beyond mortal sight and language, thus earning their mystical halo, it is important to remember that they are also rooted in the sexuate and incarnate condition of human life. The happiness that finally consists of this love does not scorn our mortality. The Mystic longs for singular, ineffable union with the divine, but he longs from within his humanity and his personal vectorial installation in the world.

Happiness as a Modern Theme

To an astonishing degree, modernity has been a series of experiments with substitutes for happiness. Unlike the ancients, who generally believed that happiness lay in the direction of individual wisdom and restraint, the moderns appear tacitly convinced that it is or ought to be a property of mass populations.

Generally acknowledged as the father of modern thought, Descartes himself was not especially "modern" in his notions of happiness but adhered closely to certain ancient dichotomies by distinguishing between *heur* (external luck or happy occurrence) and *beatitude* (inner blessedness). Honors, riches, and health are not really within our power to summon, but virtue and wisdom are. *Beatitude,* the inner state of contentment, presupposes and points to the highest good, which is essentially superior to and aloof from the exterior accidents of materiality.

For his part, Pascal saw the unbreachable limits and ultimate impossibility of happiness in this life. Only if man could confine his life to the present, foregoing imaginary anticipation of the future, could he reasonably aspire to full happiness. It is an indictment of imagination, but more than that, it is a pessimistic outlook on the human condition. Pascal observes that men do not live in the present, at least not fully, but always await life in a more or less remote and ever recessive future.

For Spinoza, desire is the very essence of man. From this premise it follows that being and happiness cannot be considered separately. To desire happiness is also to desire to live and act persistently. To exist, therefore, is to exist in action, in doing, in obedience to a will to continue in existence, as Unamuno restated so forcefully. Here, Spinoza gives expression to the modern predisposition to equate life with the increasing—and in extreme form the frenzied—sum of its activity. Naturally, even though he would have wished otherwise, Spinoza had to confront the reality of death because it loomed inevitably on the horizon of human freedom and the will to continue in existence. In the end, Spinoza's stoic disposition led him to a virtuous definition of happiness. Happiness, he concluded, is not the reward of virtue but virtue itself.

Leibniz, whose misunderstood theme "the best of all possible worlds" was satirized in Voltaire's *Candide,* considered happiness from standpoint of the primal unit, or monad, and from the perspective of God as the Author of their preestablished harmony. The higher monads, or spirits, were created in the image and likeness of God, and while they "have no windows" through which to communicate with one another, because of this likeness and out of His love God allows Himself to become humanized and to enter into happy communion with them. Insofar as this communion offers happiness, the supreme law of God is fulfilled. For "happiness is to persons what perfection is to entities." Naturally, this happiness can never be complete because the infinite God transcends this limited life. Yet for this same reason the process of discovering God and the additional possibilities of happiness unfold endlessly before us. Life in the here and now is a foretaste of future happiness. Therefore, as God's love floods us with happiness we ought to love Him in turn with "tenderness." And this love of God is happiness, Leibniz declares, adding in the rationalistic spirit of his age that it is an enlightened love accompanied by light.

From a very different vantage point, Fichte agreed that the happiness of spirits or persons corresponds to perfection in things. Human happiness consists of love, which he holds to be the condition of truth and authenticity of life. He argues that the expression "happy life" is redundant, for life is necessarily happy insofar as it is authentic. Love is the center of life, and therefore he reasons that love, life, and happiness are one and the same. Now then, the beloved object of true life is that which we call God, whereas the object of apparent life is the world. This means that life and happiness admit of degrees of authenticity and falsification.

In the English thinkers—Bacon, Locke, John Stuart Mill—there appears for the first time the notion of quantified happiness we know as utilitarianism. Bacon believed that to confine love to one or few persons was to deny or weaken the natural inclination of human love toward magnanimous and charitable expression on behalf of the many. According to Bacon, one ought to seek serenity without destroying magnanimity, and rather than the mere peace of mind obtained by withdrawal from, or indifference to, the world, one should proactively desire and enjoy. For Bacon, love must avoid the wanton and lascivious and go out instead to humanity at large, just as our desires, acts, and pleasures find their natural arena in the world.

John Locke reasoned that happiness moves these desires in the first place. But happiness also admits of degrees: the lowest level of happiness is achieved when an absence of pain combines with the presence of pleasure. Good is that which is apt to produce pleasure, and evil is that which causes pain.

This means that good and evil take on an instrumental quality. They are good or bad *for* something insofar as they produce states of being or feeling. Thus arises the notion of good as utilitarian. Going a step further, good is multiplied—if not intensified—by application of this pleasurable instrumentality to as many people as possible. For the utilitarian mind this constituted—or at least approximated—happiness.

However, it remained for John Stuart Mill to give the notion of utilitarian happiness its definitive formulation. Like Locke, he defined happiness by the antipodes of pain and pleasure. The moral basis of his doctrine is the principle of the greatest happiness, and acts are licit or illicit insofar as they promote, repectively, happiness or unhappiness. For Mill, the standard of comparison in matters of happiness is not the individual but the many who have the opportunities of experience and the habits of self-knowledge and observation. To Marías, this means, in addition to a psychological component, that "The sediment of all this is the capacity for comparison, which means that individual and immediate reaction is of no great worth. The important thing is the comparative reaction of many people with experience and the habit of comparing."[19]

Although lacking intellectual profundity, utilitarianism with its emphasis on quantification and mensurability and the reduction of happiness to plural modalities was to have an enormous impact. It gave rise, for instance, to the mania for polls and surveys, on which public policies and political parties depend so much in our time. Its summarizing slogan, the greatest good (read "happiness") for the greatest number, which was linked to an optimistic expectation of a general rise in the material welfare of the masses, has come true on a scale undreamed of in Mill's lifetime. Yet it is debatable whether the general level of happiness has ascended in tandem with this materialistic advancement. Indeed, given the poor opinion that people always seem to have about their own time, millions who by former standards would be accounted as affluent are persuaded that in the midst of abundance their lot is worse than ever.

Marías suspects that although the utilitarians spoke of happiness what they really meant was welfare. They made too much of practicality; cool to idealism, they seemed to reason that if happiness was beyond human reach, then it was better to define happiness as something within reach.

As Marías understands it, to equate happiness with welfare is to subject it to a double reduction. First, to think of happiness as merely being well, that is, free of pain and with a comfortable expectation of pleasure, is to strip happiness of its projective and dynamic character. Secondly, it mistakes the things and conditions that bear on happiness for happiness itself. In effect, from this perspective happiness becomes identical to security.

But this reasoning becomes a trap. As Marías sees it, the human condition is always uncertain and insecure. But if we think that security is happiness, then we easily believe that insecurity is unhappiness. Therefore, the very condition of our life, precarious as always, persuades us a priori and without human appeal that we are doomed to unhappiness.

The utilitarian imperative of the greatest happiness for the greatest number has legitimized a statistical view of human life in which a reasonable accuracy in dealing with enormous numbers is offset by bizarre absurdities and almost certain error when it comes to predicting the fate of small groups or individuals. Homogeneity is the underlying assumption, but in the end it turns out to be merely mathematical and not human. As the cliché states quite correctly, no two persons are alike. To put it another way, the quantitative similarities tell a story of sorts, but it is not the qualitative human narrative that offers real understanding.

The reduction of happiness to statistics favors the static. (Which explains Marías's antipathy toward the new historicism with its emphasis on formulaic models, graphs, and the like. It is essentially anti-historical, for history as the general story of human life is necessarily dynamic.) The welfare state promises a paradisical condition of stasis, in which nothing new happens and therefore nothing new is imaginable.

But Marías would agree with the poet Machado:

> *Se miente más de la cuenta por falta de fantasía*
> *también la verdad se inventa*
> ["For lack of imagination men lie to excess;
> Truth is also a creation"].

And he would add that this lack of imagination leads to a dehumanization of life. For instance, the terrorist who kills strangers mechanically and unfeelingly does not understand what it means to kill a human person, because he cannot or will not imagine the personal life of his victims.

Thus, Marías believes that before it can be lived, our life, including the next life, must first be imagined so as to be desirable, even if not clearly represented. Without this effort, our view of the future must necessarily remain featureless and probably forbidding. No wonder, then, that paradisical welfare ideologies such as utilitarianism and socialism, which think of themselves as futuristic, actually reject the future with its unexpected dimensions and surprises. The utopian State—witness Marxism—denies even the possibility of a post-utopian world. Once in place and claiming to have resolved all historical dilemmas, this ideal state then tries to extend its hegemony over all the tomorrows to come.

Naturally, in the long run the effort always fails. Although statistics and excessive planning partially domesticate and weaken the unexpected dimensions of life, eventually chance breaks through causal schemes, destroying strategies and jolting men free of their self-styled perfect, and thus limiting, ideologies.

But just as the utilitarian mind fears the unexpected and takes provision against it, so also it seeks indemnization from the inevitable. Yet where, wonders Marías, does one find compensation for an act of disloyalty, or the heartbreak of a lost love, or, most of all, the death of a loved one? The theories that presuppose happiness to be universal and life-long welfare in principle tolerate no human suffering, which, if one considers the matter thoughtfully, may be the greatest suffering of all.

These brief summaries reflect the restricted treatment of happiness in modern thought. As Marías notes, happiness ". . . has been a subterranean and almost shunned theme."[20] He goes on to point out that with the exception of the scriptural beatitudes, the history of the happiness theme can be summed up as theories of what it must or ought to be. But then Marías wonders what we will find if we set aside these prerequisites and imperatives and pay attention to what it means when one says simply "I am happy" or, equally telling, "I am unhappy."

Situation and Happiness

If happiness cannot be reduced to welfare and wellbeing, then what is lacking? Marías would begin a response by restating a defining premise about life itself: living does not mean simply to be in this or that state with or without the accoutrements of comfort and welfare. Nor is it confined merely to doing as such. Rather, living means to be engaged in doing something that fulfills one's life. From the verb "to be" [*estar*], we glimpse life's relative stability, and from the gerund "doing" [*haciendo*], we see its dynamic and moving dimensions. This is the "vectorial installation" discussed in earlier chapters.

We know this "relative stability" of life as "situations." Situations endure long enough to be recognizable as such, but because they are inherently unstable they are defined temporally or logistically by reference to other situations. This means that our time, far from being cosmic and amorphous, exhibits a fundamental situational articulation. Our life is modulated in a discontinuous series of beginnings, anticipations, and denouements, which means that instead of being an occasional or imposed quality, its drama is intrinsic and constant.

The most basic temporal situations are day and night, waking and sleeping. What is more, each day has its profile and personality. But this feature blurs in the modern trend toward homogeneity. Seldom do we acknowledge anything distinctive about a given day or bother to weigh it in our private balance when it is over. For the most part, our days are as busy as they are forgetful, and we turn to pleasures to fill the vacuum. Yet for Marías this attitude is an error. "Each day is unique and different, and one must ask of each an accounting. This is the microstructure of life."[21] Hence the Christian attention on *daily* bread and detail; the possible plenitude of each day links in structural sequence to weeks, months, years, ages, and ultimately to the final accounting we call the Last Judgment. For this reason, we live one day at a time but we project ourselves individually toward situational outcomes at varying vital distances and across the ages of our life. For the Christian, there is an additional and decisive component: this ideal displacement occurs in view of the final escatalogical *terminus ad quem.*

Waiting is the name we give to the temporal distance between our projective efforts and their fulfillment or outcome. And since we undertake these projects in the name and for the sake of happiness, waiting and happiness have been inseparably linked. Being happy, says Marías, has always meant primarily ". . . going to be happy."

For millennia, work was structured in such a way as to expect an outcome. The farmer worked his crops and awaited an uncertain harvest; the craftsman labored to produce a finished item. In other words, work made sense because it pointed to a defining conclusion. Yet modern work, like the labor of

Sisyphus, tends to be repetitive and literally pointless because at no point is it finished. It is process without outcome, labor without progress, activity without definition. Instead of a rich vital melody arising from renewable expectations, projective enterprises, and unexpected outcomes, life abates to a single tone, that is, a dull monotone, a crushing monotony, a destructive boredom.

For Marías, it is a grave fallacy to believe that one can work poorly and yet live well by seizing on other compensations. Life is unitary. Wretchedness in any dimension of our being invades and corrodes the whole spectrum of life.

Happiness finds its fulfillment in the totality of a dynamic, situational life. On the other hand, monotony seems to reduce us to a single hopeless situation, which is clearly a contradiction of life's terms. In other words, life cannot be monotonous without violating its own "eventual" surge toward "being happy." For this reason, the first certain casualty of this monotonous violation is our happiness. As Marías summarizes, "A happy life is the one that can pronounce itself so in its projective unity."[22]

Happiness, Pleasures, and Amusements

The very word "happiness" resists pluralization in most languages. We may and sometimes do say there are "different kinds of happiness," for instance, but upon reflection we realize that this is an overstatement and that what we really mean is a series of possible variations on a single underlying theme, not separate cateories or genres of happiness. This singularity ought not to surprise us if we take seriously our earlier claim that happiness is linked to the projective and structural unity of life. Happiness is one even as our life is one.

To look at it in another way, the happiness—and unhappiness—we experience relates to what we expect from life. Yet, as Marías reminds us, we are not always certain about what we desire. Socially sanctioned and inherited opinions about what constitute happiness often seduce us into seeking what we do not personally want. This is one of the greatest threats to our happiness.

Whereas happiness is singular, pleasure is thought of in both the singular and the plural. We speak generically of pleasure but also of pleasures. Furthermore, we sometimes describe certain people as "pleasure-seekers," but never, it seems, as "happiness-seekers." These linguistic distinctions put us on track of other phenomena concerning pleasure and happiness that deserve our attention.

To begin with, contemporary views on pleasure generally divide into two antagonistic categories. On the one hand, the increasing multiplicity, simultaneity, and abundance of recreational options leave no doubt that pleasure

constitutes a social norm of enormous impact in our time. Modern people believe they have a "right" to constant pleasure and feel unjustly deprived if they
do not receive their daily quota. But it remains an open question whether our
time is really more "pleasurable" than others have been. For there is little
pleasure in pleasures too often repeated.

At the same time, the glorification of work and workers, which, as
Marías reminds us, is a modern phenomenon, renders pleasure as an end in itself somewhat suspect and often censurable. We should not wonder that it
often comes disguised as other things: exercise, health, competition, personal
enrichment, etc. For the celebrated American "work ethic," now imitated on a
world scale, situates work at the moral center of life and obliges pleasure to
seem as much like work as possible in order to be respectable.

If we are sincere with ourselves, we have to acknowledge that socially
predominant pleasures—sports, for example—often are not pleasurable at all
for multitudes of people. Furthermore, in an age seduced by the economic, we
are prone to think that if it does not cost it cannot be fun. Yet the simple fact
remains: pleasure is that which produces pleasure, and the personal range in
each case may have little to do with official pleasures vouchsafed by society.
But in no case is pleasure a trivial matter apt only for idling away excess time.
"A certain dose of pleasure is necessary in life. Without it life weakens and
fades and most certainly turns out to be not very creative."[24]

If it is true that human life is inherently insipid, as Ortega observes, it
may also prove exhaustingly burdensome, as Marías states. In either case, we
look beyond ourselves for relief and find it in amusements, diversions, and entertainments. All these terms indicate a turning aside from ourselves, what Ortega calls "a vacation from our humanity." We are momentarily "entertained,"
that is, literally "held between" or "diverted" from our pathway, at liberty to
"muse" on, and thus be amused by, things beyond or beside our otherwise circumscribed life.

But these entertaining excursions away from ourselves are more than
their name implies and their effect more than momentary. Marías describes
them as "an expansion toward the unreal and imaginary." Amusements, art,
and play not only offer us a pleasurable vacation from ourselves; they also ex-
pand our life by allowing a fanciful visit to dimensions denied to us in fact.
For this reason, this unreal expansion turns out to be one of the real necessities
of life. But in order to enhance their efficacy these entertaining interludes
must be kept in a vital balance that prevents both excessive frequency and inordinate denial.

In an earlier chapter, we saw how the temper of life, male and female, is
concentrated in the human countenance. To a significant degree, it tells our
story and reveals our aim. An important dimension of this life temper appears
in the present "felicitary" context as degrees and shades of humor, momentary

and lasting, we observe in another's face. The sum of this personal temper is not happiness itself, as Marías reminds us, but rather serves as its setting. In other words, without constituting happiness as such, pleasures and entertainments incline us toward it and have a bearing on its quality.

Modes of Happiness

Marías accepts Ortega's claim that the traditional "felicitary occupations" could be summarized in four basic categories: hunting, dancing, racing, and social gatherings [tertulias]. But normally these activities belong only to what Marías refers to as "personal time" (somewhat equivalent to the American expression "quality time") and are excluded from compensated job time and the lost time we spend getting into and out of these modes. If it is true that in general we work fewer contracted hours than our ancestors did, we also lose more time waiting, driving, or attending to the increased bureaucratic complexity of our affairs.

Even though the modern era has been obsessed with the working portion of our time, Marías reminds us that normally our life begins within a felicitary setting. In childhood, nearly all time is personal, which may help account for our nostalgic attachment to it. Infants do not begin life by working but by playing, and even in the most penurious circumstances parents try to create a protected haven for their children. Adult duties and needs tend to erode this personal time, but this very reduction makes it all the more precious.

There seems little doubt that in our personal priorities we stand opposed to the modern fascination with work. We do not feel cheated if we miss a workday or spend less time in traffic, but we count it a personal loss if these categories invade our private time, perhaps curtailing our vacation or filling our weekends.

While not disputing Ortega's four basic felicitary occupations, Marías reminds us that in our time the list may need to be modified or perhaps supplemented. For example, today hunting still offers millions of hunters a "vacation" away from the usual toils and troubles of their humanity, but because of sheer numbers and limited access, others must find substitutes in such activities as sports. Reading is essentially a modern phenomenon, and the cinema and television are even more recent additions to the felicitary possibilities.

In any case, probably the supreme possibility of happiness has to do with the other sex, primarily in the modes of the intersexuate relationships described earlier. These include friendships, conversation, conviviality, flirting, and participation in the codes of conduct that regulate behavior in these areas. Naturally, love and sexual relations may occur within this intersexuate setting, but it is important to remember that, relatively and statistically speaking, they occur only rarely.

The Vital Balance

"To live," says Marías, "is to understand and to understand oneself."[25] Therefore, because we have no choice but to analyze our circumstantial world in order to live, life itself in its unitary, biographical wholeness turns out to be a comprehensive intrinsic theory and includes dimensions of clarity and insight that transcend the purely intellectual. Life can be told, and what is more, must be told in order to be understood. Thus, this intrinsic theory is narrative in its primary aspects. But it is important not to read a reductionalistic or condescending intent into this statement. We live life dynamically, that is, as vectorial movement occurring from within what we could call—using a neologism—an "installary" condition. But this does not exlude its multidimensionality, its ideal ranges and recurring uncertainties insofar as its component elements are concerned.

The analytical separation of these components is valid only in view of the unitary wholeness of life. In fact, it makes no sense to call them "components" in the first place unless we refer them to the unitary life they compose. Hence, just as it is erroneous to reduce life to its anatomical or biological structures, so it is at another level to interpret it compartmentally as profession, sex, economics, politics, and the like. "This may be done as long as we are interested only in a partial aspect of life. But if we forget the unitary connection from which they receive their reality, then we bring about the reduction of life to the level of things, which vitiates even the particularity of these zones and gives an erroneous view of them."[26] And inasmuch as happiness applies to life in its seamless entirety, this compartmentalization naturally works against our felicitary possibilities.

But we must distinguish between life in its integral wholeness and its temporal entirety, that is, between the biographical entirety of one's life at each given moment and the lifetime sum of its given earthly moments. There may be moments of happiness within a lifetime characterized by profound unhappiness, just as happiness can prevail in a life burdened by pain. The point is that these moments of happiness, fugitive and limited as they are, affect the entirety of our life at the time.

Here we find this principle which Marías repeats in one form or another throughout his writings: anything pursued abstractly at a remove from the unitary wholeness of our life is alien to our happiness. On the other hand, those pursuits that arise from our fundamental project of becoming ourselves and being true to ourselves move within the arena of happiness, making it possible or improbable.

This insistence on the centrality of unitary life emphasizes the dual hierarchies of importance that its particular dimensions and contents assume. First, there is a social hierarchy based on prevailing social norms, or *vigen-*

cias. At the same time, each person has a private hierarchy of importance. Always with individual exceptions, some eras are marked by relative harmony and minimal discrepancy between the social and the personal.

Historically speaking, the imposition and modification of this social hierarchy was a slow process that consolidated the world in such a way that it seemed predictable, true, and dependable, even though it may have been a harsh dependence. Now, however, this slow social mechanism has been replaced by artificially planned preferences that have little to do with private life or, for that matter, historical society.

This artifical acceleration of social mechanisms has brought about what Marías calls a "disorder of preferences," which in our time has vastly widened the margins of personal inauthenticity and jeopardized the relatively delicate balance of life. In order to maintain itself this vital balance requires of us an intelligence that precedes but also transcends pure intellect. In effect, it consists of an ability to know one's real feelings despite the accelerating social pressures to discount our own inclinations in favor of generic dispositions.

What Marías calls *educación sentimental* [education or refinement of sentiment] is needed to reassert or restore this personal life balance.[27] In recent times, this facet of human instruction has been ignored or vulgarized because it has not enjoyed social prestige or academic sanction. Seduced by the colossal, our time has no heart for the miniscule. The "education of sentiment" covers a range of activities, often modest and immediate but intensely human, which our stunted aesthetics and underdeveloped sensitivities do not normally appreciate or bother with. Yet as Marías concludes, "The scorn of the immediate, concrete, and objectively insignificant renders happiness impossible, because these are the contents that constitute it when they assume importance in life, when they hold a position in the effective system of our preferences."[28]

The Crisis of Expectations

Earlier, we observed attempts to gauge happiness by objective, collective, and statistical measures. The results are what Marías terms "macrohappiness," which is to say a "no man's happiness" rendered skeletal and unsubstantial by a lack of daily content and personal detail. This is warning enough not to mistake social predispositions for private happiness. Yet despite this acknowledgement we cannot overlook the telling fact that the structure of a historical epoch has a direct bearing on the intensities, expectations, and modes of individual happiness. Marías calls this historical setting the "... *material alveolus* in which are lodged the possibilities of happiness or unhappiness."[29]

Therefore, even though happiness is always a personal and ultimately immeasurable phenomenon, it reflects and presupposes a social configuration and thus a certain mean level of "macrohappiness." This level and the intensity with which it is pursued vary significantly among societies. The utilitarian society finds it expedient to substitute other things for happiness—general welfare, security, etc.—while the Romantic era idealized it and could not settle for anything less. In our own time, happiness may be privately desirable but in general it seems an inopportune topic for open discussion. Still other societies have no qualms about placing it first on their vital agenda.

The egalitarian spirit of our age decrees that all peoples and times are essentially the same and tends to dismiss differences as local ignorance. Naturally, this flies in the face of historical reality. As Marías reminds us, there are societies, as there are persons, that one could describe variously as bored, resigned, moderate, agitated, delirious, and even demented.

Instead of always creating harmony, egalitarianism may actually exacerbate hostilities. Despite what they say, people feel that their way of life is normal, and therefore all normal people ought to find it worthy of imitation. Deviations from this assumed norm are then seen as irrational, even criminal, aggressions against the egalitarian condition. The fact that other peoples feel the same way about their society creates a hostile and critical attitude. Ours, says Marías, is an extremely judgmental age.

All of which leads to the conclusion that human expectations of happiness and what Marías describes as our "tension toward happiness" are subject to wide fluctuations, and the same can be said for attitudes about misfortune. Beyond egalitarianism there emerges the vast variety of the world. In some societies, it would approach subversion not to be happy. Paradoxically, in secure societies that seek to mandate happiness for the masses and where in theory—though of course not in fact—everything is anticipated and provided for, there are formidable impediments to risking personal, unprogrammed formulas for happiness. The very proliferation of means characteristic of the modern welfare state may itself diminish the possibilities of personal happiness unless it includes freedom, leisure, and perhaps most important of all, an active desire for happiness.

If world wars marked the first half of the twentieth century, a paralyzing dread of war and universal catastrophe has characterized the second. Unlike what Ortega described as the "imperialistic" tenor of the nineteenth century, the prevailing mood of recent decades generally has been fearful and defensive. Above all, our age longs for protection and security, and it seeks this safety in colossal numbers. The swift rise of collectivism and macroeconomics has tended to displace the preeminence of private life. If personal life continues to be a sentimental priority, we think of economics as hard reality.

In the general mood of pessimism and fear that marked the Cold War era, the West came to suspect that despite unprecedented prosperity, technological advances, and relatively war-free security, this was perhaps "the worst

of all possible worlds."[30] The proof was everywhere: poverty, hunger, violence, injustice, and the like. But it was insufficient evidence for so substantial
a claim. As a rule, mankind has always been poor, and without exception has
always been exposed to dangers and always condemned to live in a harsh
world amid threatening and unfair circumstances.

As for human happiness, such attitudes have brought on a crisis of expectations. For many think that in such a world as ours one cannot be happy,
or at least that it is immoral to be happy if others are wretched. Nor are we disposed to wait, for ours is not a patient age. We are used to hearing the indig-
nant recounting of things mutilated and missing in our world. Perhaps it
would be better, Marías reminds us, to dwell less on what we lack and more
on what we have and what we can achieve with the always modest means that
timidly offer themselves up for our disposal. This implies an altered perspective, from which hope and anticipation pry open our closed horizons and
admit the possibility of happiness. But to be more precise, we find that we
must veer away from mere abstract ideals of happiness and pursue it into the
personal lives of men and women.

The Plot of Happiness

Happiness is anything but passive. Our vectorial installation causes happiness not simply to exist but to happen. (In English, the common root of
"happiness" and "happen" suggests their related dynamism.) Happiness is not
limited to a state of being but implies primarily a state of doing. We call the
sum of this doing living, and for this reason happiness exhibits the same attributes as life itself.

Both life and happiness appeal for perpetuity. To be alive and happy is
first of all to aim to go on being alive and happy. Thus we can say that one is
"installed" in happiness regardless of its subsequent instability. In other
words, happiness—and life—may end but this ending is external to their inner
vectorial and "installary" condition of projected continuity.

The vectorial character of happiness takes the experiential form of hopeful anticipation. And even though death (especially the death of loved ones)
looms as a possible threat to our happiness, it also gives time a dramatic structure by charging each moment with a rich and poignant sense of irretrievabil-
ity. Marías speaks of an "advance nostalgia" that comes over us in the midst of
happiness as we realize that this moment will not come again. Human time is
also invested with an odd mortality.

As we saw in Ortega's narrative of Soledad and "A," when happiness is
missing life exhibits the odd peculiarity of declining to a feebler level of reality. This decline is not simply a function of more pain or less pleasure but an
indication that we live, think, and love from only a fraction of our potential reality. On the other hand, happiness intensifies life; while it lasts we live mo-

ments of plenitude. During such moments, we escape our ordinary, persistent existence and catch a glimpse of that extraordinary life we recognize as our true self.

In some lives, this experience is likely, in others, improbable. We observe that some lives are well planned and executed, whereas others seem forever destined to disorder and misery. To put it figuratively but also biographically, some lives suffer from a rudimentary, unrealistic plot, while others flow nicely along a well-scripted storyline. This does not necessarily mean that our life plot must be complex in order for our lives to be happy. A very simple plot may be rich with extraordinary detail and exude a wealth of reality. While a plot of intricate twists and turns may prove to be trivially complex. Naturally, the generic components of our plot reflect the pressures of social norms, including the common notions of happiness, but the decisive element is our own imaginative creativity.

The degree of happiness, Marías tells us, has more to do with the way in which we imagine our life plot than with its range or level. The calm life may appear superficially to be monotonous if we fail to consider the degree of commitment to its fundamental passion. But in any case there is a more pernicious order of monotony: that experienced in an agitated life. The very "sound and fury" of such lives may cause us to think they are more interesting than a life of deep concentration, but if we observe closely we see how often this restlessness conceals the existential panic of the lost.

The frantic haste associated with this agitated boredom must not be mistaken for the truly dramatic life. Life is inherently dramatic insofar as our plot surpasses the generic and demands of us that we stake our lives on authentic personal causes. But this can hardly be said of those who crave excessive security, who feel no particular attachment to place or persons, and who are content to flow with the common tides. Nor is it likely that they will know happiness. "Happiness is a risk: he who exposes himself to being happy also exposes himself to being unhappy, and he who refuses to expose himself at all will be neither."[31]

The Personal Source of Happiness

All along, we have been trying to detach happiness from merely "objective" considerations so as to center it in what we could call our integral personal selfsameness. Unlike other aspects—fame, wealth, power, pleasure—which affect us in peripheral and partial areas of our life, happiness alone touches *us*. This quality makes it possible to speak of happiness in terms of the dramatic plot and its associated trajectories of which our life consists. Because it is a strictly personal matter, it comes as no surprise to hear Marías repeat that our principal source of happiness is other persons.

As we saw earlier, in the real circumstantial and social context of life to

speak of person is to include other persons. The very attributes of personhood—love, friendship, conversation, among others—call for the presence of
others. Children, for example, play a humanizing, personalizing role in the
lives of adults. Nevertheless, this does not mean that our inclination toward
others occurs easily or that it is easily sustained. The world presents formidable obstacles to human plenitude through its depersonalizing pressures, usages, and prohibitions against which there is no ready immunity. Yet,
according to Marías, this principle remains invulnerable: only those whom we
treat as persons can offer us personal happiness. And if this is true, then it follows that intense, fulfilling happiness is possible only in those human relationships defined by profound mutual intimacy.

Of course, persons also cause us the most painful forms of unhappiness.
They may disappoint us by their shallowness or deceit. We sense that they
have defrauded themselves and in doing so have defrauded us as well. But the
fault may lie in us. Perhaps we have not made the effort to know them, have
not been generous enough to credit them with hidden attractions. Most of all,
perhaps because of envy, shortsightedness, or hurt, we hasten to pronounce
them finished but deficient products, losing sight of the fact that as a "coming"
or "becoming" reality, human life is always penultimate and ever capable of
being more than it reveals. This deficiency becomes most apparent when we
view other persons as a means to serve our ambition and not as an end in
themselves.

This brings us once again, but from another angle, to the "amorous" or
"lovely" condition of life. "All personal relationships," Marías declares, "consist of the possibility of love in varying degrees and differing vectors which
may or may not come to fruition. In some cases it appears in an inverted form
as hatred, which is the aversion to reality, and primarily one's own reality."[32]

Within this amorous substratum, we discover that the person who offers
us the most happiness is the one we can love and thus the one who allows us
to fulfill our personal calling. Reciprocal love between persons who find in
each other an end and not simply a means offers the fulfillment of life, a fulfillment we know as supreme happiness. It is an irrevocable happiness, for
without it and without the beloved persons who make it possible, life is less
than life and we are less than ourselves. Thus, we desire—and require—this
love and these loved ones not for a time but forever.

The Sexuate Forms of Happiness

The supreme happiness we have been discussing is strictly personal. But
the persons we know are either men or women, and this means that despite a
common fund of similar and reciprocal attributes, happiness assumes two sexuate forms, masculine and feminine. Both must deal with certain features that

affect human life as such: uncertainty, neediness, ignorance, danger, and of course, mortality itself. But they confront these contingencies from their basic conditions of manhood or womanhood, which make sense only in defining reference to each other.

The masculine condition presupposes an essential enthusiasm for woman that invalidates all notions of sexuate neutrality. This is why it is always erroneous to exalt one's manhood at the expense of woman, as though man were a creature apart from or superior to woman. Naturally, the same could be said for woman in relationship to man. Both radical feminism and overweening masculinization are dead end frauds.

As we saw earlier, man is naturally weak, needy, and ignorant. Yet the masculine condition demands of him strength, sufficiency, and knowledge. In a word, man is an insecure creature who nevertheless must exhibit decisive strength and resolve, especially for those whom he cherishes. Man does not possess these attributes and yet, paradoxically, he has to possess them. In other words, he must make the difficult effort to achieve them. Being a man is primarily trying to be so. But this very effort, apparently so arduous and problematic, also brings a form of happiness that is proper to the masculine condition. In Marías's words: "When man strives toward all this, when he tries seriously and earnestly to be strong and certain and to know what to abide by, then he derives from the effort a certain happiness, and if successful he experiences a happiness peculiar to man as such and not to mankind in general."[33]

Man expresses much of this masculine effort vocationally and professionally. Historically speaking, men have tended to identify their profession or trade with their condition. It was not simply that one *had* a job as a butcher, for example, but rather that one *was* a butcher, shoemaker, etc.[34] This meant that men were "installed" vocationally in the formal sense in which Marías uses the term. Whereas men have nearly always been more or less dissatisfied with their work situation, the so-called "proletarization" of factory workers in the nineteenth century was a cause of unhappiness with their condition as laborers. Today men are much more likely to think of a particular job as a situation which they can and do change with relative ease. But perhaps not without paying a price; work that is revocable does not normally arouse the profound happiness associated with an irrevocable vocation.

With this mobility has come an increase in the level of competition and a corresponding decrease in what is sometimes referred to as the "comfort zone." There is a reluctance to relax and enjoy what we have earned, for fear that another will overtake us in the interval. Naturally, this attitude reduces the chances for happiness traditionally possible in the satisfactory pursuit of a profession.

This is related also to a rise in pernicious forms of ambition. Marías finds nothing censurable in the classic and possibly genetic desire of men to overcome circumstances and challenges. Indeed, meeting and overcoming such challenges has always been a particular source of happiness for men. Much more questionable, on the other hand, is a sort of unfocused and abstract ambition "to get ahead" and "make a name," but without a clear and achievable goal. Often the consequence is a restless and unhappy state of agitation that seldom has a ready cure because rarely does it have a ready cause.

The fact that men and women have tended to converge on this type of ambition in recent decades increases the likelihood of a new and unprecedented rivalry between them, especially now that both sexes are more likely than ever to work shoulder to shoulder at the same jobs. This situation leads not only to increased competition but also to a simplification in the sexuate relationships. The result for both sexes is to take each other for granted, and, having taken the measure of each other, to believe to their mutual misfortune that nothing further can be expected. And in a practical sense, so it is, for usually we see only what we foresee.

If happiness for man tends to be expressed as a function of what happens to him, for a woman it is more likely to relate to who she is. Given the fact that generally throughout history, women have shown greater kindness and higher levels of morality than men, Marías suggests as a reason the felt need to be happy with themselves, that is, within themselves. For whereas men customarily spend their lives caught up in the challenge of external or transcendental things with only sporadic visits to their inner life, women habitually dwell more immediately within themselves, and, we could add, more formally, at a superior level of immanence. And if all is not well within, then she cannot be happy with herself. In a sense her kindness is her defense; she must be good to others so as to be good to herself.

But it would be a mistake, Marías warns us, to think that while man acts woman merely abides. Man makes things; woman makes herself. This is why ambition in woman takes a different form; she is more likely to be ambitious about her person and her relationships than about power and the material stockpiling of things. Because of social pressures and example, she may adopt the masculine paradigms of ambition, but naturally they remain adoptive and therefore essentially alien to her feminine condition.

This is why Marías defends the notion of attractiveness traditionally associated with women. For feminine attractiveness means that woman is appreciated for herself and not for what she possesses. Therefore, when rivalry exists between women it tends to be deeper than the professional rivalries of men. For it is not so much a question of profession as of their very persons.

Yet despite her relative modesty, woman's attractiveness attracts, which means it is meant to be exhibitionistic so as to draw others to her. For many reasons, in our day this quality has fallen somewhat into disfavor, so that women sometimes make an effort to go unnoticed and neutral. Yet as we saw earlier, the feminine condition requires not that woman be attractive or beautiful but that she try to be so. Thus, in order to attract others woman first has to make the effort to be attractive, and this means that she has to give of herself. A certain generosity and altruism are implicit attributes of the feminine condition, which means that narcissism and miserliness are not. And because woman is predisposed to giving of herself she is also able to receive unto herself. She is natively hospitable, and radically so during pregnancy when she "houses" her tiny "guest." (Certain aspects of abortion take on interesting dimensions when viewed from this angle.) Subsequent motherhood is an extreme form of generosity, which, despite its toils and frustations, offers extreme forms of happiness.

In contrast, it is a source of considerable unhappiness for women to renounce generosity, as recent politically motivated feminism urges. Women have been told that their first priority is not to give of themselves but to demand their rights. But Marías reminds us that there also exists the right to be generous as a consequence and condition of being woman.

On the other hand, it would be wrong to restrict womanhood to the maternal. For all its importance, motherhood omits woman herself and the other dimensions of her life. These alternate considerations revolve around an implicit question: what does it take to make women happy? Marías ventures this response: "When a woman feels that she is being treated as a woman—which is not very often—she experiences a kind of plenitude which in its highest degrees may reach happiness."[35]

It is customary to think of the traditional injustice with which women have been denied or deprived of legal or social rights. But perhaps it has been a greater injustice, a personal injustice as it were, not to treat women for what and who they really are. Marías notes that many women happily endure considerable hardship provided they feel appreciated and especially if they feel they are truly loved, not as simply as females but as feminine persons.

It would be hard to exaggerate the human importance of woman's happiness. For feminine happiness is the key to all sexuate happiness. Therefore, as Marías contends, "If we men were smarter than we are, we would have tried always to see to it that women were happier than they are, because it is the primary condition for happiness in the world. To the degree that women are not happy, there is no happiness, and of course man cannot be happy either."[36]

Happiness and Human Mortality

Does death render all our happiness illusory? If we say we are happy, we really mean to say "we are going to be happy." For unlike things, life is not a static but an ongoing reality that is always going or coming to be. But since at the empirical level life is a closed structure that terminates in death, does this invalidate our hopes and our happiness? In the last analysis, if life is merely provisional, then so is our happiness, for the certainty of its ending erodes the quality of its duration. Marías puts it more bluntly: "We find ourselves in a very strange situation: happiness is necessary, but if it must end with death, then it is deceitful and illusory and possible only so long as I forget that I must die. Thus it rests on a fiction. If this were the case, then happiness would have an intrinsic element of falseness."[37]

Conversely, the hope of immortality, a hope that rises from the ongoing and open structure of life, acts as the possible guarantor of the persistence and consistence of our happiness. Yet this hope cannot free itself entirely from uncertainty, for it ranges too far from this life for us to summon incontrovertible proof from everyday experience. This is why Christian hope rests finally on revealed truth that transcends common dialectics. Therefore, even as we are thrust toward immortality we cannot be categorically sure it awaits us. This is why the Christian deals with fact but lives by faith.

But here we see also that the horizon we call death brings life into sharp focus. It forces choices upon us and neatly separates the trivial from the significant. The very limitation of our life lends an extraordinary value to time and what we do with it, or to be more exact, how we live it. Mortality forces us to choose for good what we want forever.

Our immortal hope links this life with the next, which gives a supreme importance to both dimensions of being. For what we desire in the next life must be chosen from this present mortal standpoint, and this means that this world appears to have been invested with a supreme purpose and importance. Thus, to scorn this present life is to repudiate the context and conditions of this exalted choosing. Of course, our hope and our choice may be in vain, but it gives us pause to realize that if so, we shall never know it. In the long run, skepticism, even when right, is never rewarded. On the other hand, faith is based on the premise that the world ultimately makes sense and has meaning.

Nevertheless, the modern age has long since declared the world to be absurd, alternately trivial and opaque, and, as Arnold wrote, "without help for pain." But this common rush to judgment ignores the inner "sense and sensibility" of life that cannot be wholly externalized but must be lived internally, which is to say intimately. This is why the ultimate core of personal intimacy cannot be breached even though it can be sensed. Yet life in some wise must be inherently transparent to itself as self-interpretation, else we could not manage to live it at all, could not project it in the first place, and would not even be aware of the world's alleged absurdity and indifference to our condition. This is the sense in which Marías speaks of life as an "intrinsic" and necessary theory of itself. To live is to be obliged to have a view and a preview of our general trajectory, and this vision, articulated in daily sequence, is the primary and truest meaning of "theory." In this sense and this meaning we find the prime condition for our probable happiness.

But there is an unhappines in contemplating the interruption of our projected life, and perhaps an even deeper unhappiness when we foresee the death of our loved ones. In this context, Marías declares: "We find that the urge for immortality is primarily the need for the immortality of *others*."[38]

Here, we pick up once again the theme of man's "amorous" being, which, according to Marías, constitutes the very root of the human condition. It is no coincidence, he notes, that intense love and immortal longings appear together. For to the degree that one loves, one needs to go on living beyond mortality so as to go on loving beyond death. Personal resurrection in the flesh, the most radical hope of immortal survival, appears to be rooted anthropologically in the amorous condition of mankind. The longing to experience everlasting life is first of all an altruistic acknowledgment of other cherished lives. On the other hand, it may be possible to trace the ease with which the modern age rejects immortality to the decline in the amorous condition of life.

Marias insists on the connection of this life and the next: ". . . as soon as the continuity and coherence is lost, the personal condition disappears."[39] This continuity must be understood as the continuity of life beyond death, but also as the prior connection between life and death in this world. The precise nature of this connection not only determines our view of death but of earthly life as well.[40]

This means that the projective condition of life in our circumstantial here and now must include *also* a projective anticipation of the next life. Recall how Marías has argued that the next life must be imagined at least enough to desire it. Thus, the drama that is our life includes other acts beyond the intermission of death. Death signifies the loss of many things, but perhaps not all will be lost, and possibly much will be gained in compensation. Religious thought has always dwelt preferentially on the things that one cannot take to the next life. But perhaps we have not thought enough about the dimensions of our life that *must* remain biographically with us, our memories, our plans, and especially our personal being and our loved ones. These must remain if life in the next world is to be "my life." (Whether they really remain is a different, though related, question.)

Generally speaking, we have thought of the next life as "residual" and "discarnate," to use Marías's description. If we are candid about it, we admit that in general our traditional views of the next world have been unappealing and grimly unhappy. Even though Christianity is replete with similar notions, the fault lies not in its teachings but in our lack of imagination. Christians confess that Christ was resurrected in the flesh and that he ascended bodily into Heaven, thereby offering us the assurance that we shall finally do likewise. Embedded in this belief is the implication that the next life will be a personal continuation, with a different empirical structure in which we shall know the plenitude of living without suffering our present deficiencies. This would be the ultimate and eternal fulfillment of Christ's promise of the "abundant life."

But what, other than sheer presumption, would lead us to think that we are able to project life beyond mortality, when previous generations would not even try? In earlier times, this formidable task would have been impossible. Now, however, for the first time in history, Marías argues, discoveries made in the Ortegan species of philosophy afford knowledge of what life is in its human, personal, and biographical dimensions. For the first time, he tells us, we have a controllable idea of "my life." Traditional thought, including theological thought, failed to identify the requisites of personal life that are universally applicable because they are universally necessary. Not until Marías have there existed the analytical, anthropological, and theoretical means to attempt to understand the plot-like structures of biographical life in this world, and perhaps in the next as well.

As we saw earlier, at best, perfect happiness is impossible in this world because our life is successive and lacks simultaneity. To choose is also to renounce, for life is successive and "eventual," and we must forego or cut short countless possible trajectories for want of "world and time." Thus, the life to come can best be thought of as the fulfillment of our authentic trajectories which in this life we have pursued or abandoned. And if this is so, then the life to come will be more truly, personally, and happily ours.

Our full happiness demands an unmutilated reality. But this is not simply our old mortal reality now guaranteed survival and safe from decay in its present form. We shall not be merely "saved" but raised to new life. For whatever God touches He exalts. Marías declares, ". . . our love of God will intensify our reality in such a way as to cause our love for His creatures to multiply. They will be more beloved and more interesting because we shall be overflowing with God's love for us and our love for Him . . ."[41]

Conclusion

The title of this chapter, "The Pursuit of Happiness," with an oblique salute to the celebrated phrase in the American Declaration of Independence, refers to the ongoing, protean life enterprise. It also implies that the pursuit is worthwhile, that it is alluring and enticing. Life is indigent and incomplete, and so is the happiness that attends our living. But the hope of life is for more and fuller life. Thus, we look forward with what Marías calls *ilusión,* a term that finds no easy translation in other European languages but which we may render loosely as "hopeful anticipation."[42]

Most of all, we live in hopeful anticipation in reference to those we love as a supreme function of our amorous condition. And since personhood is always an emerging and inexhaustible reality, this amorous task requires the continuation of this life in the next. We can be happy with nothing less.

This *ilusión*, or hopeful anticipation, is a way of taking full possession of our human and personal condition. We could say that it is a strategy for promoting happiness. Not that this possession is ever complete in this present world. Happiness is a "pursuit," which means among other things that it proves to be elusive and incomplete because our own reality is tentative and utopian. Happiness often dances out of reach and sight, and our hopes culminate modestly in parcels, moments, and glimpses of happiness. But we continue our pursuit, discovering as we do so another strain of happiness in the very expectation of finding it.

12

A LIFE RECALLED

On July 14, 1988, just past his seventy-fourth birthday, Marías began to write his memoirs. By August 26, he had finished the first book of nearly four hundred pages; by February 6, 1989, the second and even longer work; and, incredibly, by July 9, 1989, he had completed the third and only slightly shorter volume of his twelve-hundred-page *Una vida presente* [A Present Life], subtitled simply *Memorias*.

This breathtaking pace is itself a part of the story of his *Memorias*. Marías describes the experience: "I did not know whether I could write this book. As soon as I began, I realized that I *had* to write it. In almost complete solitude during the hot summer, without notes or papers, I wrote swiftly, swept along by the book itself."[1] Most likely, the volume of work produced in such a short time can be considered proof that his style and his life converge in the *Memorias* in a seamless and dramatic harmony. Juan López-Morillas adds this insight: "To the conceptual unity one must add necessarily the biographical unity. For what sets the philosophy of Marías apart is the fact that in addition to being a conceptual system, it is a temporalized and vitalized thought: in a word, biography."[2]

I have remarked elsewhere about this congruency in Marías's intellectual production. Unlike those who experience radical conversions that necessitate a renunciation or denial of whole phases of their lives, Marías exhibits no such painful embarrassments or abrupt swings in his. This consistency allows him to reprise his life autobiographically at its several junctures, as an actor might slip easily again into perfectly mastered roles. Marías has often stood at odds with certain circumstances; never, it seems, with himself. His posture in the *Memorias* is, however, far more than the common retrospective sentimentality of the mature for what they remember fondly—and perhaps erroneously—to be the gilded years of their youth. Instead, the reader has the impression that without remaining as he was in younger years, Marías has never stopped being who he was. Of course the objection could be raised that neither has anyone else. But many are only tentatively and uncertainly committed to themselves, only dimly aware of who they really are and forever condemned to second-guess their life. As Marías himself teaches, human life admits of degrees of authenticity and levels of falsification. In his case, the degree of fidelity to his original life project has remained uncommonly high.

The *Memorias* presented Marías with a new challenge as a writer. All his earlier books had been works of theory intended to describe the true configurations of reality. Now he was confronted with the prospect of *narrating* in novelesque fashion his own life and the interlaced lives of many others. Far from being an impressive tour de force, however, this venture into a new genre was really a function of the direction his philosophy had taken. Following his watershed work *Metaphysical Anthropology* (1970), in which he described the empirical structure of human life, Marías realized that henceforth his efforts would veer toward the consideration of concrete dimensions of this newly elaborated anthropology. It was a direction implicit in the Ortegan species of philosophy since the days of Ortega himself. Biography, novel, and memoirs were tempting possibilities. That he eventually settled for the latter was not, therefore, merely a matter of choice but an acknowledgment of the internal demands of his philosophy. As we saw earlier, this push toward the concrete, specific dimensions of life represented the third phase of his thought. Naturally, the supreme test of his method would devolve on the understanding of his own life. Philosophy itself, he tells us in his *Razón de la filosofía* [Reason of Philosophy], is always a personal matter, and whenever this condition has been overlooked or forgotten, philosophy has either declined to an abstract caricature of itself or been abandoned altogether.[3]

If style is the man, as Buffon wrote, in the *Memorias* it is at the same time an impressive case in point of Marías's doctrine that literary style has a revelatory value not unlike the physiognomic expression of a face. Modulated by generic "installation" in the circumstantial and historical world—nationality, culture, language, historical time, etc.—one's style is a visible or verbal expression, or in some cases misrepresentation, of a prevailing but variable personal life temper. Thus, style is, as Marías puts it, the "substratum" of all philosophical doctrine and, equally important, it allows us to gauge the degree to which a doctrine or a life has been rendered authentic. Vigorous, clear, and unlabored, the literary style of the *Memorias* exhibits a facility of expression by the author that can only come from a wholehearted solidarity with all dimensions of his doctrine. As Madariaga writes, "As in the case of Ortega, it can be said of Marías that his style reminds one of clear water that sparkles in its transparency." And he adds: "In him thought springs forth with such graceful facility that it seems that he is not saying anything new, and yet everything is new and happy."[4]

It is important to realize that even the most replete memoirs are at best sketchy. In a double sense they are marked by omissions. First, one forgets or perhaps chooses to ignore certain moments, names, and episodes. But even if one enjoys total recall along with the procedural freedom granted by a clear conscience, as Marías does, there remain those unrealized dimensions, relationships, and pathways that were possible but passed over at given moments of life. The road travelled acquires its full significance only if we consider also the other roads not taken. To use Marías's terminology, our definitive "trajectory" must be seen in the context of all our possible trajectories, realized or not.

At the same time, if we are subject to lapses of memory, we may also remember too much. This was the situation which confronted Marías. The problem was to keep the flood of memories inserted in what he calls a "complex and intricate concatenation." What he meant was that instead of straying anecdotally and extemporaneously, he had to stick to the dramatic structure of his life. Only by staying with his personal "plot" was he able to express his life in its historical and hierarchical reality. Indeed, only within this plotted sequence do we glimpse the way life appeared to him.

The *Memorias* tell the story of a Marías *desde dentro* ["from within"], which is to say within the drama of his life and circumstance as he saw and felt it. Marías is able to reconstruct the internal necessities and justifications of his life, yet at the same time this faithfulness to plot also saves him, if saving he needed, from the subjective self-indulgence so common in memoirs. It was personal proof that the system he had spent half a century developing and refining had passed perhaps the hardest test of all. No doubt this is why the reader senses in Marías the satisfaction of the great writer as he demonstrates a fine mastery of his themes.

Within this dramatic structure, the "protagonist" and his cirumstances surge forth with all their originality, urgency, and problematicity. His zest for life is contagious. The reader is swept up in an unfolding story rendered dramatic by the lively march of coming events. In the period covering the Spanish Civil War, for example, we are able to sense at critical moments the potential historical trajectories and celebrate wise choices or share consternation over erroneous decisions.

Marías does not "evoke" his past in the manner, say, of an Azorín, but instead restores or recalls it to "presence," so that it becomes virtually relived and relivable. He says of the experience: ". . . as I observed my life I found it to be *present*. But at the same time, it appeared before me in an orderly fashion with its connections in a complex and intricate concatenation."[5] Along with this presence is reborn the original eagerness to find out what tomorrow holds. Despite many things gone wrong, Marías does not rail against reality, does not yield to the temptation to condemn or discount what can be, or could have been. Even in the bleakest of moments we hear no anguished protest against the world's unfairness, no angry outcry over his situation, no whimperings of self-pity. He makes no ethical concessions to the second-rate, and this ethical resolve exerts in turn a powerful moral tug on the reader.

To use a uniquely Spanish term on which Marías has insisted so much, an *ilusión,* or "hopeful anticipation," permeates the *Memorias.* Things often go wrong, of course, but they begin from what poet Jorge Guillén calls a "well-made world"; the error of men's ways is always to be understood in reference to the possibility of being on target, what Marías would probably call with a more efficient Spanish expression *acierto.*

It would be presumptuous to try to restate the contents of the *Memorias.* It is unlikely that anyone could tell as well what he has already told. Hence the disproportionate brevity of these comments when compared to other chapters of this book. The intention is strictly complementary to what Marías himself has said about his life, the only possible advantage being a relative detachment that permits certain observations pertinent to his "philosophical story" and to our purpose in this writing.

Ortega considered it a moral imperative and an act of generosity to return to life what life has given us, but only after we have refined it through long and responsible meditation. But in order to give we must first take possession. Naturally, there is a form of possession in being itself, but the act of taking possession occurs only through the word, the *logos.* Man comes into his own—and comes into possession of his own—through language. This is why, says Marías, the radical aspects of human life are loquacious. We have heard it repeated many times in this book: human life must be told in order to be understood. And this is first true of our own life. What we cannot utter we do not really understand, and what we do not understand we cannot express, and what we cannot express is not fully humanized.

Memorias is a tale of immense energies and daunting problems. Marías emerged *persona non grata* from the Civil War. We saw earlier how the doors of the University were closed for good and access to the media denied him for many years. At best, his intellectual career seemed precarious. Because of this same official animosity, even his doctorate was withheld until 1951.[6]

This intellectual marginalization was precisely the fate Marías's enemies had wished for him. Yet in a paradoxical way it becomes apparent in *Memorias* that there have been notable if not altogether satisfactory compensations for these restrictions. Denied vocational access to the university in his own country, Marías turned to a larger world forum. If generations of students in Madrid were not permitted to benefit from his teaching, others in such faraway places as Yale, Indiana, Oklahoma, and Puerto Rico have been his pupils, and many of these have remained his friends and disciples.

Marías often speaks of the brilliance of University of Madrid in its halcyon days during the early thirties. There is no doubt that it was a very hard blow for him not to be able to help continue its intellectual splendor. Yet if he could not hold a professorship in Spain, he was able to devote himself all the more to his other essential vocation as a philosophical writer. Because of these early constraints and extended restrictions, Marías was not to experience the personal *éclat* and immediate national following of an Ortega. He comments at length on these circumstances in *Memorias* and offers ample facts for the reader to draw conclusions, one of which must surely be that if Marías himself was treated unjustly, so were the generations of students deprived of his teaching.

For earnest readers, many of those lost lessons survive in retrievable form in his writings. In this sense, his teaching was only deferred not denied. By narrating his own life, Marías also tells the broader tale of a historical epoch, and as we come to understand his story we also begin to understand the promises and lament the failures of a time that often seems incomprehensible, even, and perhaps particularly, to those who lived through it.

In *Memorias,* Marías takes "expressive possession" of his biography through personal adherence to the philosophical and anthropological doctrine he has spent his life developing. This is why he suggests that it may serve others as a broadly applicable method of biographical understanding. In this literal and personal way with himself as the "protagonist," he has obeyed with his characteristic generosity the Ortegan imperative to return to life in enhanced and purified state what life has given to him.

Memorias is part of a protracted effort by Marías to develop a comprehensive anthropology. Consider finally his own testimony: "Aside from their narrative significance as a real 'novel,' as I have conceived and carried them out, these memoirs are another step, and perhaps the greatest, in the series of efforts I have made to understand human reality."[7] This is why the *Memorias* must be understood not as an example of authorial self-indulgence but as an example of the responsibility, freedom, and devotion to truth that have always characterized his life and his doctrine. In a word, the *Memorias* represent an act of generosity by Marías. And we could add, intelligence. For as Marías has said himself, we think not with our minds only but with our life, and if we do not live generously we cannot really think intelligently.

Marías once observed that in his discovery of irreducible human life Ortega had discovered "a new continent" of philosophy. Perhaps the metaphor is too generous. Would it not be more accurate to say that Ortega undertook the voyage and reached the outliers of the new main? For it was Marías who first entered this unknown geography, plotted its empirical *mapamundi,* and, in the *Memorias,* described essential coordinates.

CONCLUSION:
A WATCH OVER MORTALITY

If it is true that the speculations of thinkers eventually translate into the public policies and general epistemological norms of peoples, then can we not conclude that the most grievous legacy of modern philosophy has been its failure to formulate an adequate anthropology? The genocidal wars and crude ideologies of the modern age usually are cited to support this thesis.

But there is a closer testimony of this failure in our local and private confusion over what constitutes right and wrong conduct, moral and immoral postures. We try to placate both the sacred and the profane and thus find ourselves stretched to the snapping point between irreconcilable images of human life. The more we bend in tolerance, the more unyielding the world becomes. Perhaps if we were more reflective, we might conclude that when all is said and done, philosophy is both deeply necessary and supremely risky, because all the ideas we live by can turn malignant. We know the process: it only requires malignant men.

Writ large, this anthropological failure may have rendered our societies too frantic, and some suspect now too uncivil, for harmonious life and yet too timid to consider substantial remedies. They fear the worst but place no trust in the best. The world of late has begun to wrestle with the gloomy conviction that far from being the measure of things good and beautiful, mankind will likely prove to be their ruination. Those who consider themselves most enlightened often take the dimmest view of our future. They decided some time ago that mere mischief defines the human condition.

It is true that an older optimism about humanity still lingers in political clichés and nostalgic pronouncements about our purported innate goodness and good sense. Yet the newer pessimism declares it passé and urges on us the embarrassing persuasion that human life has become too calamitous, too prolific, and thus too cheap to justify this old enthusiasm. The simple exuberance of life seems a social misfit in our dour time. Even as we still repeat the old refrain that people, particularly children, are our most precious resource, we are privately sure that the world has too much humanity. Many of the same people who struggle for more rights for mankind wish there were fewer men to exercise them. More and bigger is the general rule in every other sphere of our world; only when it comes to humanity do we argue that less is better.

All his life and in all his writings, Marías has confronted these two conflicting interpretations of human life. On the one hand, we find the Greco-Judeo-Christian anthropology. Twenty-five centuries ago the Greeks discovered human reality. Man, they reasoned, is someone who lives in both mind and body, who understands the world in one way or another, who embraces everything with thought and language, who is free and therefore responsible, who chooses his life ("as the archer chooses his target," said Aristotle), who may be good or evil, happy or unhappy, and who desires to go on living forever beyond death.

With the Greeks dawned the insatiable human curiosity about the world, so different from anything else on Earth, that gave rise to arts, ethics, science, academies, universities, manifestations all of their irrepressible calling to discover truth and beauty. (It is a telling fact that because of this Greek legacy of universal curiosity in the West, non-Westerners can pursue universally respected degrees in their particular culture in Western universities, but probably no Westerner could do the same in a non-Western university. Non-Western curiosity still appears to be limited largely to utilitarian and parochial interests.)

In time, this Greek brilliance merged symbiotically with the Judeo-Christian belief that man was created by an effusive act of the Creator's love and, unlike things, "in His image and likeness." Mankind is therefore "like" God (though not perfect or "godlike" despite that likeness). Still possessing the endowments inherited from the Greek mind, the Judeo-Christian also claimed a personal relationship with the divine Persons of the Trinity. For he was a *child* of God, and if child then *brother* or *sister* to all others, great and lowly, men *and* women.

The Judeo-Christian believes in faith that he is destined to personal resurrection. For God will call him by name and in that calling sustain his life forever. He will know and be known as the person he is. Redeemed by the sacrificial Christ and strengthened by the Paraclete, he is free and responsible. He can and must choose who he is to be forever.

If the Greeks transcended polytheism by sheer intellect, and came to think of God as the supreme mind and mover of the universe, the Judeo-Christian knew Him by revelation as the personal God whose unimaginable majesty and might were expressed to the believer as love, compassion, forgiveness, and salvation.

Because the Christian believed that in Christ ". . . lie hidden the mighty, untapped treasures of wisdom and knowledge," Greek learning, now sanctioned and refocused by Christian faith, was adapted to new forms and institutions, giving rise to yet another cycle of humanities: art, music, literature, and science. Learning rested on the foundational belief that all human life was precious to God and therefore worthy of supreme consideration. In time this exalted Judeo-Christian view of human life gave rise to a whole cycle of humane codes of civil governance, intellectual enlightenment, and individual rights.

But even as what Marías calls the "first theory" of human life was reaching its zenith in the Renaissance, the "second theory" was preparing to supersede it. Just as in the new cosmography the earth was removed from its privileged place at the center of the universe, so in the new anthropology a movement began to strip man of his exalted status in the general economy of reality.

It took hundreds of years, but by the end of the nineteenth century the deconstruction of human reality was essentially complete. Like a once privileged aristocrat now fallen from grace, human reality was reassigned to a lowly zoological order and now stood in democratic classification with other animals. Mind, soul, and invention were defined as evolutionary by-products. Mother Nature replaced God the Father as the creator of life, and man, who once had stood only a little lower than angels, now rose no higher than apes. He was an animal, or alternately a thing—difficult and peculiar, to be sure— among other animals and other things. The proper question was no longer *who* is man?, but *what* is man? By the Nazi era in our century, we had a definitive answer: it was said that individual human worth amounted to a few dollars worth of chemicals.

Naturally, in order to achieve this reduction great portions of human reality had to be simplified. Hence the deterministic appeal to the collective, the unconscious, or the primal. The old utilitarian maxim, the greatest good for the greatest number, was reinterpreted to mean the greatest good *is* the greatest number. Marxism, psychologism, Darwinism were logical and aggressive subsets of this general theory of human life.

The second theory of human life denies *a priori* any transcendent destiny for mankind and presupposes instead that *whatever is lower is truer.* Hence the modern resentment of superiority and the mania to reduce the excellent to the ordinary, the advanced to the primitive, the intelligent to the torpid. By stages, individual rights became subservient to group rights, as the demands of the masses began to overwhelm the leadership of the gifted.

For his part, Marías has always looked on this humanistic reductionism as a primary phenomenological transgression, for nothing we see, nothing we sense in human life gives us the intellectual and moral right to demean personal reality. Yet it would be a mistake to interpret the philosophy he has spent so many decades developing to be solely or even primarily a reaction against the perceived errors and consequent disenchantment of modernity. Both Ortega and Marías have stated in their writings that by their reckoning the modern age was already over by about 1900, by which they mean that its creative force had dwindled and that a new order was called for. Naturally, its presence, moribund or otherwise, would linger indefinitely in deficient and probably grotesque forms. First Ortega and then Marías responded to the call to begin shaping the intellectual framework for the age to come.

But others—Kierkegaard, Nietzsche, Unamuno, for example—had also sensed the waning of modernity and had devised their own strategies against its excesses. Kierkegaard's *Either/Or,* Nietzsche's *Thus Spake Zarathustra,* and Unamuno's *The Tragic Sense of Life* were typical expressions of the revolt against rationalism. For Ortega, who first basked then labored under the shadow of Unamuno during his earlier years, these melodramatic and popular versions of *Lebensphilosophie* were particularly disturbing. Their objections to rationalism were well-founded, and this justification endowed the irrationalists with considerable rhetorical power. The problem was that they were unable to transcend the rational-irrational dichotomy, which meant that instead of overcoming modernity they might cause it to linger in its alter ego form as mere irrationalism long after its creative life functions had ceased. We saw how Ortega's *Meditations on Quixote* constituted both a response to Unamuno and an outline of the new species of narrative, historical reason, that henceforth was to be the Ortegan instrumentality of inquiry.

By Marías's time, this early alarm over Unamunean irrationalism had subsided, translated in part into a concern for a world embroiled in virulently irrational wars. Anyway, Unamuno's doctrine was too much a property of his own personality to be taught to others. Consequently, he left no direct disciples, though there have been generations of admirers. From a greater historical distance and with a calmer disposition in the matter than his mentor Ortega, Marías proposed to "save" Unamuno rather than confront him, that is, to sort out his genius and preserve what was sound in his doctrine.

For Marías, it was never a matter of simply supplanting one doctrine with another. We shall not cease to be "modern," for we shall continue to pursue knowledge by the scientific method and to think by means of Cartesian reason. And we shall always be in some wise Medieval, Classical, and Judeo-Christian so long as we incorporate the truth of these legacies in our way of thinking and living.

On the other hand, neither can we confine ourselves to modernity. We come from it, which means that we are heading somewhere else. Nor, as Marías sees it, does the task at hand consist of returning to early versions of the "first theory" of human life; rather, it is to explore with enhanced methodologies and insights the new philosophical "continent," so that life may be the richer. For after all, it is not really a question of metaphorical continents but of how well and happily we and our loved ones live and understand our life.

All the efforts Marías has made in a now-lengthy life have been to keep a watch over our common mortality, which by a curious twist of meaning also means our life. The modern age saw very clearly that our bodily life is a closed mortal structure and in rationalistic fashion concluded that physical death was the end of our story. By denying immortality as a human possibility, the moderns stripped life of its final enchantment. If they succeeded in convincing most men that immortality was a vain hope, they eventually failed in their manifold campaign to satisfy mankind with substitute dreams. Intransigent to our final hopes, the world naturally turns indifferent to our deeper life. Through science, modern men gained mastery over the material world, but they could not remedy the loss of their soul.

Perhaps there is more to our story after all. Wordsworth cites a ". . . faith that looks through death." Marías shares this faith, but as a philosopher he also gives a reason, a new kind of reason, for the plausibility of personal transcendence. We are mortal and we die, yet we discover biographically and structurally that our life opens not to mere biological destruction but to indefinite projectiveness. We can imagine and dream and discuss rationally our own physical death, but this does not stop us from projecting our imagination beyond that moment to see what the world will be like afterwards. To the chagrin of the ages, our bodily life contains death; it is mortal. Yet to contain something is to be in some sense greater than that something. The minimal paradigm would be this: death happens but life contains it, exceeds it, and goes on. Each portion of this statement refers to what Marías has been saying, and the full significance depends on this context.

The drama and movement of life points to—but naturally does not prove—this personal continuation. The world shows itself to be not a fixed point but a scenic circumstance that hinders and helps our dramatic journey through it. Nowhere can we stop and make our life a static rest, for our destiny moves always before us, perhaps as annihilation—who can deny the possibility?—but also as a reasonable anticipation, as a final hope arising from the restored splendor and mystery of our radical life. In this world and time we are eccentric, at odds with things and in search of an excellent center so as to be whole and wholly ourselves. Yet there is surrender in our effort, and every choice of things good is also a forfeit of things worthy. Through experience, we discover this truth: we are never quite ourselves here, never quite fulfilled, never completely happy.

Here, finally, we come to the ethical core of our life. As Marías sees it, we move not in the ambit of the good, as traditional ethics has claimed, but with our view fixed on the best.[1] Because ethical (and unethical) conduct is possible only within the possibility of freedom and free choice, it follows from Marías's argument that our life is intrinsically moral. Thus, no ethical system can remain a mere set of rules; rather it fleshes out into reality only as freedom exercised, as responsible spontaneity of action. In other words, everything we do appears within an awareness that we could have done something else. Hence, we live with the possibilities of error and repentance. Furthermore, in the light of what has been said, this is meaningful only if we go beyond the abstract and analytical planes of life and come to the empirical world of men and women. For this reason, it is possible to speak of moral and immoral conduct only within our anthropological and biographical condition as persons, that is, within the forms of actual installation such as bodiliness, worldhood, and our social and sexuate condition. This is why Marías believes true morality to be the intensification of life, and by implication the intensification of things human. Far from codified rules, negative dogmatisms, and the dull, craven forms of *vita minima* of our time, true morality, and thus the best of our available choices, consists of the maximum affirmation of personhood. On the other hand, immorality could be defined in this context as the negation of personhood—human and divine.

Finally, it must be said that if Marías's exploration of human personhood is far advanced by contemporary standards, it is also far from finished. The zoological vision of man still fascinates most contemporary thinkers, almost hopelessly so it seems in Anglo-American circles, and only timidly do we begin to approach again the great matters of human transcendence. Among other possibilities, Marías's thought offers the hope, or so I believe, of engendering new species of theological thought. But the chances of this coming to pass depend after a certain point not so much on the personal efforts of Marías as on the willingness of other thinkers, particularly theologians, to acknowledge and put to good use his discoveries.

And there are other themes in Marías's work which, if cultivated, could shed much light on contemporary dilemmas. Consider, for instance, the almost untapped resources in both Marías and Ortega for new methodologies of literary criticism. The sociological possibilities of his and Ortega's social theories remain untested outside of a few Spanish thinkers. Almost the same could be said for establishing a general aesthetic theory.[2]

But in all these areas and others not included, the fundamental step has already been taken: his work, still unfolding, is available, the truth as he understands it has been spoken and proclaimed, and thus its liberating action begins, which means that in the long run it will make itself heard in many unforeseeable good ways. Probably this is why, in the face of our world's terrific falsehoods, Marías himself remains unmoved by their allure. Unlike Aladdin's mother, he has never been tempted to exchange real magic lamps for worthless substitutes.

Not that his way has been easy. With this line of thought Marías has assumed one of the most audacious and humbling of human tasks. For error and possible failure can never be discounted. Then why make the attempt? Why philosophize about such things in the first place? Because, as Marías sees it, this is the direction, and destiny, and splendor of our mortality. For the sake of happiness and at the risk of failure, it is worth an alert watch, even a lifetime watch, for ourselves certainly, and even more for those we love.

NOTES

Introduction

1. In "Compás," *Nuestra Andalucía,* p. 12. A collaborative work by Julián Marías (theoretical commentary), Alfredo Ramón (water colors), and Enrique Lafuente Ferrari ("compás" [tempo]).

2. In discussing Marías's links to French philosophy, Alain Guy describes the Latin and Mediterranean spirit as ". . . fait de souci de clarté, de sens de la mésure, de la précision rationelle, d'amour de beau . . ." [consisting of a concern for clarity, a sense of moderation, a rational precision, (and) a love of beauty]. This and subsequent translations, unless otherwise noted, are by the author.

3. ". . . la filosofía es *teoría dramática,* intrínsicamente personal y biográfica; desligada de la vida efectiva del filósofo, no es inteligible; y, si se toman las cosas en rigor, *no es filosofía.* La filosofía no tiene sentido más que como algo que mana de una vida concreta, con una *libre forzosidad* que sólo la teoría de la vida humana hace inteligible" (*Ortega. Las trayectorias,* p. 23).

4. "La indiferencia por lo lejano ha sido sustituida por un vivo sentido de *solidaridad* con todo lo humano" (*Razón de la filosofía,* p. 209).

5. Patrick Dust speaks of the "realistic reenchantment of the world" in Ortega as a possible means of transcending modernity. However, neither Ortega nor Marías would agree that the world was ever devoid of essential enchantment, even though the various philosophies from positivism to existentialism to deconstructionism came to such conclusions. Marías says simply: ". . . reality is marvelous. Its inexhaustible richness presents itself before the eyes of him who dares to look upon it . . ." (. . . que la realidad es maravillosa. Su inagotable riqueza se presenta ante los ojos del que se atreve a mirarla . . .) (*Razón de la filosofía,* p. 256). For Dust's commentary on Ortega see "On Reading Ortega for our Time," *Ortega y Gasset and the Question of Modernity,* pp. 50–66.

6. See Eugen Rosenstock-Huessy, *Out of Revolution* (Norwich, pp. 453 ff.; 594 ff.), and Julien Benda, *Trahison des clercs.* Ortega's views on intellectual desertion are most spectacularly summarized in his *Revolt of the Masses.*

7. "Hay que *revivirla, repensarla* . . . es decir, incorporarla a la propia vida, verla desde la perspectiva irrenunciable de ésta, a la altura del tiempo de cada cual. Esta es la única forma de fidelidad libre que permite la apropiación de la creación

ajena, que deja de ser ajena al seguir viviendo en los demás" (*Ortega. Las trayectorias,* p. 506).

Chapter 1

1. The most complete biographical account of Marías's life is his own three-volume work *Una vida presente. Memorias.* Other helpful summaries are Juan del Agua's "Introducción," *Homenaje a Julián Marías;* Juan Soler Planas's "Perfil biográfico-intelectual de Julián Marías" [Biographical-Intellectual Profile of Julián Marías], *El pensamiento de Julián Marías;* Anton Donoso's "Biography," *Julián Marías;* and Domingo Henares's "Apunte biográfico de Julián Marías" [Biographical Note on Julián Marías], *Hombre y Sociedad en Julián Marías.*

2. "No podía ser profesor—una vocación vivísima, irrenunciable—en las instituciones oficiales españolas. Podía, acaso, escribir algún ensayo en las escasas revistas que podrían aceptar a una persona en mis condiciones; los periódicos me eran inaccesibles—lo fueron por doce años, hasta 1951—. ¿Qué quedaba? Mi vocación filosófica era imperiosa; no menos, la de escribir. La única salida auténtica era escribir libros de filosofía" (*Memorias,* I, p. 292). On the basis of a false accusation made by a former friend and classmate, Marías was arrested and imprisoned May 15, 1939. He was released provisionally—and, as it turned out, permanently August 7, 1939. His comments about his prison experiences are included in *Memorias,* I, pp. 267–78.

3. "Tomé en serio sus consejos: reedificar España, levantar de nuevo la propia vida" (*Memorias,* I, p. 281).

4. "En rigor, cuando pude verdaderamente volver a escribir lo tuve que hacer desde la más profunda intimidad, no desde las zonas periféricas de la persona, sino desde su mismo centro, después de entrar en últimas cuentas conmigo mismo. Podría decir que nunca había sido tan radicalmente escritor como desde que recuperé la posibilidad de serlo, en estos últimos años" (*Memorias,* III, p. 151).

Chapter 2

1. In this context, the following comment by Marías is illuminating: "Ortega had read my writings, except my book on Unamuno, which he always refused to read. 'I cannot read a book by you on Unamuno,' he told me. 'For you he is a theme. You do not realize that I have spent my life struggling with him. It would affect me too much'" (Ortega había leído mis escritos, salvo el libro sobre Unamuno, que nunca quiso leer. "Yo no puedo leer un libro suyo sobre Unamuno—me dijo—; para usted es un tema; no se da cuenta de que me he pasado la vida luchando con él; me afectaría demasiado") (*Memorias,* I, 351 [my translation. Unless otherwise indicated, subsequent translations are by the author.]). Elsewhere, Marías writes: "As for *The Tragic Sense of Life* it is ev-

ident that it signified the most intense and vibrant formulation of irrationalism, the most urgent, energetic, and penetrating opposition between reason and life. An impassioned, cordial book, full of insights and truths and of enormous persuasive power, it was capable of launching Spanish thought along a pathway that to Ortega seemed closed. It was the most forceful and unavoidable challenge to the certainties in which little by little Ortega was beginning to establish himself. I believe that the impact of *The Tragic Sense of Life* was one of the strongest stimuli that 'precipitated' the personal philosophy of Ortega" (En cuanto al *Sentimiento trágico de la vida* es evidente que significaba la formulación más intensa y vibrante del irracionalismo, la oposición más apremiante, enérgica y aguda, entre la razón y la vida. Libro apasionante, entrañable, lleno de aciertos y verdades, de enorme fuerza persuasiva, capaz de lanzar al pensamiento español por un camino que a Ortega le parecía cerrado. Era el más energico reto, el insoslayable *challenge* a las evidencias en que poco a poco empezaba a instalarse Ortega. Creo que el impacto, del *Sentimiento trágico de la vida* fue uno de los más fuertes estímulos que "precipitaron" la filosofía personal de Ortega) (*Ortega. Circunstancia y vocación,* p. 335).

2. Even though Unamuno did not carry the debate with Ortega and rationalism beyond the positions taken in 1912–14, others have attempted to link his name with more recent versions of irrationalist postmodernism. In his *Miguel de Unamuno: Bipolaridad y síntesis ficcional. Una lectura posmoderna,* Gonzalo Navajas claims to find important similarities between Unamuno and the deconstructionism of Jacques Derrida, Paul de Man, Wolfgang Iser, and others. The reasoning is indeed "irrational" and not the least convincing.

3. "En 1914–16 posee Ortega el núcleo de su filosofía. Su expansión, dilatación, articulación, serán la obra del resto de su vida, de cuarenta años de esfuerzo creador" (*Ortega: Las trayectorias,* p. 122).

4. See Chapter 4, "The Generations of Marías," for a generational interpretation of the Generation of 1898 epoch.

5. These are the predominant themes of Ortega's *El tema de nuestro tiempo* (1923), included in *Obras completas,* III, pp. 141–203. It should be noted, however, that in his extended analysis of Spain, *España invertebrada,* Ortega himself did not make use of the historical reason on which Marías has insisted. In this sense, the latter's *España inteligible* may be seen as a corrective to what he saw as Ortega's failed analysis. See Chapter 9, "Understanding Spain."

6. ". . . la fenomenología no fue para nosotros una filosofía: fue . . . una buena suerte" (*Obras completas,* VIII, p. 42). Here Ortega associates himself with his German classmates Nicolai Hartmann and Heinz Heimsoeth and makes clear their dissatisfaction with the neo-Kantianism imposed on them at Marburg by Paul Natorp and Hermann Cohen. I have traced Ortega's subsequent break with Husserlian phenomenology over the issue of "bracketing" (*epoche*). Ortega, and later Marías, argue that life does not reduce to Cartesian consciousness and cannot be set aside for the convenience of prior meditation but must be lived in its always immediate and urgent emergence.

See "Husserlian 'Reduction' Seen from the Perspective of Phenomenological 'Life' in the Ortegan School" (*Analecta Husserliana,* Vol 36 (1991), pp. 371–85); and "Phenomenological 'Life': A New Look at the Philosophic Enterprise in Ortega y Gasset" (*Analecta Husserliana,* Vol. 29 (1989), pp. 93–105).

7. "Al hacerme la ilusión que *quito* la posición de mi anterior 'conciencia primaria' no hago sino *poner* una realidad nueva y fabricada: la 'conciencia suspendida,' cloroformada" (*Obras completas,* VIII, p. 256).

8. ". . . en suma, *la vida* en su incoercible e insuperable espontaneidad e ingenuidad" (*Obras completas,* VIII, p. 53).

9. "De hecho, inevitablemente, las cosas aparecen *en la vida.* Mi vida es el área o ámbito en que encuentro todas las cosas, e incluso a mí mismo en cuanto hombre, realidad radicada en mi vida como realidad radical" (*Razón de la filosofía,* p. 59).

10. See Ortega, *Meditaciones del Quixote,* pp. 321 ff. A more extensive discussion of perspectivism is to be found in his "La doctrina del punto de vista" (*El tema de nuestro tiempo,* [*Obras completas,* 111], pp. 197–201).

11. For an illuminating discussion of Ortega's views on modernity see Rockwell Gray, *The Imperative of Modernity: An Intellectual Biography of José Ortega y Gasset.* Among other things, Gray explains (pp. 16–20) Ortega's notable polemic with the nineteenth century by pointing out that to Ortega the recent past had lost many of the virtues and exacerbated the vices of the modern age.

12. "La vida humana es estrictamente personal, no un *que* sino un *quien,* algo proyectivo—en expresión mía *futurizo*—, real e irreal a la vez. Es drama, lo que yo hago con las cosas para ser quien pretendo ser" (*Razón de la filosofía,* p. 103). Although this and similar statements are arguably *implicit* in Ortega's writings (in *El hombre y la gente* and *El tema de nuestro tiempo,* to my knowledge, nowhere in his works are they formulated with the rigor Marías gives them.

13. Juan López-Morillas, *Intelectuales y Espirituales,* pp. 219–20.

14. "Ortega ist alles andere als ein blosser Schuler and Ableger oder Fortsetzer der deutschen Philosophie. Er hat sie als Reiz in sich aufgenommen, von Leibniz bis Husserl, von Kant bis Scheler, wobei ich Reiz im physiologischen Sinne nehme. Der Reiz provoziert eine Reaktion, eine Antwort des Organsystems. Ortegas Denken ist durch den Zusammenstoss mit der deutschen Gedankenwelt zu sich selbst gekommen." (*Ortega. Merkur* [Mai 1949], p. 419).

15. "En esos ocho años en que no lo vi ni recibí orientaciones suyas, en que me quedé solo con sus libros, los cuadernos de notas de su cátedra, sus recuerdos, en que tuve que movilizar mi pensamiento personal, . . . Cada día me iba sintiendo más hondamente instalado, a nivel distinto, en una filosofía repensada, revivida, prolongada hacia las direcciones a que mi propia vocación me llevaba" (*Ortega. Circunstancia y vocación,* pp. 30–31).

16. *Obras,* VIII, pp. 530–31; English version from *Philosophy as Dramatic Theory,* p. 105.

17. "Geometría sentimental," Vol. II, *Obras completas,* pp. 471–72.

18. "La 'dramatización' de este pasaje es la forma teóricamente adecuada de 'vivificación' de la doctrina" (*Ortega: Las trayectorias,* p. 148).

19. "Nos sentimos individuales merced a esta misteriosa excentricidad de nuestra alma. Porque frente a la naturaleza y espíritu, alma es eso: vida excéntrica" ("El alma como excentricidad," *Vitalidad, alma, espíritu, Obras completas,* II, p. 469).

20. "¿Y no es esto—la mujer como norma—el gran descubrimiento de Dante?" (*Obras completas,* III, 320).

21. ". . . exigir la perfección al hombre" (*Obras completas,* III, 330).

22. "Bastaría para ello tomar en serio la idea de *proyecto* y llevarla a sus últimas consecuencias cuando la vida individual está irremediablemente ligada a otra, también en su plena individualidad. Esto requeriría un uso a fondo de la *razón vital.* Pero ése es precisamente el gran hallazgo filosófico de Ortega: la teoría que sólo se constituye como tal precisamente en su ejercicio, en su función de *dar razón* de las diversas realidades. . ." (*Ortega: Las trayectorias,* p. 138).

23. In his meditation on the question of God Marías notes that the traditional insistence on intelligence and rationality may be a case of "professional distortion" by theologians, philosophers, and intellectuals: "But if we look closely at things we see that man is defined by a strange and primary *amorous* condition in which his manner of confronting reality and projecting his life consists. If to this we add the Christian view that God *is love* this dimension stands out in both instances in an extraordinary way" (Pero se se miran de cerca las cosas se ve que el hombre está definido por una extraña condición *amorosa,* que es primaria y en la que consiste su manera de habérselas con la realidad y de proyectar su vida. Si a esto se añade que el cristianismo dice de Dios que *es amor,* esta dimensión aparece con extraordinario relieve por ambas partes) (*Razón de la filosofía,* p. 291).

24. *Philosophy as Dramatic Theory,* p. 301.

25. In "Love and Human Finalities," "In Consideration of Women," and "The Pursuit of Happiness," Chapters 7, 10, and 11, respectively.

26. ". . . *mi* vida aparece desde luego como convivencia con 'otras vidas', y por esto me descubro como *yo* frente a un *tú,* tropiezo con el carácter *disyuntivo* de la vida (ser ésta *o* ésta *o* ésta), y esto remite a una nueva noción, 'la vida', que no es una especie o género, sino *la vida de cada cual.* Resulta, pues, que *mi vida* como realidad implica una 'teoría intrínseca', sin la cual no es posible, una interpretación y proyección imaginativa de sí misma como *tal vida*" (*Razón de la filosofía,* p. 25).

27. "¡Grave olvido, mísera torpeza, no hacerse cargo sino de unas pocas circunstancias, cuando en verdad nos rodea todo!" (*Obras completas,* I, p. 564).

28. "Tras el momento inicial, el filósofo encuentra que hay una filosofía, pero que, por uno u otro motivo, no le basta; tiene que hacer *otra*. La suya está definida por una relación de *alteridad*. Parte de una filosofía existente, pero precisamente para apartarse de ella y buscar otra. Para hacerlo así, no se olvide, tiene que tener presente la anterior y comprobar su insuficiencia" (*Razón de la filosofía*, p. 61).

29. Because authentic philosophy is a function of dynamic life, to think, for Marías as it was for Ortega, is to have to go on thinking. In one of his latest writings Marías observes: ". . . philosophy can never be an accumulation of results, as occurs in other kinds of knowledge. It must be renewed over and over, in a personal way, although also specifically in essential continuity" (*Razón de la filosofía*, p. 293).

Chapter 3

1. "Julián Marías es uno de los españoles que más firmemente decidieron no renunciar a los hallazgos de una España que los hombre del 98 comenzaron a desplegar. Su vasto esfuerzo intelectual va dirigido a dar cuerpo a una posibilidad española, . . . en la línea de una tradición que, desde nuestro tiempo, bien podemos ya calificar de clásica" (*Cinco aventuras españolas*, p. 191).

2. ". . . constantes ajustes de la filosofía o la amistad, y siempre proyectos, proyectos, proyectos" (*Ortega: Circunstancia y vocación*, p.31).

3. "A mí me parece importante, me parece necesario, ir más allá de los dos, justamente plantear el problema, el problema de Unamuno—que no sólo es suyo—a la luz de los recursos intelectuales que debemos principalmente a Ortega" (Lecture delivered August 12, 1973, in Soria [my italics]).

4. In addition to earlier mention of the theme in 1914 (*Vieja y nueva política*), 1917 (*Obras completas*, III), and 1922 (*Obras completas*, VI), Ortega's principal writings on the theory of generations include "La idea de las generaciones," *El tema de nuestro tiempo* (1923); "La idea de la generación," *En torno a Galileo* (1933); and *Papeles sobre Velázquez y Goya*. (The work on Velázquez was first published in German in 1943 with an introduction by Ortega in that language. The combined works appeared in Spanish in 1950 [*Obras completas*, VIII].) Major writings by Marías on the generations theory include *El método histórico de las generaciones*, 1949 (translated into English [*Generations: A Historical Method*], Italian, and Portuguese; amplified several times, most recently in 1989); *La estructura social: teoría y método*, 1955 (translated into English as *The Structure of Society*), *Literatura y generaciones*, 1975. The applied (or implied) theory appears in many of his works, including *La biografía de la filosofía*, 1954; *La España real*, 1976; *La justicia social y otras justicias*, 1979; *España inteligible*, 1985; and *Cervantes clave española*, 1990. The study by Jaime Perriaux, *Las generaciones argentinas* (Buenos Aires, 1970), is an impressive attempt to apply the generational method to Argentinean society.

5. "Como la teoría de las generaciones es intrínsecamente metódica, esto quiere decir que se modifica y enriquece al contacto con la realidad histórica-social. Es

siempre la realidad la que decide, es ella la que impone las rectificaciones si son necesarias, la que reclama los complementos de una teoría siempre en desarrollo, que no es sino un instrumento para aprehender y dominar conceptualmente esa misma realidad" (*Literatura y generaciones*, p. 179).

6. ". . . ha desarrollado muchos de los temas de Ortega sólo iniciados o insinuados en los escritos o en las ensenanzas de éste . . ." (*Diccionario de filosofía*, Section "Marías").

7. In a moment of obvious exasperation over the carelessness with which the generations concept was being used in 1949, Marías remarked: "It is as if the theory had been conceived on Sirius or Alpha Centauri rather than in Madrid!" (*Generations: A Historical Method*, p. 150).

8. *Generations: A Historical Method*, p. 133.

9. What may appear to us to be fairly constant has varied considerably over the ages. Montaigne, for instance, believed that thirty-three was the average life span (as it may have been in the sixteenth century) and that by the age of twenty "our souls . . . promise all that they will be able to do." But what seems to set Montaigne and the ancients most apart from us was their forthright expectation of death and the idea that extended life was a rarity. Montaigne was of the opinion that regardless of one's age, to reach it was a rarity, for most did not. To die in old age of natural causes, he goes on to say, is the rarest of deaths and therefore the least "natural." Compare this attitude to our modern notion that life may be prolonged indefinitely and that death is somehow a statistical "accident." For Montaigne's comments see "De l'aage," *Essais*, Livre Premier, Chapitre LVII).

10. "Paradójicamente, el hombre puede poseerse a lo largo de su vida y ser él mismo porque no se posee íntegramente en níngun momento de ella" (*Razón de la filosofía*, p. 149).

11. *Generations: A Historical Method*, p. 71.

12. ". . . aprehende la realidad en su conexión" (*Obras*, II, p. 171).

13. Juan Zaragüeta and Rodríguez Aranda (among others) have criticized the claim by Ortega and Marías that their approach transcends the old dichotomy of realism and idealism. Zaragüeta notes, for example, that "Marías takes pride in resolving this problem (Realism-Idealism) 'with magical simplicity,' by including in reality the cognitive subject itself which with the object constitutes life. . . . However, the matter does not appear to be so simple. Because the coinciding of the subject with the object is rigorously [certain] in the perception or *sense-based* intuition of the latter by the former, in mutual presence in time and space. But this coinciding is gradually released in the *imaginative* representation of objects spatially absent or temporally past or future, in conditional objects (those that 'would happen') and merely possible, in fictitious objects, in ideal objects, i.e., supraspatial and supratemporal. . . . It would be fitting to ask what is meant by 'idealism' in view of these extremes . . . , and to answer such a question would constitute its greatest task. But this would not exactly amount to a denial of

the same. Realism and idealism mutually present themselves as immediately evident."
(Marías se precia de resolver este problema (Realismo-Idealismo) 'con mágica simpli-
cidad,' incluyendo en la realidad el propio sujeto cognoscente que con el objeto constituye la vida. . . . El asunto, sin embargo, no parece tan sencillo. Porque la coincidencia
del sujeto con el objeto es rigurosa en la percepción o intuición *sensible* de éste por
aquél, bajo la mutua presencia en el espacio y en el tiempo. Pero dicha coincidencia se
va relajando gradualmente en la representación *imaginativa* de los objetos espacial-
mente ausentes o temporalmente pretéritos o futuros, en los objetos condicionales (que
'sucederían') y meramente posibles, en los objetos ficticios y, finalmente, en los objetos ideales, o sea, supraespaciales y supratemporales. . . . Cabría hacer al idealismo un
interrogatorio de lo que quiere decir en orden a todos estos extremos . . . , y en contes-
tar a él estribaría su mayor compromiso. Pero ello no constituiría precisamente su
refutación. Realismo e idealismo se tienen por inmediatamente evidentes" (cited by
Juan Soler Planas, *El pensamiento de Julián Marías,* p. 221).

14. *Generations: A Historical Method,* p. 72.

15. "Por otra parte, si el mundo ha sido creado por Dios, es inteligible *que sea
inteligible . . ."* (*Razón de la filosofía,* p. 287).

16. ". . . lo decisivo es que estos hombres funcionan como centros de otras
vidas, de cuyas circunstancias formo yo parte; es decir, yo encuentro en mi circunstancia y originariamente, a otros hombres que también me encuentran a mí y que, como
yo con ellos, cuentan conmigo; por tanto, yo cuento con ellos de un modo peculiar, que
incluye su contar conmigo; por esto nuestra recíproca conducta se orienta de modo
muy distinto de como acontece cuando se actúa en vista de las cosas, porque si bien yo
estoy en éstas, ellas no están, en último rigor, conmigo . . ." (*Introducción a la filosofía,
Obras,* II, p. 231).

17. "Una sociedad está definida por un sistema de vigencias comunes—usos,
creencias, ideas, estimaciones, pretensiones—; no basta, pues, con agrupar a los hombres de cierta manera para obtener una sociedad; si dentro de una agrupación arbitraria
rigen distintos repertorios de vigencias, hay más de una sociedad . . ." (*La estructura
social, Obras,* VI, p. 173 [English version from *The Structure of Society,* p. 6]).

18. "La historia . . . afecta a los hombres en cuanto son una pluralidad coexis-
tente y sucesiva a la vez; la vida histórica es, pues, convivencia histórica" (*Introducción a la filosofía,* p. 320 [cited in *The Structure of Society,* p. 6]).

19. In "Circumstance and Vocation" (Chapter 2).

20. ". . . son a la vez 'actos' y 'personajes', es decir, los 'quienes' y los 'pasos'
de la historia. El movimiento histórico no es continuo, como el de un vehículo que
rueda o un avión, sino discontinuo, como el de un cuadrúpedo o el andar de un hombre;
esto es, procede *gradualmente,* o sea por pasos; por sus pasos contados; y estos
pasos—aproximadamente de quince años—son los intervalos de las generaciones. La
historia se puede contar por generaciones, que son el *presente elemental* histórico: el

plazo de relativa establidad de una figura del mundo . . ." (*La estructura social, Obras,* II, p. 194 [*The Structure of Society,* p. 25]).

21. "Una generación es una zona de quince años durante la cual una cierta forma de vida fue vigente. La generación sería, pues, la unidad concreta de la auténtica cronología histórica, o, dicho en otra forma, que la historia camina y procede por generaciones" (*Obras completas,* VI, p. 369).

22. See *Generations: A Historical Method,* pp. 95–106, for Marías's extended commentary on this generational paradigm.

23. For clarification of these and other points see *Generations: A Historical Method,* pp. 96–106 and *The Structure of Society,* pp. 25–45.

24. For a full explanation of the method see *Generations: A Historical Method,* pp. 172–177. The generational series established by Marías for Spain in the nineteenth and twentieth centuries are: 1811, 1826, 1841, 1856, 1871, 1886, 1901, 1916, 1931, 1946, 1961, 1976, 1991. Marías has applied this procedure to his study of Spanish Romanticism and the Generation of 1898. See "Un escorzo del romanticismo," *Generaciones y constelaciones,* pp. 221–242, and "El centenario de la generación del 98," *Literatura y generaciones,* pp. 100–109, respectively.

25. "Este esquema ha dejado de ser válido. Los hombres mayores de sesenta años y plenamente activos son hoy legión" (*Literatura y generaciones,* p. 180).

26. See his "Solencia e insolencia," *Obras,* VI, pp. 496–500; also *La mujer en el siglo XX,* pp. 92–94.

27. See especially "Human Relations," *The Structure of Society,* pp. 168–208.

28. Marías goes on to say in the same passage: "This strange precociousness cannot but cause us to suspect that the development of the theory was a matter of necessity, for the early germination of an idea is usually an indication that it is urgently needed to meet some intellectual, and in general, historical, situation" (*Generations: A Historical Method,* p. 69).

Chapter 4

1. See for instance *Literatura y generaciones,* pp. 101, 175.

2. "En un banquete en su honor en 'Pombo,'" *Obras completas,* VI, p. 226.

3. Remember that Marías follows Ortega's suggestion that generations begin their historical activity around the mean age of thirty. Thus the so-called Generation of 1898, born in a "zone of dates" centered on 1871, would be expected to begin its historical activity in 1901 (which it did). The generation of 1886 (Ortega's generation)

began its rise around 1916. (Note that Ortega published his first major work, *Meditations on Quixote*, in 1914, when he was thirty-one. Following this paradigm we can see that Marías's generation (1916) would begin its rise to prominence in 1946. Marías's own work may be cited as evidence for the validity of the generations theory. His first major work, *Introducción a la Filosofía*, was begun in 1945 and completed early in 1947 (published in February of that year).

4. *"Nuestro tiempo* empieza con ellos y ha seguido, por lo menos, tres generaciones más: la de 1886, la de 1901, la de 1916. ¿Y las siguientes? Ha podido parecer que estaban ya en otra cosa: pero no es seguro" (*Literatura y generaciones,* p. 109).

5. See Marías's work on Spanish Romanticism in "Un escorzo del Romanticismo," *Obras,* III, 206 ff.; also included in *Generaciones y constelaciones,* pp. 221–42.

6. *José Ortega y Gasset: Circumstance and Vocation,* p. 31.

7. *Historia de los heterodoxos españoles,* book 8, chapter 1, *Obras de Menéndez Pelayo,* p. 275; *José Ortega y Gasset: Circumstance and Vocation,* p. 35 (note).

8. "Andrés Hurtado, los primeros días de clase, no salía de su asombro. Todo aquello era demasiado absurdo. El hubiese querido encontrar una disciplina fuerte y al mismo tiempo afectuosa, y se encontraba con una clase grotesca, en que los alumnos se burlaban del profesor. Su preparación para la ciencia no podía ser más desdichada" (*El árbol de la ciencia,* p. 15).

9. "Esta que creíamos nación de bronce ha resultado ser una cana hueca" (*Reconstitución y europeización de España,* p. 3).

10. "Lo que el 98 significa es la patentización de la inanidad de los supuestos básicos de las generaciones anteriores, el descubrimiento de la falsedad en que se había fundado la vida española, bajo una película de apariencias favorables" (*José Ortega y Gasset: Circumstance and Vocation,* p. 49).

11. ". . . es posible una situación extremadamente anormal y paradójica, que es la de vivir *contra la verdad.* Y es—no nos engañemos—la dominante de nuestra época. Se afirma y quiere la falsedad a sabiendas, por serlo; se la acepta tácticamente, aunque proceda del adversario, y se admite el diálogo con ella: *nunca con la verdad* (*Introducción a la Filosofía, Obras,* II, p. 97).

12. "Las vigencias más fuertes, sólidas y profundas no se presentan como tales, no se anuncian ni enuncian . . ." (*The Structure of Society,* p. 63).

13. See Ortega, *Meditaciones del Quixote,* p. 336 (*Obras completas,* I).

14. "—Yo sé quien es usted—le decía—y quiero tener el gusto de saludarle. Es usted uno de los hombres del porvenir . . ." (*Antonio Azorín,* p. 147).

15. *The Generation of 1898 in Spain,* p. 14. One problem with this paradigm, as Shaw himself concedes, is that it excludes such figures as Benavente and Valle-Inclán. For Shaw the term "Generation" is purely arbitrary, for he understands it to mean a

handful of famous writers who lifted Spain to the "forefront of modern cultural development." In other words, from our point of view the flaw of Shaw's work is that he fails to treat the "Generation" of 1898 as a generation.

16. *La generación del noventa y ocho,* p. 254–55.

17. "Ninguna razón externa—conveniencia económica, prestigio social, facilidades políticas, automatismo de las instituciones—los lleva a la vida intelectual; ésta emerge en ellos desde dentro, desde los senos más profundos de su autenticidad, porque la necesitan *para ser ellos mismos en esa realidad española que han aceptado"* (*José Ortega y Gasset: Circumstance and Vocation,* p. 51).

18. *José Ortega y Gasset: Circumstance and Vocation,* p. 53. See "Calidad de página," *Ensayos de conviviencia* (*Obras,* III, 241–43).

19. See the previous discussion in "The First 'Generation of 1898.'"

20. Cited in *José Ortega y Gasset: Circumstance and Vocation,* p. 53; originally in "Calidad de página," *Obras,* III, p. 241.

21. See his "Introducción," *Meditaciones sobre la literatura y el arte,* pp. 7–40.

22. In his *Práctica del saber en filósofos españoles: Gracián, Unamuno, Ortega y Gasset, E. d'Ors, Tierno Galván,* p. 31, Jiménez Moreno notes: "The aspect of each and all of the philosophers considered herein finds its concrete expression in the *practice of knowledge* which is not content to speculate on well-behaved intellectual and abstract forms but rather centers on reflections on life . . ." (El aspecto de todos y cada uno de estos filósofos que aquí se considera se concreta en *la práctica del saber,* que no se contenta con especular sobre formas intelectuales y abstractas muy bien conformadas, sino que se centra en la reflexión sobre los problemas de la vida, . . .).

23. "Para España, el hombre ha sido siempre *persona;* su relación con el Otro (moro o judío en la Edad Media, indio americano después) ha sido personal; ha entendido que la vida *es misión,* y por eso la ha puesto al servicio de una empresa transpersonal; ha evitado, quizá hasta el exceso, el utilitarismo que suele llevar a una visión del hombre como cosa . . ." (*España inteligible,* p. 421).

24. Specifically, Marías has written of Unamuno's use of the novel as a hermeneutics of the "only question" of ultimate human and personal destiny. See "La novela como método de conocimiento," *Miguel de Unamuno, Obras,* V, pp. 67–76.

25. "De estos experimentos políticos los intelectuales del noventa y ocho sacaron una misma conclusión: la urgencia de buscar en zonas de pensamiento y actividad ajenas a la política los medios de rescatar a España de su progresiva catalepsia" (*Hacia el 98: literatura, sociedad, ideología,* pp. 242–43). López-Morillas goes on to note that what appears to be merely an apolitical attitude turns out to be a surly distrust of political formulas as well as in the men and methods of politics.

26. "La segunda generación . . . nace a la vida histórica y a la vida literaria cuando los hombres del 98 no están todavía en disposición de *padrear* a nadie. Su formación cultural, que es uno de sus caracteres decisivos, no debe nada a los hombres del

98, cuya influencia, por entonces, era casi nula" (*Literatura española contemporánea*, p. 155).

27. "¿Cuántas de sus cualidades no han sido conscientes para los del 98 precisamente gracias a Ortega?" (*Literatura española contemporánea*, p. 157).

28. *José Ortega y Gasset: Circumstance and Vocation*, p. 122.

29. Particularly in two articles: "Phenomenological 'Life': A New Look at the Philosophic Enterprise in Ortega y Gasset," *Analecta Husserliana*, Vol. XXIX, (1989), 93–105, and "Husserlian 'Reduction' Seen from the Perspective of Phenomenological 'Life' in the Ortegan School," *Analecta Husserliana*, Vol. XXXVI, (1991), 371–85.

30. Nevertheless, according to Marías this "Spanish Europeanism" has very ancient European antecedents. In a recent article, "La España europea y la unidad de Europa" [European Spain and the Unity of Europe], he repeats his belief that instead of being less European than other European countries, Spain is actually *more* so. Spain chose to be European and Christian even though it could have become Islamic. In addition, the European character and centrality of Spain were demonstrated throughout the Middle Ages by the pilgrimages to the shrine of Saint James in Santiago de Compostela. The isolation of Spain was a much later and essentially modern phenomenon. See *Cuenta y Razón*, February–March 1993, pp. 13–16.

31. Father Benito Feijóo (1676–1764) and Gaspar Melchor de Jovellanos (1744–1811). Eighteenth-century Spain is discussed in Chapter 9.

32. "Es la primera . . . que tuvo maestros españoles, en un doble sentido: maestros universitarios creadores, dueños de métodos plenamente actuales, y modelos literarios válidos, sin arcaísmo y frente a los cuales no se sintieran en actitud de discordia y ruptura" ("¿Generación de 1927?", *Generaciones y constelaciones*, p. 273).

33. "El defecto fundamental de la generación es su apartamiento de la vida, de la realidad" (*Literatura española contemporánea*, p. 165).

34. "Confesémoslo sin reparo: nuestro espíritu es insoportablemente letrado y pedantesco" (*La generación del noventa y ocho*, p. 19).

35. "Se radicalizaron, pues, las pretensiones de sus antecesores . . . Los hombres nuevos traerán a la política igual actitud que a la ciencia o el arte. . . . Razón pura en la ciencia, en la política, y casi me atrevería a decir que pureza racional e irracional en poesía . . ." (*Cinco aventuras españolas*, pp. 20–21).

36. "Esta generación comienza proclamándose *minoritaria;* admite, desde un principio, la existencia de formas populares de arte, que rechaza por vulgares e indignas" (*Literatura española contemporánea*, p. 166).

37. "Esta generación, comparada con las demás de nuestro tiempo, muestra un predominio de las facilidades sobre las dificultades. . . . Las hadas madrinas han solido acompañar fielmente al equipo de la generación de 1901" ("¿Generación de 1927?," *Generaciones y constelaciones*, p. 274).

38. "... esa solidaridad se resquebraja un poco en la generación de 1901, que es 'muy suya' y un poco menos ligada a las anteriores y posteriores ..." ("¿Generación de 1927?," *Generaciones y constelaciones,* p. 275).

39. "Estaban demasiado bien dotados, tenían demasiadas destrezas y gracias—piénsese en Lorca—, se les ofrecían demasiados caminos, tenían delante y al lado tantas incitaciones de sus demás compañeros, tantas facilidades. No tenían—por lo general—urgencias; podían esperar, aplazar la adscripción definitiva, ensayar, probar, gustar" ("¿Generación de 1927?," *Generaciones y constelaciones,* p. 276).

40. "Para ellos, más aún que para los de la generación precedente, la guerra va a ser una realidad vigente que condicionará desde la raíz de su propia vida, que facilitará o amenazará su futuro" (*Cinco aventuras españolas,* p. 21).

41. "Nuestra solidaridad con esas tres generaciones anteriores ha sido radical, irremediable, a prueba de reservas y descontentos. Hemos sentido que en ello iba la vida futura de España y la salvación de todo lo que nos parecía valioso, estimable, original, insustituible en un milenio de vida española, en medio milenio de creación universal, transespañola" ("¿Generación de 1927?," *Generaciones y constelaciones,* p. 276 [my italics]).

42. Luis Martín Santos, *Tiempo de silencio,* p. 133 (translated by Rockwell Gray in *The Imperative of Modernity. An Intellectual Biography of José Ortega y Gasset*).

43. "... nuestra situación no es comparable a la de hace un siglo. Está definida por la existencia de una filosofía llena de posibilidades creadoras, presente; por un fenómeno de arcaísmo, suplantación del comienzo del presente por algo resueltamente pretérito; finalmente, por un abandono de la perspectiva filosófica, de las cuestiones mismas que constituyen el nervio de esa ocupación milenaria ..." (*Razón de la filosofía,* p. 68).

44. "No se pierda de vista que de lo que se trata, sobre todo, es de la eliminación de las *preguntas* que el hombre, y desde cierto momento la filosofía, se han hecho por íntima necesidad" (*Razón de la filosofía,* p. 76).

Chapter 5

1. *José Ortega y Gasset: Circumstance and Vocation,* p. 11.

2. Both Marías and Ortega allude to the "Jericho Method" of philosophizing which Ortega describes: "The great philosophical problems require a tactic similar to that used by the Hebrews in the taking of Jericho with its inner rose gardens: without a direct attack, circling slowly about it, tightening the circle at each turn, and filling the air with the sound of dramatic trumpets. Thus in the ideological siege, the dramatic melody consists in always maintaining the awareness of problems, which are the ideal drama" (*Obras completas,* VII, 279).

3. In the most exhaustive compilation of Ortegan studies to date, over four thousand secondary sources were listed. See Anton Donoso and Harold C. Raley, *José Ortega y Gasset: A Bibliography of Secondary Sources.*

4. ". . . en lugar de invitarme a quedarme en esa obra realizada y acaso gozarla, me impulsaba a ir más allá." "No es casual que desde este momento, y a pesar de factores de extrema gravedad que parecerían haberlo impedido, mi producción intelectual haya sido mucho mayor que en cualquier otra época" (*Una vida presente: Memorias 2*, pp. 352–53).

5. *Metaphysical Anthropology,* p. 17.

6. *Metaphysical Anthropology,* p. 48.

7. *Metaphysical Anthropology,* p. 48. Translator Frances M. López-Morillas correctly translates the generic *el hombre* into its English equivalent "man," and I see no compelling *linguistic* reason to substitute cumbersome, politically coded equivalents (for example, "persons," "individuals," or worse, "she-he," etc.). Moreover, Marías himself is aware (even if most protesters are not) that in its generic meaning the English "man" corresponds to the German *man* and to the French *on* (one, a person of either sex) and not to *Mann* (a male).

8. *Metaphysical Anthropology,* p. 50. For a comprehensive treatment of "complication" see Antonio Rodríguez Huéscar, *José Ortega y Gasset's Metaphysical Innovation.*

9. Some confusion has persisted over the respective meanings of "vital reason," "historical reason," and "narrative reason." Historical reason may be understood as the *concrete* form of vital reason, inasmuch as life is intrinsically historical. To put it another way, vital reason in theory becomes historical reason in practice as soon as it begins to function in real time with real people. And since anything human must be told in order to be understood, according to Ortega, then in practice historical reason takes the form of a narrative. Hence the term "narrative reason." See *Obras,* V, p. 230.

10. *Metaphysical Anthropology,* p. 60.

11. *Metaphysical Anthropology,* p. 69.

12. "Geometría sentimental," *Obras completas,* II, pp. 471–72.

13. *Obras completas,* II, p. 472.

14. See Chapter 2 ("Circumstance and Vocation").

15. *Metaphysical Anthropology,* p. 74.

16. *Metaphysical Anthropology,* p. 76.

17. *Metaphysical Anthropology,* p. 78.

18. *Metaphysical Anthropology,* p. 88.

19. *Metaphysical Anthropology,* p. 89.

20. *Metaphysical Anthropology,* p. 96. In my earlier study, I argued that the analysis of "my" life permits me to arrive at certain propositions concerning being as such. However, at the empirical level I find things "slanted" in a precise "posture of being," as it were, because *I am living* as I am, installed in a certain desiderative way in a certain historical world. Being, it seems, occurs at two levels, the analytical and the empirical. See *Responsible Vision,* p. 263. The point seems less convincing now but perhaps still worth making.

Chapter 6

1. As we shall see later, the *Memorias* of Marías, the masterful three-volume exposition of his own life and times, stand as the first and final test of his dialectical method. In this context the subtitle, *Una vida presente* ["a present life"] is especially revealing.

2. *Metaphysical Anthropology,* p. 28.

3. *Metaphysical Anthropology,* p. 35.

4. *Metaphysical Anthropology,* p. 137.

5. *Metaphysical Anthropology,* p. 141.

6. Marías refers to this sphere of life as the "domain" of woman. Although woman has tended to lead a less "expressive" life than man, she has also been more substantive. While man has a disturbing tendency to become caught up in the surface instability of life, woman shows a greater concern for basic things. In other words, men are interested in change, while women tend to be interested in what it is that changes. Ordinarily, this propensity is misinterpreted as a drive for security. Marías argues that woman concerns herself with the routine and the mediocre in those circumstances that do not permit her anything better. See "La intrahistoria, dominio de la mujer," *La mujer y su sombra,* pp. 63–71.

7. *Essais* (Livre Troisième, v), p. 74.

8. ("La mujer, en toda la historia de Occidente, ha tenido que vivir en un mundo que ha sido fundamentalmente el mundo del hombre, en el que la mayoría de las invenciones—al menos las visibles, las referentes a 'cosas'—eran masculinas. La mujer ha tenido que instalarse en ese mundo, y labrarse dentro de él su mundo particular" [*La mujer en el siglo XX,* p. 172]). The reader is directed to other writings on the topic, for instance, "Vital Reason: Masculine and Feminine," *Metaphysical Anthropology,* pp. 170–78, and "Human Relations" (Section 50, "Persons, Men and Women"), *The Structure of Society,* pp. 168–70.

9. *Metaphysical Anthropology,* p. 176.

10. However, the matter of clothing is far more complex than it may first seem. How much of the body one must clothe—and in what fashion—in order for "proper" concealment to occur seems to be largely a matter of social convention. On the beach or at a pool we would probably consider a woman or man clad in the briefest swimsuit to be dressed adequately. But were these same individuals to appear in their underwear, which probably covers more of the body than the swimsuits in question, we might well be shocked at the perceived "impudence." This alone is enough to begin the argument that our contemporary attitudes about clothing, which usually takes the form of slouchiness, slovenliness, and semi-nudity, amount to a naive and simplistic misunderstanding of its *humanizing* significance.

11. *Metaphysical Anthropology,* p. 156. Here Marías refers to man as male. See Note 7, Chapter 5.

12. *Metaphysical Anthropology,* p. 163.

13. *Metaphysical Anthropology,* p. 165.

14. *Metaphysical Anthropology,* p. 166.

15. "Habría que alumbrar todas las formas posibles de amor, sobre todo todas las *composibles,* biográficamente conciliables, que pueden coexistir en diferentes dimensiones y planos. Si se toman las cosas así, en toda su complejidad y riqueza, la mujer resulta el continente misterioso cuya exploración puede ser asunto de toda la vida; y espero que también de la otra" (*La mujer y su sombra,* p. 216).

Chapter 7

1. In *La felicidad humana* [Human Happiness], p. 25, he states: "This seems to indicate that man is impossible, and so he is. Man consists of trying to be what cannot be, and this is what we call with an excellent verb *living.* This word does not have the same meaning when applied to a plant, an animal, or to man. There is an internal contradiction in the very condition of man: he moves in the element of happiness and inevitably unhappiness belongs to him."

2. "Las pretensiones son más definitorias que la realidad. Pero sería mejor corregir esto y decir que *la realidad humana es primariamente pretensión, proyecto,* y en esto consiste su extraño carácter de ser a la vez real e irreal" [Strivings are more defining than reality. But it would be better to correct this and say that human reality is primarily aim, or project, and its odd quality of being at once real and unreal consists of this feature]. *La felicidad humana,* p. 38.

3. Marías makes the argument repeatedly in his writings that philosophy must be defined and guided by the unavoidable human problems it encounters and is not to be intimidated into silence by possible dilemmas. Nor should this be a cause for alarm for the genuine philosopher. "Uncertainty accompanies the philosopher as a shadow

follows a body" (*Razón de la filosofía*, p. 293). From this it follows, Marías goes on to say, that philosophy cannot rest on a corpus of prior results but must consist in essential continuity and constant renewal.

4. *Metaphysical Anthropology*, p. 180.

5. *Metaphysical Anthropology*, p. 182.

6. "No creo que este amor sea una 'especie' de aquel 'género', sino que todas las demás formas de amor brotan de esa raíz que es el amor intersexuado como forma fundamental de la necesidad personal" (*La mujer en el siglo xx*, p. 219–20). See also *La escuela de Madrid. Obras*, V, pp. 319–20; *Metaphysical Anthropology*, pp. 186–87; and *La mujer y su sombra*, pp. 123–25. In *Metaphysical Anthropology*, Marías states: "I believe . . . that all 'loves' are biographical forms derived from love in the strict sense, human realities whose ultimate root lies in the possibility of love in the strict meaning of the term" (p. 185).

7. "Este amor entre hombre y mujer es el núcleo concreto de la amplísima condición amorosa; quiero decir que toda ella se ordena en torno de él, de manera que todos los demás 'amores', en el sentido más lato de la palabra, no es que sean modificaciones o transformaciones de ese amor heterosexuado, sino que su *raíz* se encuentra en él; es decir, que, dentro de la estructura empírica, todo amor radica en esa estructura, que es precisamente heterosexuada" (*La mujer y su sombra*, p. 126).

8. It would be a fascinating task to relate the anthropological basis of human love to a theological consideration of divine love. Obviously this lies beyond the boundaries of this writing.

9. *Metaphysical Anthropology*, pp. 193–94.

10. See *Mapa del mundo personal*, p. 147.

11. *Metaphysical Anthropology*, p. 195.

12. ". . . la suma delicia para el hombre es ver como la mujer se va manifestando, descubriendo, revelando su intimidad, hasta llegar a acoger en ella al varón en su propia personalidad" (*La educación sentimental*, p. 279).

13. "El problema es si se llega al núcleo personal o no. Cuando se logra, se tiene la plenitud de percepción o, si se prefiere, intuición de una persona. Es una experiencia que no tienen muchos . . ." (*Mapa del mundo personal*, p. 145 [my translation]).

14. See "El amor en nuestro tiempo," *La educación sentimental*, p. 273.

15. ". . . la sexualidad indiferenciada, múltiple, pasajera y *sin importancia*" (*La educación sentimental*, p. 276).

16. ". . . es la forma más profunda de decadencia, porque no es económica, política o cultural, sino que afecta a la realidad misma" (*Mapa del mundo personal*, p. 204).

17. ". . . yo no soy nada que pueda encontrar, porque *yo soy quien encuentra* todo eso. Incluso cuando me encuentro a mí mismo, el propiamente 'yo personal' es el que encuentra y no el encontrado" (*Razón de la filosofía*, p. 269).

18. *Metaphysical Anthropology*, p. 265.

19. "El hombre hace su vida, ciertamente con las cosas, condicionado por su circunstancia, que impone lo que es, pero tiene que imaginar, elegir, decidir *quien* pretende ser, como vio Ortega desde el comienzo de este siglo" (*Razón de la filosofía*, 273).

20. ". . . si el mundo ha sido creado por Dios, es inteligible *que sea inteligible*" (*Razón de la filosofía*, p. 287).

21. *Metaphysical Anthropology*, p. 267.

Chapter 8

1. ". . . ese plus de realidad que los españoles solemos tener" ("La figura del sacerdote," *Innovación y arcaísmo*, p. 301).

2. ". . . se fue decantando en mí la resolución de llenar el tiempo que me quedase con algunas obras que me eran 'propias', que si no las llevaba a cabo era probable que se quedaran sin hacer" (*Una vida presente*, 3, p. 81)

3. "No es extraño que mis pensamientos se orientaran hacia lo que desde mucho tiempo atrás había sido objeto de mi reflexión: la religión, y muy concretamente el cristianismo, su significación, su consistencia, si se permite usar esta palabra, sus realizaciones históricas, sus riesgos" (*Una vida presente*, 3, p. 100).

4. "El cristianismo no da soluciones; da luz para buscarlas" (*Innovación y arcaísmo*, p. 292).

5. ". . . se lo toma como 'punto de partida' para ir a otras cosas, que son las que de verdad interesan" (*Problemas del cristianismo*, p. 5).

6. "Hay que partir de las cosas, de la realidad creada—precisamente cuando se descubre en ella su carácter de 'criatura' . . ." (*Problemas del cristianismo*, p. 6).

7. ". . . la evaporación de la religión como tal, la proyección del cristianismo sobre otros planos, que pueden no serle ajenos, que pueden serle esenciales, pero precisamente como religión, en una perspectiva religiosa. Desde ella, pueden reaparecer justificadamente las cuestiones que hoy afanan a los hombres; sin ella, el cristianismo queda desvirtuado, exangüe, ineficaz, sin interés. Que es, tal vez, lo que se trataba de demostrar" (*Problemas del cristianismo*, p. 11).

8. Commenting in 1945 on *Naturaleza, Historia, Dios* [Nature, History, God] by Xavier Zubiri, Marías spoke of an "unfortunate tendency" to restrict the area of Christianity by eliminating mention of the very thinkers that make it possible to think, or perhaps to dream, of a "Christian philosophy." At the same time Zubiri stirred in him the hope ". . . that perhaps some day there may exist in our world something that with full rigor deserves the illustrious and problematic name *Christian philosophy*" [". . . que algún día exista en nuestro mundo algo que merezca con pleno rigor el nombre ilustre y problemático de *filosofía cristiana*"] ("La escuela de Madrid," *Obras*, V, p. 473). According to his later description, his own work would qualify for the title. "For a long time I have thought that the only acceptable meaning of the expression 'Christian philosophy' is that of philosophy of Christians as such, that is, [philosophy] done from the perspective in which they find themselves by virtue of this religious condition which causes them to 'look' in certain directions and from which they must exercise their thought with the scrupulousness and rigor that philosophy demands" [Hace largo tiempo he pensado que el único sentido aceptable de la expresión 'filosofía cristiana' es el de filosofía de los cristianos en cuanto tales, es decir, hecha desde la perspectiva en que se encuentran por esa condición religiosa, que los hace 'mirar' en ciertas direcciones, y desde la cual tendrán que ejercitar su pensamiento con la escrupulosidad y el rigor que la filosofía reclama] (*Razón de la filosofía*, 284–85). Even before the publication of *Problemas del cristianismo*, José Luis Abellán included him in the movement of Christian Spiritualism that grew out of Orteganism. See his "Panorama de la filosofía española," *Razón y fe* (1977), p. 140.

9. "La enseñanza en los seminarios se ha reducido, con contadas excepciones, a un enquistamiento en formas de escolástica que dejó de ser creadora a mediados del siglo XIV . . ." (*Problemas del cristianismo*, p. 24).

10. In an interesting aside in the same passage, Donoso reasons that "It evidently hurt Marías to see in print what Jacques Maritain, one of the world's most influential Thomists, had said of his friend, the French existentialist Gabriel Marcel, a convert like Maritain to Catholicism, namely, that only those Catholics are Thomists who are sufficiently intelligent to be such" (*Julián Marías*, p. 141).

11. In his latest writings, Marías advances the thesis, already implicit in his earlier thought, that the *religious* origin of the "problem of God" (existence, attributes, relationship to mankind, etc.) is unavoidable precisely because it is not fundamentally a philosophic problem at all but, prior to philosophy and its methods, appears as a human problem, that is, a function of the human drama we call living. This leads him to question the priority of so-called pure intelligence and rationality in dealing with questions about God. If we begin from the only accessible starting point, my life and my circumstance, we find that man is defined by the "amorous condition" discussed in an earlier chapter. Within it we come to grips with reality and project our life. This leads at once to the Scriptural definition of God as love and suggests a new way (which is also the Biblical way) of understanding the Divine from a human reference point. Intelligence and rationality newly converted to instrumentalities of man's "lovely" condition now

reemerge to pursue their discoveries *within* this context. See *Razón de la filosofía*, pp. 291–92.

12. "Sin duda excede de nuestras posibilidades, en el sentido de que no será como la imaginamos; claro que no. Pero será porque no lleguemos a imaginarla adecuadamente, porque nos quedaremos cortos; no, ciertamente, porque imaginemos algo *superior* a la realidad. ¿Es pensable que el hombre pudiera llegar adonde Dios no llega?" (*Problemas del cristianismo*, p. 29).

13. *Metaphysical Anthropology*, p. 267.

14. *Metaphysical Anthropology*, p. 266.

15. ". . . consiste en *inventar una panacea y negar todos los males que es incapaz de curar*" (*Problemas del cristianismo*, p. 33). The problem is further complicated by what Marías calls ". . . a curious reluctance to acknowledge that wickedness exists . . ." He goes on to discover the ultimate causes of this attitude in the generalized movement toward the elimination of the notion of personhood with its concomitant freedom and responsibility and the reduction of everything human to natural and cosmic phenomena. Marías is concerned that no distinction is made or even understood to exist between the genocidal ferocity in Ruwanda or Yugoslavia and an earthquake or a flood. Both are treated as "humanitarian calamities, that is, simply as an "ill" *(mal)* of the world and not in the first case as a consequence of human wickedness *(maldad)*. See "La maldad existe"[Wickedness exists], *ABC* (August 4, 1994).

16. For Marías, the term not only contains justice but also conceals a multitude of wrongs. See his *La justicial social y otras justicias* (1974).

17. ". . . la justicia *social* es sólo una forma particular de la justicia, y que mas allá de la justicia hay legión de cosas que importan" (*La justicia social y otras justicias*, p. 36).

18. ". . . *justicia social es aquella que corrige una situación social que envuelve una injusticia previa que invalida las conductas justas, los actos individuales de justicia*" (*Problemas del cristianismo*, p. 38), an idea expressed previously in *La justicia social y otras justicias*, p. 11.

19. "Esto me parece lo peor, porque además de perder el horizonte han perdido la conciencia de lo que es *vivir,* esto es, necesitar seguir viviendo *siempre;* y, lo que es más, necesitar que sigan viviendo siempre las personas amadas, cuya aniquilación, si verdaderamente son amadas, resulta insorportable" (*Problemas del cristianismo,* pp. 41–42).

20. "Como se ve, estamos en el curso de una gigantesca operación que consiste en *invertir* el orden de las cosas tal como lo impone una perspectiva cristiana. Ahora bien, esa inversión es intelectualmente una falsificación, moralmente una perversión" (*Problemas del cristianismo*, p. 43).

21. *The Structure of Society*, p. 207.

22. "The Mind of Julián Marías. A Catholic Disciple of Ortega," *Tablet* 197, no. 5 (June 30, 1951), p. 516a.

23. ". . . el cristiano, por muy firme que sea su certidumbre personal, debe presentar como incierto lo que para otros muchos hombres lo es, y tiene que justificar su ciertidumbre hasta donde sea posible" (*Problemas del cristianismo,* p. 56).

24. "But it is not easy for a 'provisional' marriage with reservations to be *fully* real and happy, and personally I believe this possibility is worth the effort" [Pero no es facil que un matrimonio con reservas y 'provisional' pueda ser *plenamente* real y feliz, y personalmente creo que esa posibilidad vale la pena] (*Problemas del cristianismo,* pp. 58–59).

25. Marías has not changed his personal opinion, stated in 1978, that ". . . the social acceptance of abortion is morally the gravest thing, *without exception,* in the twentieth century" (*Problemas del cristianismo,* p. 62). In his article "La cuestión del aborto" [The Question of Abortion] (ABC [Sept. 10, 1992]), Marías presents his objections to abortion from his promised anthropological premises. In it, he begins by distinguishing between the notion of the child as derivative of its parents or a part of its mother and the view of human life as a radical "innovation of reality." He rejects the concept that human life corresponds to a "what" and is therefore susceptible to reduction and depersonalization. As Marías has stated time and again, life corresponds—and responds—to a "who." Only the "what" of our life derives from our ancestors; "who" we are is someone unique, irreplaceable, and irreducible to lesser realities.

Chapter 9

1. ". . . nadie, ni él mismo, había aplicado a la investigación de España" (*Una vida presente,* III, p. 256).

2. According to Ortega, "The illness is not confined to the country's political life. It is society itself which is sick. It is the head and the heart of almost every Spaniard that are ailing" (*Invertebrate Spain,* p. 64). I have examined Ortega's views of Spanish society in the chapter "Ortega and Spain," *José Ortega y Gasset: Philosopher of European Unity,* pp. 188–213.

3. In *The Spaniards: An Introduction to Their History* and *The Structure of Spanish History.* In his zeal to render justice to Jewish and Moslem influences in Spain, which he claims orthodox historians have concealed because of their antisemitic and "Islamophobic" sentiments, Américo Castro goes to the opposite extreme by becoming prosemitic and an Islamophile insofar as Spanish history is concerned. He seems able to find Jewish and Moorish presences under almost every stone and behind every bush in the Spanish historical landscape.

4. In *A qué llamamos España* (1970), notwithstanding his acceptance of Américo Castro's concept of Spain as an ethnic and geographical mosaic, Pedro Laín Entralgo veers in the general direction of Marías's view of an overarching and defining

collective project when he includes as the first of five fundamental "Spanish" characteristics "The ardent hope of rising to very lofty heights and destinies, humanly exemplary and prefigured in the heart of a divine or human belief" (p. 69). For the most part, however, the work rides parasitically on Castro's earlier theses and offers scant theoretical advances, even though it deserves attention because of its impressionistic personal and emotional interpretations.

Although their dialectical approaches differ greatly, Marías likely would agree with portions of the statement by Manuel García Morente (*Idea de la hispanidad* [1947]: "The deep meaning of the history of Spain is the consubstantiality of country and religion," adding that "to serve God is to serve Spain" (p. 211). Therefore, "The Christian knight summarizes in his Cervantine silhoutte the most exquisite and purest character of the immortal Spanish spirit [*hispanidad*]" (p. 218).

5. *Understanding Spain*, p. 4.

6. *Obras completas*, VI, pp. 44–45.

7. *History as a System*, p. 231.

8. Marías rejects with equal vigor and for similar reasons the related doctrines of progressivism and evolution. He objects to the first on the grounds that it empties each succeeding age of substance, for each is thought of as mere preparation for a better age to come. The present is sacrificed to an ever-unrealized "futurism." But this does not mean, on the other hand, that human history ends in some utopian final version, such as we find in Hegel or Marx. There is never a final option, which in itself is a contradiction not only of terms but of the human condition itself.

Over against the Hegelian idea of history as the unfolding of a destiny implicit from the beginning, Marías argues that human history is necessarily innovative in the most radical way because beyond natively inert resources nothing is foreordained as destiny.

9. *Understanding Spain*, p. 22.

10. *España inteligible*, p. 52 (my translation). The passage in *Understanding Spain*, an excellent translation on the whole, was inaccurately rendered.

11. *Understanding Spain*, p. 50.

12. *Understanding Spain*, p. 46.

13. *Understanding Spain*, p. 64.

14. *Understanding Spain*, pp. 94-95.

15. *Understanding Spain*, p. 102.

16. *Understanding Spain*, p. 117.

17. *Understanding Spain*, p. 118.

18. *Understanding Spain,* p. 120.

19. *Understanding Spain,* p. 135.

20. *Understanding Spain,* p. 146. The remark by Sánchez-Albornoz is cited in the same passage.

21. Pero de toda Spanna Castiella es mejor,/por que fue de los otrros el comienço mayor, . . . (*Poema de Fernán González,* p. 48). The anonymous poet adds: "Even Old Castile, to my understanding, is better than the rest because it was the foundation . . ." [Avn Castiella Vyeja, al mi entendimiento, mejor es que lo hal por que fue el cimiento].

22. *Understanding Spain,* pp. 157–58.

23. *Understanding Spain,* p. 163.

24. The reason for this, Marías believes, was that medieval man did not base his life primarily on *ideas,* which are notoriously unstable, but on a compact system of *beliefs.* Christians, Jews, and Moslems shared a system of beliefs: monotheism, creation, salvation, divine revelation in a Book. They did not have the same faith, which explains their wars and rivalry, but they shared the same belief, or at least, the same kind of belief. "They did not have the same faith, . . . but they have the same belief, that is the same type of belief; they do not believe the same things, but believed the same way; that is why they understood one another—all too well—and fought among themselves"(*Understanding Spain,* p. 172).

25. *Understanding Spain,* p. 173.

26. Una fe y un pastor solo en el suelo,
    un monarca, un imperio y una espada.

27. *Understanding Spain,* p. 201.

28. *Understanding Spain,* pp. 242–43.

29. *Understanding Spain,* p. 272.

30. *Understanding Spain,* p. 283.

31. *Understanding Spain,* p. 325.

32. *Understanding Spain,* p. 327.

33. *Understanding Spain,* p. 328.

34. *Understanding Spain,* p. 345.

35. *Understanding Spain,* p. 351.

36. See Chapter 3, "Metaphysical Reality and the Theory of Generations."

37. *Understanding Spain*, pp. 364–65.

38. *Understanding Spain*, p. 423.

39. *Understanding Spain*, p. 424.

40. *Understanding Spain*, p. 444.

41. *Understanding Spain*, p. 452.

Chapter 10

1. Ortega discusses the concept of *vigencia* most notably in *En torno a Galileo* (*Obras completas*, V, pp. 37 ff.), and *El hombre y la gente* (*Obras completas*, VII, pp. 259 ff.); also in *Ideas y creencias* (*Obras completas*, V, pp. 383 ff.). The best summary, however, is to be found in Marías, *The Structure of Society*, pp. 46 ff.

2. *La mujer*, p. 14. No English translation of this work exists. This and subsequent translations are mine.

3. *La mujer*, p. 10.

4. As Ortega puts it, "To comprehend anything human, be it personal or collective, one must tell its history. This man, this nation does such a thing and is in such a manner, *because* formerly he or it did that other thing and was in such another manner" (*History as a System*, p. 214). The idea of vector was added by Marías. See his *Antropología metafísica*, pp. 107–15.

5. *La mujer y su sombra*, p. 191.

6. *La mujer*, p. 17.

7. *La mujer*, pp. 97–98.

8. *La mujer*, p. 102.

9. *La mujer*, p. 111.

10. *La mujer*, p. 124.

11. *La mujer*, p. 118.

12. *La mujer*, p. 122.

13. *La mujer*, p. 135.

14. *La mujer y su sombra*, p. 22.

15. *La mujer y su sombra*, p. 55.

16. *La mujer y su sombra*, p. 71.

17. *La mujer y su sombra*, p. 82.

18. *La mujer y su sombra*, p. 92.

19. See Note 42, Chapter 11, for commentary on the meaning of *ilusión*.

20. *La mujer y su sombra*, p. 145. Insofar as his own "biography" is concerned, recall Marías's earlier statement that his book *La mujer en el siglo xx* owed very little to other books but an immense amount to many women. In his prologue to *La mujer y su sombra* he reminds us that in addition to these many real friendships with women of several cultures and conditions, there is an imaginary dimension to be considered also: the women of movies and fiction. It is interesting to note that one of the few points of disagreement between Ortega and Marías was over this very theme of intersexual friendship. See *La mujer y su sombra*, p. 146.

21. *La mujer y su sombra*, p. 174. Marías goes on to say that "Where there is no woman there can hardly be a home and if there is its artificiality is easily discovered." This pleasing "woman's touch" has little to do with the luxury or modesty of fixtures and furniture. The inhospitable home is usually the sign of a harsh and inhospitable woman. Unlike Marías, for whom woman is the other radical form of human reality, Ortega argues that the appearance of woman is ". . . a particular case of the appearance of the Other" and that she is less impressive than man (See *El hombre y la gente, Obras completas*, pp. 168–72).

22. *La mujer y su sombra*, p. 176.

23. *La mujer y su sombra*, p. 179.

24. *La mujer y su sombra*, p. 211.

25. *La mujer y su sombra*, p. 214.

26. *La mujer y su sombra*, p. 216.

27. The Pope goes on to say that "One cannot think adequately about man without reference, which for man is constitutive, to God" (p. 35).

Chapter 11

1. For an illuminating discussion of the theme of happiness see Antonio Rodríguez Huéscar, "Sobre la felicidad," *Revista de Occidente*, No. 168 (May 1995), pp. 122–43.

2. Ortega once noted: "Aunque parezca mentira, falta por completo una historia de la imagen que los hombres se han forjado de la felicidad" [Even though it seems unbelievable, there is no history whatsoever of the image of happiness men have shaped for themselves], *A veinte años de caza major, Obras completas*, VI, p. 424. Ortega goes on to sketch a theory of human activity divided between *ocupaciones felici-*

tarias, or "felicitary activities," and work. Painfully submerged in his obligatory work, man dreams of another program of activities in which life itself would be realized as delight and happiness—if only there were enough time. For this reason, Ortega says that life as such is dull or "insipid," a mere "being there" or "showing up." Thus, man has no choice but to convert his life into a "poetic task" by creating a more attractive plot. A theme that will stand forth in *La felicidad humana* is that certain generations and societies have shown a greater talent or "vocation" for happiness—and thus un-happiness—than others.

3. *La felicidad,* p. 17. No English version of this book exists; this and subsequent translations are mine.

4. *La felicidad,* p. 21.

5. *La felicidad,* p. 25. In *Metaphysical Anthropology,* Marías expounds: "Aspiration to happiness is unrenounceable, because it coincides with the aspiration which constitutes our life. It is, to begin with, the realization of the aspiration; consequently, every aspiration is an aspiration to happiness; and therefore, instead of 'flowing' normally, like biological life, it has a coefficient or success of failure which varies at every moment. Man feels himself successively at a certain 'level' of realization of his aspiration, at a certain altitude of happiness" (pp. 239–40).

6. *La felicidad,* pp. 27–28.

7. *La felicidad,* p. 43.

8. *La felicidad,* p. 56.

9. *La felicidad,* p. 59.

10. *La felicidad,* p. 60. Marías goes on to explain: "I mean that a person who is sad ends up a little happier if the street is cheerful, and if a happy person goes through gloomy, sordid, deathly, or simply boring streets, he feels his happiness slipping away little by little."

11. *La felicidad,* p. 66.

12. *Nicomachean Ethics* (Book 1: Ch. 3), *The Basic Works of Aristotle,* p. 937.

13. *La felicidad,* p. 76. Marías adds: ". . . all this shows that beneath this somewhat abstract set of ideas lies an intuition or experience of happiness."

14. *La felicidad,* p. 106.

15. *La felicidad,* p. 110.

16. *La felicidad,* p. 130.

17. *La felicidad,* p. 143.

18. *La felicidad,* p. 143.

19. *La felicidad,* p. 153.

20. *La felicidad*, p. 128.

21. *La felicidad*, pp. 174–75.

22. *La felicidad*, p. 179.

23. Spanish permits the expression *felicidades* [literally "happinesses"] but in the sense of "congratulations." When one speaks of *la felicidad* the meaning is singular and unitary, as it is in English and other languages.

24. *La felicidad*, p. 191. Pursuing this argument, Marías goes on to assert that attitudes of renunciation, ascetism, and austerity must be justified, perhaps as the price one must pay for the achievement of a higher good. Otherwise, they would seem to have very little moral ground.

25. *La felicidad*, p. 217.

26. *La felicidad*, p. 213.

27. As he has so often, Marías himself responded to this need with his *La educación sentimental* (1992).

28. *La felicidad*, p. 218.

29. *La felicidad*, p. 221.

30. In his "¿El peor de los mundos posibles?" [The Worst of Possible Worlds?], published in *Esquema de nuestra situación* (1970) and republished in *Innovación y arcaísmo* (1973), Marías notes several destructive ironies evident in or underlying this pessimism. One is the insistence on seeking illegally what has already been granted legally and saying clandestinely what everyone can say publicly. Another is the distortion of the real world by the so-called daily "news." Nothing of substance, says Marías, can be summarized as a sound bite. Imagine how ridiculous and meaningless it would be if someone had reported twenty-five centuries ago that "Philosophy has begun in Ionia" or, equally silly, "Medicine has been invented." Consequently, "The man of today, bombarded by news from the time he wakes up until he goes to bed, cannot escape the impression that life is an uninterrupted succession of errors, misfortunes, and violence" (*Esquema*, p. 33).

31. *La felicidad*, p. 266. Marías refers to this reluctance to run the risk of happiness as "the temptation of Limbo."

32. *La felicidad*, p. 293.

33. *La felicidad*, p. 300. The reader will recall that the anthropological foundation of these ideas was discussed in Chapter VI ("Men and Women").

34. Despite a great deal of internationalization, significant cultural differences in attitudes about professions still exist. Marías points out that Spaniards tend to have a sort of "monogamous marriage" to their profession. It may delight or bore them, but they seldom abandon it. Americans, significantly enough, often refer to a job as a "situation" and are quick to switch to another if it pays more or proves more appealing.

These differences appear linguistically in English and Spanish. In the United States to inquire about a man's profession one normally asks, "And what does he do?," whereas in Spain the question would likely be," *¿Y qué es el?* [And what is he?].

35. *La felicidad*, p. 316.

36. *La felicidad*, pp. 318–19.

37. *La felicidad*, p. 324.

38. *La felicidad*, p. 344.

39. *La felicidad*, p. 354.

40. For a fuller discussion of the various views of death (cismundane, transmundane, etc.) see *The Structure of Society*, pp. 201–08.

41. *La felicidad*, p. 372.

42. Comments Marías: "The best example of *ilusión* is the life of a child, indeed here it assumes its characteristic form, for a child without *ilusiones* is not, properly speaking, a child, but rather an offspring, a 'cub' or an incomplete adult" (*Breve tratado de la ilusión*, p. 39).

Chapter 12

1. *Una vida presente*, I, p. 400. This and following translations are mine.

2. *Intelectuales y Espirituales*, pp. 219–20.

3. See p. 13.

4. *Homenaje a Julián Marías*, p. 445. Madariaga adds: "This writer lived for years on a plateau open to all the abysses and never lowered his eyes, never lost hope, never lost heart, never consented to anything that was not the clear water of an artistic and independent soul."

5. *Una vida presente*, I, p. 13. Upon reflection, I chose the title "A Life Recalled" instead of "A Life Remembered" as I had first intended. Even though the terms are often interchangeable in common speech, "recall" has a vocative value, at least etymologically; things "recalled" can simply mean "remembered," but we may also "recall" things so that they come back to stand in our presence, as it were. This seems closer to the idea of "A Present Life."

6. Marías's doctoral thesis, "La filosofía del Padre Gratry," was disapproved in 1941 even though it was published immediately (*La filosofía del Padre Gratry, Obras*, IV, pp. 147–314. He recounts the circumstances of his doctoral defense and the awarding of his doctorate in 1951 in *Una vida presente*, I, pp. 319–23; 383–84.

7. *Una vida presente*, III, p. 409.

Conclusion

1. In *Tratado de lo mejor* (1995), Marías observes that the comparatives "good" and "best" (*bueno* and *lo mejor*) involve more than simple linguistic irregularities. He argues that whereas traditional ethics has looked to the good, the real norm of conduct is to be found in the "best."

2. See for example my study, "Hacia una teoría estética en Julián Marías," *Hispanófila*, no. 41 (1970), for an outline of his aesthetic thought. Marías has on occasion expressed the hope of elaborating on the theme.

WORKS CITED

Abellán, José Luis. "Panorama de la filosofía española." *Razón y fe* 947 (1977), 140.

Anonymous. *Poema de Fernán González*. 4th Edition. Ed. Alonso Zamora Vicente. Madrid: Espasa-Calpe, 1970.

Aristotle. *Nicomachean Ethics. The Basic Works of Aristotle*. Ed. Richard McKeon. New York: Random House, 1941.

"Azorín" (José Martínez Ruiz). *Antonio Azorín*. Madrid: Biblioteca Nueva, 1939.

Baroja, Pío. *El árbol de la ciencia*. Madrid: Alianza Editorial, 1967.

Carpintero, Heliodoro. *Cinco aventuras españolas*. Madrid: Revista de Occidente, 1967.

Castro, Américo. *The Spaniards: An Introduction to Their History*. Berkeley and Los Angeles: University of California Press, 1954.

Costa, Joaquín. *Reconstitución y europeización de España*. Madrid: Martín Retortillo, 1981.

Curtius, Ernest Robert. "Ortega." *Merkur*. Jahr 3, no. 15 (1949), 417–30.

Donoso, Anton. *Julián Marías*. Boston: Twayne, 1982.

———. *José Ortega y Gasset: A Bibliography of Secondary Sources*. With Harold Raley. Bowling Green, Ohio: The Philosophy Documentation Center, 1986.

Dust, Patrick. *Ortega y Gasset and the Question of Modernity*. Minneapolis: The Prisma Institute, 1989.

Fox, E. Inman. *Meditaciones sobre la literatura y el arte*. Madrid: Castalia, 1987.

García Morente, Manuel. *Idea de la hispanidad*. Madrid: Espasa-Calpe, 1961.

Gray, Rockwell. *The Imperative of Modernity: An Intellectual Biography of José Ortega y Gasset*. Berkeley: University of California Press, 1989.

Guy, Alain. "Julian Marias et la pensée française." *Homenaje a Julián Marías*. Madrid: Espasa-Calpe, 1984.

Henares, Domingo. *Hombre y sociedad en Julián Marías*. Albacete, Spain: Diputación de Albacete, 1991.

Jiménez Moreno, Luis. *Práctica del saber en filósofos españoles: Gracián, Unamuno, Ortega y Gasset, E. d'Ors, Tierno Galván*. Barcelona: Anthropos, 1991.

Laín Entralgo, Pedro. *A qué llamamos España*. Madrid: Espasa-Calpe, 1970.

―――. *La generación del noventa y ocho*. Madrid: Espasa-Calpe, 1983.

López-Morillas, Juan. *Hacia el 98: literatura, sociedad, ideología*. Barcelona: Ediciones Ariel, 1972.

―――. *Intelectuales y Espirituales*. Madrid: Revista de Occidente, 1961.

Madariaga, Salvador de. "Julián Marías, escritor." *Homenaje a Julián Marías*. Madrid: Espasa-Calpe, 1984.

Marías, Julián. *A Biography of Philosophy*. Translated by Harold Raley. University, Alabama: The University of Alabama Press, 1984.

―――. *Breve tratado de la ilusión*. Alianza Editorial, 1984.

―――. *Cervantes clave española*. Madrid: Alianza Editorial, 1990.

―――. *Esquema de nuestra situación*. Buenos Aires: Editorial Columba, 1970.

―――. *Generations: A Historical Method*. Translated by Harold Raley. University, Alabama: The University of Alabama Press, 1970.

―――. *Generaciones y constelaciones*. Madrid: Alianza Editorial, 1989.

―――. *Innovación y arcaísmo*. Madrid: Revista de Occidente, 1973.

―――. "La cuestión del aborto." *ABC*. (September 10, 1992).

―――. *La educación sentimental*. Madrid: Alianza Editorial, 1992.

―――. "La España europea y la unidad de Europea." *Cuenta y Razón*, (February–March, 1993), 13–16.

―――. *La España real*. Madrid: Espasa-Calpe, 1976.

―――. *La felicidad humana*. Madrid: Alianza Editorial, 1987.

―――. *La justicia social y otras justicias*. 2nd Edition. Madrid: Espasa-Calpe, 1979.

―――. "La maldad existe." *ABC*. (August 4, 1994).

―――. *La mujer en el siglo XX*. Madrid: Alianza Editorial, 1980.

―――. *La mujer y su sombra*. Madrid: Alianza Editorial, 1986.

―――. *Literatura y generaciones*. Madrid: Espasa-Calpe, 1975.

―――. *Mapa del mundo personal*. Madrid: Alianza Editorial, 1993.

―――. *Metaphysical Anthropology: The Empirical Structure of Human Life*. Translation of *Antropología metafísica. La estructura empírica de la vida humana,* by

Frances M. López-Morillas. University Park and London: The Pennsylvania State University Press, 1971.

———. *Nuestra Andalucía.* With Enrique Lafuente and Alfredo Ramón. Madrid: Díaz-Casariego, 1966.

———. *Obras.* 8 vols. Madrid: Revista de Occidente, 1958–70.

———. *Ortega. Circunstancia y vocación.* Madrid: Revista de Occidente, 1960; in English: *José Ortega y Gasset: Circumstance and Vocation.* Translated by Frances M. López-Morillas. Norman: University of Oklahoma Press, 1970.

———. *Ortega. Las trayectorias.* Madrid: Alianza Editorial, 1983.

———. *Philosophy as Dramatic Theory.* Translated from various works by Marías by James Parson. University Park and London: The Pennsylvania State University Press, 1971.

———. *Problemas del cristianismo.* Madrid: Biblioteca de autores cristianos, 1979; amplified second edition, 1979.

———. *Razón de la filosofía.* Madrid: Alianza Editorial, 1993.

———. *The Structure of Society.* Translated by Harold Raley. University, Alabama: The University of Alabama Press, 1986.

———. *Una vida presente. Memorias.* 3 vols. Madrid: Alianza Editorial, 1988–89.

———. *Understanding Spain.* Translated from *España inteligible,* by Frances M. López-Morillas. Ann Arbor: The University of Michigan Press and the University of Puerto Rico Press, 1989.

Martín Santos, Luis. *Tiempo de silencio.* Barcelona: Seix Barral, 1965.

Menéndez Pelayo, Marcelino. *Historia de los heterodoxos españoles. Obras de Menendez Pelayo.* Madrid: Edición Nacional, 1948.

Montaigne, Michel E. *Essais.* 3 vols. Ed. Maurice Rat. Paris: Garnier Frères, 1958.

Navajas, Gonzalo. *Miguel de Unamuno: Bipolaridad y síntesis ficcional. Una lectura posmoderna.* Barcelona: PPU, 1988.

Ortega y Gasset, José. *History as a System, and Other Essays Toward a Philosophy of History.* Translated by Helene Weyl, with an Afterword by John William Miller. New York: W. W. Norton, 1961.

———. *Obras completas.* 11 vols. Madrid: Revista de Occidente, 1961–69.

———. *The Revolt of the Masses.* Anonymous Translator. New York: W. W. Norton, 1930 (1960).

Perriaux, Jaime. *Las generaciones argentinas*. Buenos Aires: The Universitaria de Buenos Aires, 1970.

Pope John Paul II. *Crossing the Threshold of Hope*. Ed. Vittorio Mesori. Translated from the Italian by Jenny McPhee and Martha McPhee. New York: Alfred A. Knopf, 1994.

Raley, Harold. "Hacia una teoría estética en Julián Marías," *Hispanófila*, no. 41 (1970).

————. "Husserlian 'Reduction' Seen from the Perspective of Phenomenological 'Life' in the Ortegan School." *Analecta Husserliana*, Vol. 36 (1991), 371–85.

————. *José Ortega y Gasset: Philosopher of European Unity*. University, Alabama: The University of Alabama Press, 1971.

————. "Phenomenological 'Life': A New Look at the Philosophic Enterprise in Ortega y Gasset." *Analecta Husserliana*. Vol. 29 (1989), 93–105.

————. *Responsible Vision*. Clear Creek, Indiana: The American Hispanist, 1980.

Rodríguez Huéscar, Antonio. *José Ortega y Gasset's Metaphysical Innovation*. Albany: SUNY Press, 1975.

————. "Sobre la felicidad." *Revista de Occidente,* no. 168 (May 1995), 122–43.

Rosenstock-Huessy, Eugen. *Out of Revolution*. Norwich, Vermont: Argo Books, 1938 (1966).

Sarmiento, Edward. "The Mind of Julián Marías. A Catholic Disciple of Ortega." *Tablet* 197 (June 30, 1951), 515–17.

Shaw, Donald. *The Generation of 1898 in Spain*. London: Ernest Benn Limited, 1975.

Soler Planas, Juan. *El pensamiento de Julián Marías*. Madrid: Revista de Occidente, 1973.

Torrente Ballester, Gonzalo. *Literatura española contemporánea*. Madrid: Afrodisio Aguado, 1949.

Zubiri, Xavier. *Naturaleza, Historia, Dios*. Madrid: Editora Nacional, 1963.

INDEX